The Road To

Radical Riches

YOU ARE DESTINED FOR OUTRAGEOUS WEALTH

DAVE WILLIAMS

YOU ARE DESTINED FOR OUTRAGEOUS WEALTH

Unless otherwise indicated, all Scripture quotations are taken from the Authorized King James Version of the Bible.

Scripture quotations marked (NLT) are taken from the Holy Bible, New Living Translation, ©1996. Used by permission of Tyndale House Publishers, Inc. Wheaton, Illinois 60189. All rights reserved.

Scripture quotations marked (NIV) are taken from the HOLY BIBLE, NEW INTERNATIONAL VERSION, ©1973, 1978, 1984 by International Bible Society. Used by permission of Zondervan Publishing House, Grand Rapids, MI 49506. All rights reserved.

Scripture quotations marked (TLB) are taken from The Living Bible, ©1971. Used by permission of Tyndale House Publishers, Inc., Wheaton, Illinois 60189. All rights reserved.

The Road To Radical Riches
You Are Destined For Outrageous Wealth

Hardback and paperback editions published simultaneously for distribution throughout the United States, Canada, United Kingdom, Australia, New Zealand, and South Africa.

First Edition 2000

ISBN 0-938020-55-2

Although a great deal of care has been taken to provide accurate and current information, some of the practical concepts expressed by the author may change due to changes in local, state, or federal laws governing investments, pensions, and tax sheltered vehicles. The spiritual principles expressed in this book, however, are eternal and unchanging. Some information, such as telephone numbers, addresses, and web pages may have changed. All information is believed to be current at the time of this writing. The reader is urged to consult legal counsel regarding any points of law. This publication should not be used as a substitute for proper, competent legal or financial investment advice. The author is not engaged in rendering legal, accounting, or other professional services.

Published in the United States by:
Decapolis Publishing
202 S. Creyts Road
Lansing, Michigan 48917 USA

In Canada, write:
P.O. Box 6800-181
Agincourt, Ontario M1S3C6

DECAPOLIS
PUBLISHING

Printed in the United States of America

MHC 10 9 8 7 6 5 4 3 2

To all my precious pastor friends who want the very best for their flocks.

And I will give you pastors according to mine heart, which shall feed you with knowledge and understanding.

— Jeremiah 3:15

And I will set up shepherds over them which shall feed them: And they shall fear no more, nor be dismayed, neither shall they be lacking, saith the Lord.

— Jeremiah 23:4

For Pastors Only:
Please read Chapter Twenty Five first

Contents

Acknowledgements

Dr. Oral Roberts
who taught the world
The Miracle of Seed-Faith Living

Dr. Rex Humbard
who taught me how to be a soul
winner and who took the time to
pray for me when I was facing
criticism for my faith in
God's Promises

Kenneth Copeland
who, over the years,
uncompromisingly stood up and
persistently proclaimed God's will
concerning prosperity

Dr. Joe Gandolfo
who taught me the power of
staying devoted to God

Dr. David Yonggi Cho
who taught me the power of
having vision

Dr. E. Glenn Snook
who first taught me about the
miracle power of making
supernatural faith promises

Dr. Leroy Thompson
who has taught the body of Christ
how "Money Cometh"

Dr. Bob Harrison
who is helping business people
to learn the secret of
spiritual warfare in finances

Dick Fabian
who first taught me how to use
the telephone to set up
and prosper
in my storehouse accounts

Doug Fabian
who taught me how to be a
"Maverick Investor"

Dr. Dick Mills
my dear friend
who has brought the prophetic
word to my life on many occasions

Dr. John Avanzini
who has relentlessly taught the
Church God's powerful
principles of increase

John M. Cummuta
who is teaching his listeners how to
live debt-free and prosperously

Steve and Patsy Brock
who have always stretched my faith
and taught me how to enjoy
some of the good things in life

Richard & Lindsay Roberts
my dear friends
who have become
Master Debt-Blasters!

Rev. Neville McDonald
my dear friend
who always inspires me to reach
higher in my faith, and who
showed an entire generation
how to come out of poverty

Foreword

What a joy it is for me to be able to write a few words about Pastor Dave Williams' new book *The Road To Radical Riches.*

The word "radical" can be found in the Greek New Testament in the words of Matthew 11:12. Paraphrased it reads, "The Kingdom of Heaven is a prize to be seized. Only the ***radical*** forcefully press in and seize the prize." The Greek word for "radical" is "biastes"(pronounced bee-as-tace). It is defined by grammarians and lexicographers as "the persistent, the determined, the energetic, the aggressive, the fervent, the forceful, and the radical."

Reading this book will stir you up to a new spiritual dynamic. It is a sure cure for apathy, complacency, mediocrity, indifference, and "business as usual" — read it and get ready for a turbo-prop acceleration of your personal faith.

Dick Mills, STD, D.D.

Hemet, California

"God created you for outrageous wealth, but it won't come from rainbows, lotteries, casinos, or schemes. It comes from power — the power God gives you to get wealth."

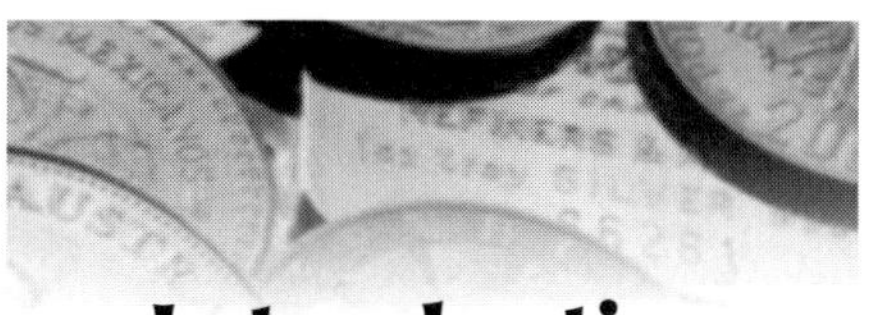

Introduction

Have you ever chased a rainbow?

When I was eight years old, someone told me that if I could get to the end of a rainbow I'd find a pot of gold. That sounded pretty good to me, and at eight years old you typically believe what you're told. So I shared the news with all my neighborhood friends.

It was around the fourth of July in 1959 when my first opportunity appeared — a beautiful rainbow in the western skies. I gathered up all my buddies and we set out to find the gold. We all needed money to buy some fireworks for upcoming celebrations and we figured this would be the quickest way. We had to get our hands on that gold.

The end of the rainbow looked like it was only a few blocks away, so we initiated our expedition. We crossed the busy street our parents told us to never cross. We cut through a car wash, marched through the back of the Bell Telephone property, through the park at the Cascades, and across the football field at the junior high school. It seemed as though that fickle rainbow was moving away from us as fast as we were moving toward it.

But we marched on with gold-dust fever.

Finally when we reached the Jackson County Airport, eight miles from home, the rainbow silently faded into the blue sky. Gone. It disappeared. And we were disappointed that we missed finding that pot of gold.

As I recall, we all got in quite a bit of trouble with our parents over that adventure, but at least they explained to us that the "pot of gold" story was just a myth. All that work for a lie. What a let down.

Lotteries, Casinos, And Schemes

Today many adult lives reflect my life as a eight-year old. I was chasing a rainbow, but today they are chasing the lotteries, the casinos, and the greed-based get-rich-quick strategies that seem to come along in everybody's life. The Bible has something to say about these schemes.

> **Wealth from get-rich-quick schemes quickly disappears; Wealth from hard work grows.**
>
> **— Proverbs 13:11 (NLT)**

God created you for outrageous wealth, but it won't come from rainbows, lotteries, casinos, or schemes. It comes from power — the power God gives you to get wealth (Deuteronomy 8:18).

Wealth Is A Blessing

Wealth is a blessing. Solomon said, "The blessing of the Lord makes a person rich, and he adds no sorrow to it (Proverbs 10:22 NLT). The word "rich" in the Hebrew language means "an accumulation of steadily growing wealth." It's speaking about material prosperity — yes, it's talking about real hardcore riches; money.

If it's true that the blessing of the Lord brings riches, then our key to wealth is *not* in searching for wealth directly, but in searching for ways to experience the blessing of the Lord. It's the blessing of the Lord that makes a person rich. I don't think anybody really wants to be poor. Everybody has a built-in desire to be wealthy. God put that desire there just like He put other desires into the human soul.

Have you wondered why you can look at two men's lives who have worked thirty years at the same place, are paid basically the same amount of money, yet one ends up wealthy and one ends up with barely enough to get by on? What's the difference? It's really simple. It's not how much money you make that determines whether or not you are wealthy, or will become wealthy. It is the blessing of the Lord and the activating of the power to get wealth that determines your financial destiny.

Some people know the right things to do to become radically wealthy. But *knowing* the right things will not bring you riches. It is *doing* the right things that speeds you up the road to radical riches. Wisdom is the right application of knowledge. When you do the right things; take the right actions, that is called "wisdom." Wisdom says, "Those who love me inherit wealth, for I fill their treasuries" (Proverbs 8:21). In this book I'm going to give you lots of knowledge. But only you can change it to wealth-producing wisdom by applying the knowledge I share with you.

The General Overview

In the first few chapters, I will talk with you about your attitude toward money. On some points I may seem a little harsh, but I have to be sure to tear out any old false foundation that may have been established in your thinking concerning wealth. I need to help you to annihilate covetousness, greed, and the love of money. These things actually deactivate the power to get wealth.

Once we have covered the basic attitudes about money, I will give you a step-by-step plan for accumulating steadily growing wealth. There is a natural progression in the wealth process, so you must not skip over any chapters. Read them all.

"Wows And Whoas"

I have carefully written each chapter to give you at least three "wow's" or three "whoa's." "Wow's" are the points that may be new to you. "Whoa's" are the points where you will see something you've been missing or some principle you may have been violating.

Each chapter will give you at least three revelations; three insights. Look closely and carefully and the Lord will speak to your heart. Quickly write in a notebook every "wow" and every "whoa" you receive.

You'll find as you read this book that it's more about radical obedience than anything else. Radical obedience brings outrageous wealth.

Back in the same year I was chasing that rainbow, a simple man, who was earning barely above the minimum wages, was listening to God. He was a man who loved Jesus Christ and always sought to obey God. One day God spoke to him about buying a small parcel of land out in the middle of nowhere. He didn't understand why, but he obeyed and bought a couple acres of dirt-cheap property. Within a year, he discovered that a new airport was being planned but couldn't go in because his property was right in the middle. Overnight, he became a millionaire when he sold his cheap property to the airport authority.

Radical obedience, even when you don't understand, brings shameless riches.

There are certain practices I will discuss that will attune you to the voice of the Lord. Your job is to listen and obey. That's all.

We first learn to listen to God by listening to His Word, the Bible, then acting upon it. When we start here, soon we'll find, like the simple man who bPought the "worthless" piece of property, that the Holy Spirit will begin to speak to us about specific actions that will bring us into the wealthy place (Psalm 66:12).

There are at least 78 revelations for you in this book. All 78 revelations are activation switches for the power to get wealth. Why don't you get a notebook now and begin to write down all the "wows" and "whoas" you find as you read? Then go a step further. Write out an action plan — what you plan to do about it. What do you plan to do about "wow" number one? What do you plan to do about "whoa" number one? Remember, in each chapter there will be three specific things about which God will speak to you.

Are you ready? Are you prepared to enter into the place of radical riches?

Okay, then, let's get started…

Dave Williams
Lansing, Michigan

"God is not interested in cheating you out of anything. He wants to put you into a position that will catapult you into 'the wealthy place.'"

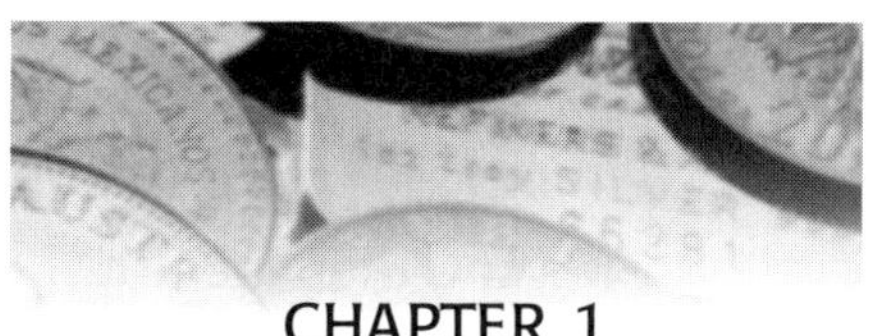

CHAPTER 1

Destined For Outrageous Wealth

Oops!

"OOPS" is what you say when you make an awkward mistake. "OOPS" is what many people are saying these days about their clumsy mistakes with money.

This Book Is About Money

This is a book about money. Actually, it's about wealth — radical wealth. I know there are more important things in life than money. I hear that statement all the time. But it seems that God felt that money was significant enough to discuss it in nearly every book of the Bible, so I guess it must be at least *among* the important things in life.

Money Isn't Important?

We try to tell ourselves, "money isn't important." But it is. Think about it. Lack of money causes misery, worry, concern, anxiety, and even an early death in some cases. Lack of money prevents children from eating properly and ruins their health. Look at the television programs that show the malnourished children. They are diseased, bloated, weak, and die young.

Lack of money causes fights in the home. Nearly sixty percent of all divorces have their roots in money problems. Lack of money prevents us from wearing proper clothing. Every year our church gives away 4000 coats to children who would normally have to walk to school in their tee-shirts in the middle of winter.

Lack of money stops us from getting the education we really want because we can't afford the tuition to the best colleges and universities.

Yes, we try to convince ourselves that money isn't important, but deep down, we all know that to experience a halfway decent life, we need money. I think one of the reasons why God talked so much about money is because He knew people would have some of their biggest problems with money. One in every six verses in the New Testament relates somehow to money.

Good News To The Poor

Jesus announced that He was anointed to preach the gospel to the poor.

> **The Spirit of the Lord *is* upon me, because he hath anointed me to preach the gospel to the poor; he hath sent me to heal the brokenhearted, to preach deliverance to the captives, and recovering of sight to the blind, to set at liberty them that are bruised,**
>
> **— Luke 4:18**

Gospel means "good news." What could possibly be good news to the poor? It had to be that, through Jesus Christ, they wouldn't have to be poor anymore. Poverty was under the curse of the law (Deuteronomy 28:14-68). Jesus redeemed us from the curse of the law (Galatians 3:13). That means that Jesus Christ has paid for our freedom from poverty and lack.

But many of God's children do not know all the marvelous provisions He has made for their deliverance from lack, and for their trek into the world of radical riches.

Jesus said, "Ye shall know the truth, and the truth shall make you free" (John 8:32). You have to ***know*** the truth before it can make you free. In this book, I am going to give you the truth about wealth.

And yes, I am talking about money.

We could talk about the spiritual riches we have inherited as believers. We could talk about the richness of love, joy, and peace that Christ brings into our lives by His Spirit. But in this book, I'm going to talk to you about material wealth. You know, the kind of wealth that so many Christians scorn, revile, and even curse.

Is something in you recoiling right now? Are you thinking, "Oh, another one of those health and wealth preachers is trying to get my money?" If so, think again, and read this book with an open heart. I am one key to your radical wealth right now (2 Chronicles 20:20). I do not say this in arrogance or pride. I just know what God has called me to do, and what God has anointed me to share with you at this very moment.

The Blessing Of Wealth

Many Christians are not enjoying the blessing of wealth. In fact, many reading this book right now have their finances in a mess. If you will take a long, hard look at your financial messes, and if you will be torturously honest, you'll have to admit that each mess can be traced back to a time when you ***didn't*** do something according to God's plan, or when you *did* something *not* according to God's plan.

God clearly instructed us in the way of living prosperously and debt-free, but we have often ignored God's Word. He said, "Give and it shall be given unto you, good measure, pressed down, and shaken together ..." (Luke 6:38). Perhaps we didn't give when we were supposed to, so we didn't receive the wealth when it was scheduled to arrive for us.

A Trip To Hawaii

A lady ran up to me, all excited a few years back. She could hardly breathe she was so ecstatic. "Pastor Dave," she began, "When you were taking pledges for the new youth center, God spoke to my husband and me about giving the money we had saved up for a second honeymoon. We had been saving for the past few years to take a dream trip to Hawaii. Instead, we obeyed God and applied the money toward the new building project. Two weeks later, I received a notice telling me that I had won a luxury trip for two to Hawaii, a vacation package many times better than what we had planned for ourselves."

I rejoiced with this lady and her husband. They gave a few thousand dollars to God's work, thinking they were sacrificing their second honeymoon. God however, is not interested in sacrifice. It is obedience He's looking for. Their sacrifice doesn't look at all like a sacrifice now that they are on the other side of their obedience. They gave to God's work, and got their vacation too. It turns out the trip was actually quadruple the luxury they had planned for themselves. And it was free, as a blessing from the Lord.

God's not interested in cheating you out of anything. He wants to put you into a position that will catapult you into "the wealthy place" (Psalm 66:12).

No matter who you are, or the messes you've made with your money, or how broke you are now, I'm going to show you a step-by-step plan for radical riches. This plan requires you to be serious about getting out of debt and stepping into the prosperity God has promised you (3 John 2). You can't be double-minded or indecisive (James 1:5-8).

Plenty Of Wealth For You

There has always been plenty of wealth around you, and available to you. I will show you how to get more than enough for all your needs, dreams, and desires. Like anything else there are some rules. They are simple rules … but they aren't easy rules.

For example, what would you do if the Lord spoke to your heart about giving $10,000 you didn't even have? What would you do? Would you fluff it off and forget it because, after all, you can't give what you don't have? Think about that for a moment.

I'm going to reveal some astonishing wealth secrets in this book. Yes, I'm going to unveil a magnificent secret to you in the chapters ahead; a secret that others have missed, or overlooked. This secret will launch your life into the realm of radical riches.

It's so simple. God seems pleased to take simple things to confound those who profess to be wise, but are really fools.

Read this book all the way through. Finish it entirely. The principles I will share with you work synergistically to provide a road map to your radical wealth. Don't pick and choose. Read everything. Meditate upon every Scripture I quote for you in this book. You are destined for outrageous wealth. Don't miss your destiny.

Are you willing to be corrected in your attitude concerning money?

> **Anyone willing to be corrected is on the pathway to life. Anyone refusing has lost his chance.**
>
> **— Proverbs 10:17 (TLB)**

Will you accept my instructions?

> **Poverty and shame *shall be to* him that refuseth instruction: but he that regardeth reproof shall be honoured.**
>
> **— Proverbs 13:18**

You bought this book. You have read this far. That tells me that you are willing to get the knowledge you need to come into the place of radical wealth. Knowledge is important. But *power* is more important. God has given you the *power* to get wealth (Deuteronomy 8:18). I'm going to shed some light on how to activate the power that is already available in you (Ephesians 3:20).

What Is Your Attitude Toward Money?

Your attitude about money is critical. If you think money is evil, filthy and deceptive, you will probably never have much. God is not against you having prosperity. He is against you developing covetousness. God is not against you having radical riches. He is against you harboring filthy greed. God is not against you having lots of money. He is against your loving that money. God is not against you having earthly treasures. He simply wants you to place a higher priority on your heavenly treasures.

A Story Of Prosperity

Doug and Terry both had developed a good attitude about money. They never criticized preachers who taught about wealth and prosperity. Instead they listened and learned. Doug and Terry, longtime friends, felt called to attend Bible School, so they left their homes and traveled to a northern state to get their education. It was 1974, right in the heat of a big recession. Money was tight and jobs were scarce.

Students were dropping out of college because they couldn't find jobs to earn the money necessary to pay their way. They were going back home by the droves. It seemed like almost everyone was saying, "There just aren't any jobs out there." It wasn't uncommon to hear words like, "Times are really hard." They seemed especially hard for those students who were depending on the local economy to put them over, instead of depending upon God to put them over.

Doug and Terry knew they were called by God to attend the college, but, like the others, they couldn't find any work. Instead of dropping out and going home, they prayed and asked God what they should do. They reminded the Lord that they were tithers and had always given generously to Him. It wasn't long before a prayer thought came to them. "Trust Me, I will show you exactly what to do."

One day as Doug and Terry were walking down the streets of this large northern city where the college was located, they noticed a "For Sale" sign on an old, run-down home. They felt impressed by the Lord to investigate. So they did, and discovered that hardly anyone was buying property because money was so tight. It was a buyer's market.

With the favor of the Lord, they were able to work out a "no down payment" deal with the owners, and they bought the old house. Every night after school, they would work fixing the old place up, replacing fixtures, painting, and cleaning. Before long, the old house became a gorgeous mansion. With God's favor, they found a buyer who paid them twice as much as they had originally paid for the house.

They had their tuition, plus enough money to buy another old home. They did the same thing over and over. During their four years of college, Doug and Terry earned over $250,000 just fixing up old houses and selling them. They loved doing it and when they graduated, they had no school debts hanging over their heads, and plenty of cash to get started in their ministries. While others believed the faithless words of the world, Doug and Terry believed the faithful Word of God, and as a result, they prospered.

It all has to do with faith and attitude.

You Are Destined For Radical Wealth

As you read this book, your faith will be affected, and your attitude will come into alignment with

God's attitude about money. When you act on what you learn, you will be activating your *power* to get wealth.

There is outrageous wealth available today. Someone recently bought a hotel and paid $30 million in cash. Do you know how much $30 million is? If you stacked up $30 million in thousand dollar bills, the stack would be 30 feet high. Someone I know purchased a private jet aircraft and paid cash for it. Money is never a problem. The problem is attitude and faith. And that's exactly what I want to touch in your life as you read this book about radical riches.

You are destined for colossal riches. You won't need to apologize to anybody for your abundance. You are about to enter into the domain of shameless wealth. But only if you qualify. That decision is yours.

"The 'hundred-fold return' seems to be reserved for those who have the faith to give everything they have at the moment."

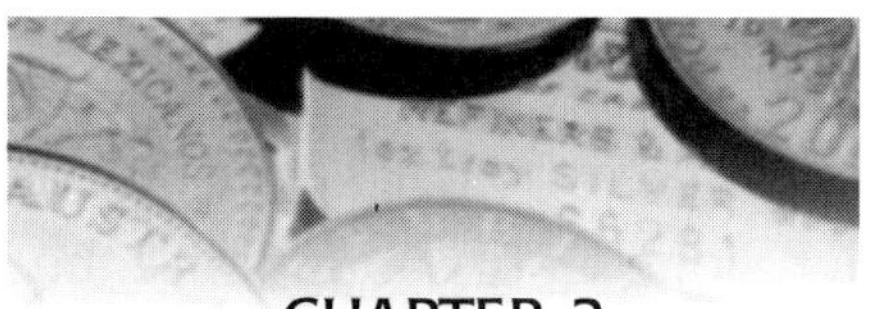

CHAPTER 2

Radical Blessings

I couldn't believe it as I read the prayer request that came into my office.

> "Dear Pastor Williams, Please pray for me. I need some dental work. If God doesn't do something about it, I'm going to use my tithe money to get it done."

That saddened my heart as I read it. It was difficult to even pray for the person, knowing that the message was more of a threat than a prayer request. The person was saying in essence, "I'm going to rob from somebody else in order to provide for my own personal needs." That is sad indeed.

Why do I say that is sad? Is it because I feel sorry for God that He's not going to get His ten percent? No, it's not that at all. It's sad because whenever a person steals from God to meet a personal need or to fill a personal desire, that person slams the door closed to God's unlimited supply and inexhaustible provision. In fact, even the attitude of thinking about robbing from God makes me shudder.

There are people who will never experience God's provision, let alone God's abundance, because they view themselves as having the right to do with "their" money just as they please. Notice, the person wrote, "my tithe money." Nobody who understands the intentions of God will ever refer to the "tithe" as theirs. It is God's tithe, and it is holy.

> **And all the tithe of the land, *whether* of the seed of the land, *or* of the fruit of the tree, *is* the LORD'S: *it is* holy unto the LORD. And if a man will at all redeem *ought* of his tithes, he shall add thereto the fifth *part* thereof. And concerning the tithe of the herd, or of the flock, *even* of whatsoever passeth under the rod, the tenth shall be holy unto the LORD.**
>
> **— Leviticus 27:30-32**

Unlike the person who threatens to withhold "their tithe" if something doesn't happen the way they think it should happen, there is another breed of Christian being raised up today. This new breed is a committed army of God-seekers, who give radically and receive radically, trusting in God as their source of supply.

> **Honour the LORD with thy substance, and with the firstfruits of all thine increase: So shall thy**

> **barns be filled with plenty, and thy presses shall burst out with new wine.**
>
> **— Proverbs 3:9-10**

Take Ellen for example. Some time ago we had an urgent need of $500,000 for new television equipment. We televise on a syndicated network of secular broadcasting stations. Infomercials and even psychic hotlines were vying for our time slots. We needed to stay on the air, but most of our twelve-year old equipment had unexpectedly broken down.

At that very moment, we faced a genuine challenge. The largest employer in our city, General Motors, was on strike. In addition, it was the middle of the summer when typically our church attendance is a little lower and the income is down to some extent. So I simply and honestly told the people of our church about the situation.

Ellen's Miracle

Ellen had just received her paycheck on Friday and hadn't even cashed it yet. She listened to my appeal, and God spoke to her heart about giving her entire check for the television ministry.

"Lord, how can this be?" Ellen wondered. "I don't have any groceries, and many of my payments are due this week." Nonetheless, she obeyed the Lord even if it meant she'd have to go without food for the next two or three weeks. She signed over the entire check and put it in the offering as a "money seed." Nobody knew except God.

> **Give, and it shall be given unto you; good measure, pressed down, and shaken together, and running over, shall men give into your bosom. For with the same measure that ye mete withal it shall be measured to you again.**
>
> **— Luke 6:38**

The next week, Ellen was joyously surprised to learn that someone had anonymously paid all of her bills. Not only that, an entire load of groceries was delivered to her house. Then to top it off, she went to the mailbox the following Thursday and discovered a check made out to her in the amount of $4,170. Needless to say, she didn't have to go without food for two or three weeks like she had originally thought. God supplied a quick harvest on Ellen's seed.

Do you think Ellen would want her little paycheck back now? Of course not. She was moving into a fresh realm of God's abundance. She learned that nothing radical happens until we give in a radical way. Not many people dare to move into this realm of radical giving. Consequently, they never procure the radical, supernatural release of God's provision and abundance into their lives.

How My Son Received His Miracle Harvest

My son was determined that God wanted him to go to Oral Roberts University in Tulsa, Oklahoma. My wife and I had always been radical givers over the years. This particular year, we had made some unusually large faith financial commitments, and now we were staring at perhaps over $18,000 a year in tuition, room and board, books, and lab expenses. How could we do it?

I told my son that he needed to plant a seed of money and to aim that seed for a desired result. He took half of his paycheck and gave it to Oral Roberts University. My wife and I wrote out a seed check of $1,000 for Oral Roberts University. We needed to plant our seed where we needed our harvest. Nobody knew my son gave half his paycheck or that my wife and I gave a seed offering of $1000. Only God knew.

> **But this *I say*, He which soweth sparingly shall reap also sparingly; and he which soweth bountifully shall reap also bountifully.**
>
> **— 2 Corinthians 9:6**

Within just a couple of weeks, a man walked up and said to me, "Dave, while I was stepping into my airplane this afternoon, God spoke to me. He told me to provide David with a full four-year scholarship to Oral Roberts University."

What? Did I hear him correctly? I began to dance, jump, and do cartwheels on the inside. Now, do you think I want that $1,000 back? No way! Do you think my son wants that half of his paycheck back? Not a chance. He is enjoying a top quality education at Oral Roberts University.

A Few Good Questions

Why is it that some people just never seem to be able to advance into God's principles of outrageous provision? Could it be that they have never taken God at His Word? Could it be that some professor of religion has turned them against the principles of God's Word? What is it? Let's find out together as we explore the exciting concept of radical riches.

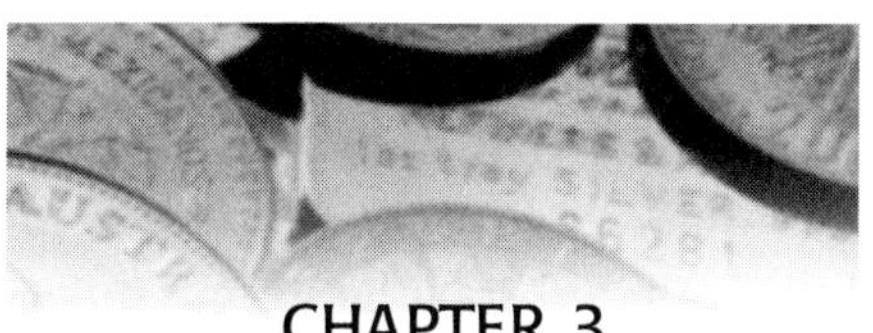

CHAPTER 3

Lord, Send Prosperity Now!

David cried, "Oh Lord, I beseech thee, send prosperity now," (Psalm 118:25b).

Haven't you ever felt like screaming those words yourself? "Oh Lord, send me some prosperity ***now***!"

You need prosperity ***now***. You have bills to pay ***now***. You have children to support ***now***. You have pledges and commitments to pay ***now***. You have needs and desires ***now***.

David did not say, "Oh Lord, send prosperity next year." He cried, "***Now!***"

Two verses later, David said that he would bring his sacrifices to the altar and lay them down. In other words, he was saying, "Lord, I need something from You ***now***. So I'm going to give You what I have ***now***. I'm going to do what I can do ***now***, trusting You to do what only You can do for me." David knew that radical wealth only comes after radical giving. God said, "Prove me ***now***," (Malachi 3:10).

Fear and excuses focus on the future. Faith is always ***now***.

> **Now faith is the substance of things hoped for, the evidence of things not seen.**
>
> **— Hebrews 11:1**

Now is the day of your salvation! *Now* is the day of your deliverance from financial bondage.

Some assert that when we teach people to give in order to receive, it does nothing more than to foster greed. Let me ask you a question. How in the world can you foster greed through giving? It's impossible. Giving is the only known antidote to greed. Greed hoards. Faith gives, and faith is what pleases God.

> **But without faith *it is* impossible to please *him*: for he that cometh to God must believe that he is, and *that* he is a rewarder of them that diligently seek him.**
>
> **— Hebrews 11:6**

The Mammon Principality

Let's look at the major contributor to the lack of prosperity and wealth. It's called idolatry or covetousness, otherwise known as the principality of mammon. Some believe that mammon is just another word for money, but the Jewish people had a deeper insight. They viewed mammon as a demonic personality — a powerful satanic being; a high-ranking demon-like creature in Satan's army.

Keep Yourself From Idols

There is a little book in the Bible called First John. John was a beloved apostle who outlived all the other apostles. He was known as the Aged Apostle of Love. The very last thing he wrote to the precious believers he was addressing in his first epistle was this:

> **Little children, keep yourselves from idols. Amen.**
>
> **— 1 John 5:21**

It's simple. It's direct. It's right to the point. Keep yourselves from idols. I love the way the Living Bible says it, "Dear children, keep away from anything that might take God's place in your hearts. Amen."

There is a powerful principality at work in the world that has drawn away more Christians, shipwrecking their faith, than perhaps any other demonic creature from the forces of hell. Outside of the devil himself, this principality is one of the most powerful of all demonic creatures. He has the power, if allowed, to pull a believer's heart away from God and into idolatry.

This demonic principality is the satanic creature that actually lays careful strategies to lead God's people into idolatry. He stubbornly prevents increase, multiplication, and abundance from coming to the believer's life. His strategy succeeds only when he can lead them into unrealized, subtle idolatry. This creature steals and blocks many Christians from experiencing the prosperity God wishes for them.

> **Beloved, I wish above all things that thou mayest prosper and be in health, even as thy soul prospereth.**
>
> **— 3 John 1:2**

This creature has a name. The Jewish people called him "Mammon." The Hebrews believed he was the hideous principality over greed, covetousness, the love of money, and the deceitfulness of riches. He's one of the cleverest and subtlest of all the personalities of darkness.

God vs. Mammon

> **No man can serve two masters: for either he will hate the one, and love the other; or else he will hold to the one, and despise the other. Ye cannot serve God and mammon.**
>
> **— Matthew 6:24**

Jesus said you cannot serve God and Mammon. The principality of mammon is persistently, and relentlessly tempting you to make decisions based upon money rather than upon God's Word and the voice of God's Spirit. If your decisions are solely based upon money, then the demonic principality called Mammon is probably controlling you. That's why some people never accomplish much in life. They listen to the god of mammon instead of the God of Heaven.

Some Christians have actually moved out of their God-given assignment in life with the purpose of pursuing wealth. They have come under the delusion of Mammon. He teases them for a season with increased wealth then suddenly springs his hidden trap. Poverty ensues like a flood as if some kind of invisible dam has abruptly broken. It's awful. It comes as one attack after another; one relentless blow after another.

I've seen this time after time. A believer will unknowingly be deceived by the motivation of money. He then enters a never-ending pursuit for more money, always looking for new ways of making ends meet. He becomes dissatisfied in his present position and, without consulting God, he makes a move outside of his assignment in life. He doesn't realize that he has been enticed by the spirit of mammon. Over time his spiritual life deteriorates, his family starts having problems, and "whack!" His world falls apart. This is exactly what happened to the children of Israel over and over again until they would repent, serve God alone, and get back into their God-given assignment and purpose in life.

You can only move into the arena of radical wealth when you refuse to listen to the spirit of mammon and obey only the voice of God.

Radical giving is the starting point to radical wealth.

How I Gave $10,000 I Didn't Have

I was sitting in a meeting with 200 ministers and their wives listening to a presentation on how we could effectively reach the people of Kosovo with the good news of Jesus Christ. It seemed that Muslims were opening up their lives to the gospel after the cruel, genocidal war. Christian teams were going into this war-torn land, rebuilding homes, and reaching children with gospel toys and presentations. These dear people had experienced so much suffering and pain, but now they were expressing a sincere openness to authentic Christian love and concern.

The superintendent of the meeting said he needed $1 million to take some teams into Kosovo to help reach the displaced Muslims. At that moment, God spoke to my heart and said, "Make a faith promise of $10,000."

"What?" I thought. "How can I make a faith promise of $10,000 when I already have a $55,000 faith promise to other missions projects this year?" Nonetheless, based on the impression of God's Spirit to my heart, I wrote a note to the superintendent saying I would give $10,000!

My wife and I have always been radical givers, but now we were making faith promises that amounted to "impossible," at least in the natural.

I had a retirement account (IRA) and another account where we placed some money to complete some parsonage remodeling and other designated projects. I wondered if I'd have to take the money out of those accounts in order to keep my faith promise. But something amazing happened.

I just happened to be talking on the phone with a lady from a charitable foundation, getting some advice and help for my new Strategic Global Missions Ministry.[1] She worked for an energy company, and I noticed a lot of commotion going on in the background. I asked her what was happening. She told me that the company had lowered its dividend, and many people on fixed incomes were selling off their stocks, driving the price of the stock from nearly $50 a share down to $16 a share. That sparked my thoughts, so as soon as we hung up, I started investigating the company.

I discovered the company was valued at $23 a share but was selling for $16 a share. I did a little research and found out the company was financially solid and moving in the right direction. So I moved some money within my retirement account and bought a few thousand shares. Then I moved some money from within our parsonage account and bought a couple thousand more shares. I never took any cash out of these accounts. I purchased the stock right within these "storehouse" accounts.

What happened next was a miracle. In fact, it was a miracle that I just happened to be on the phone with the lady as the stock was dropping. Within one month, I had earned over $10,000 in growth and dividends, more than enough to make my faith promise for the Kosovo project. Not only that, after a few more months, the stock steadily went up bringing an extra $80,000 for me personally. All this happened *after* I had made that radical commitment of $10,000 in obedience to the impression of God's Spirit on my heart.

Again, let me ask you a question. Do you think I want that $10,000 back? Certainly not. It was the catalyst that brought me an additional $80,000 in a few short months. Radical wealth always begins with radical giving. When you don't have it to give, wait for God to speak, and then make a faith promise. After that, do everything you can to pay that faith promise, trusting God to work all the miracles necessary to bring it to pass.

The Cycle Of Wealth

Now here's something really special, too. God put it on my heart to give $10,000. I made the faith promise in writing and gave it to the superintendent of the Kosovo project. I didn't know how God would do it, but I knew I couldn't remove money from my retirement account without severe penalties and grave tax consequences. I didn't want to use the money we had designated for the parsonage. It was up to God to provide. He did provide, and I gave the $10,000. Now, even though God, through a series of circumstances, brought me that $10,000 to give, He still counts it as seed for my next miracle harvest because I planted it. The "seed time and harvest"cycle of wealth continues.

Now, what if I had listened to the voice of Mammon instead of the voice of God? I would have missed out on a $10,000 seed and an additional $80,000 blessing. Mammon says, "You can't give radically. You have bills, payments, and things you want in life. You'll be broke and poor if you give radically." But if I had listened to Mammon, I would have not only missed an opportunity to help many people find Jesus Christ, but I also would have passed up the opportunity for God to bless me financially.

When God impresses you to give in a radical way, it's not because He's trying to cheat you out of something. It's because He is preparing an open door of opportunity for you. He is getting you into a faith position for radical wealth.

The Motivation Of Mammon

Nobody can serve two masters. You cannot serve both God and money. Many try, but it cannot work. Jesus Himself said it. Money issues are more likely to cause a spiritual breakdown than perhaps anything else in life. Mammon says, "Hoard for yourself." God says, "Give, so I can give you a bigger harvest."

Look at the lottery ads on television. Listen to the commercials for the gambling casinos. The spirit of mammon motivates these advertisements. Greed, covetousness, and the love of money are the pernicious weapons of this hideous, evil personality called Mammon. Mammon glorifies and deifies money.

This evil, dark spirit forcefully strikes to induce God's people to step into idolatry which is covetousness. That's right. When covetousness is dominating a person's life, that is idolatry. The first Commandment is "Thou shalt have no other gods before me."

But Mammon, the god of covetousness, greed, and the love of money is deceptive, and works hard to convince its victims that they can have both God and money as the master passions of their lives. But it cannot be done.

> **Mortify therefore your members which are upon the earth; fornication, uncleanness, inordinate affection, evil concupiscence, and covetousness, which is idolatry:**
>
> **— Colossians 3:5**

Money has a spiritual significance. How we handle it will largely determine our spiritual success or failure.

> **He that is faithful in that which is least is faithful also in much: and he that is unjust in the least is unjust also in much. If therefore ye have not been faithful in the unrighteous mammon, who will commit to your trust the true *riches*? And if ye have not been faithful in that which is another man's, who shall give you that which is your own? No servant can serve two masters: for either he will hate the one, and love the other; or else he will hold to the one, and despise the other. Ye cannot serve God and mammon.**
>
> **— Luke 16:10-13**

Satan abhors it when preachers talk about money. It is absolutely nauseating and damaging to him when a preacher will have the courage to speak on the subject of money. That is why the devil causes carnal Christians to criticize the preacher when he tries to raise money for a mission, a church program, or an evangelistic outreach. The devil does not care if the president of "Porno Smut Pictures, Inc." is wealthy. He does not care if the whiskey makers of America are wealthy. He does not care if Harry's Bar and Grill franchise is raking in the wealth. But, he sure does not want you to have any kind of wealth. And he doesn't like it when pastors start preaching about prosperity or radical wealth.

So what does Mammon do? He maneuvers you into a corner, hoping to pressure you into making a decision based solely upon money. This is how the mammon creature gets a foothold in the believer's life. If he can deceive you into making a decision independent of God's desires and instead, base your decision upon the "bottom financial line," then he can stop the flow of prosperity, abundance, and radical wealth into your life.

Some preachers are even controlled by Mammon. This evil creature tells them not to preach about money or prosperity. So they obey the spirit of mammon, keeping their people in the dark concerning God's promises of radical wealth.

Ungodly Wealth Will Evaporate

In Matthew 6:19, Jesus warned us to not store up for ourselves treasures upon the earth, but store them up in Heaven where they won't deteriorate. The person who is not laying up treasures in Heaven, but following after the god of mammon, will one day weep as he sees his hard-earned wealth evaporate into thin air.

> **Go to now, *ye* rich men, weep and howl for your miseries that shall come upon *you*. Your riches are corrupted, and your garments are motheaten. Your gold and silver is cankered; and the rust of them shall be a witness against you, and shall eat your flesh as it were fire. Ye have heaped treasure together for the last days.**
>
> **— James 5:1-3**

> **And the fruits that thy soul lusted after are departed from thee, and all things which were dainty and goodly are departed from thee, and thou shalt find them no more at all.**
>
> **— Revelation 18:14**

A person, who says, "I am not going to give ten percent to God because I have other bills to pay," is the person who is worshipping the god of mammon. That's idolatry. The Bible tells us the tithe is the Lord's not ours (Leviticus 27:30-32).

> **Will a man rob God? Yet ye have robbed me. But ye say, Wherein have we robbed thee? In tithes and offerings. Ye *are* cursed with a curse: for ye have robbed me, *even* this whole nation. Bring ye all the tithes into the storehouse, that there may be meat in mine house, and prove me now herewith, saith the LORD of hosts, if I will not open you the windows of heaven, and pour you out a blessing, that *there shall* not *be room* enough *to receive it*. And I will rebuke the**

> **devourer for your sakes, and he shall not destroy the fruits of your ground; neither shall your vine cast her fruit before the time in the field, saith the LORD of hosts. And all nations shall call you blessed: for ye shall be a delightsome land, saith the LORD of hosts.**
>
> **— Malachi 3:8-12**

Notice verse eleven. After commanding His people to give tithes and offerings, the Lord said, "I will rebuke the devourer for your sakes." Many homes and many families know what it means to have the devourer rebuked by God Himself. Others are clueless. They can't understand why money goes as fast as they earn it, and sickness is a regular feature in their home. It's simple. The devourer is *not* rebuked over the family, home, or business that does not practice bringing tithes and offerings to God's storehouse. The windows of Heaven are not open to their homes, their businesses, and their families because they have not obeyed God in money matters.

Every once in a while I will receive a prayer request like this:

> "Please pray that this business deal will go through, so I can start tithing."

Frankly, I won't pray for this one. If you aren't personally tithing (ten percent of your gross income), your business doesn't deserve to prosper. You are a thief and a betrayer, like Judas Iscariot, a disloyal disciple, who was stealing from Jesus' treasury (John 12:4-6). You will never activate the power of radical wealth until you understand and begin to practice radical giving.

It all begins with the tithe. That's where you start. Then it goes on to offerings. From there, it will progress to faith offerings and radical giving. You will begin to see progressive changes in your situation over the months and years *if you don't give up.* People who claim Jesus as their Lord, then go following the spirit of mammon, are in a constant struggle. They don't know why this "prosperity thing" just doesn't work for them. They don't recognize that it is the greed, covetousness, and idolatry that has robbed them of God's best. Maybe that's why John the apostle said, "Little children, keep yourselves from idols." He understood how the idol of mammon has the power to eventually destroy your abundance.

Believers must make decisions based upon the voice of God, not the voice of Mammon.

Mammon Controlled Churches

I have seen entire churches controlled by the spirit of mammon. A pastor will have a vision from God, along with a mandate to achieve something of significance, then a mammon-controlled board or committee will protest and argue over money until eventually the plan of God is frustrated.

I know a church that was experiencing great growth under the leadership of a fiery young pastor. The income went up tremendously as new believers were added to the church. It came time to build a new facility, so the controlling board members lowered the pastor's salary in order to "have more money for the building program." As a result, God blessed the pastor by calling him to another mission, and the church spiraled downward until it was almost bankrupt. That was twelve years ago, and the church has never recovered from the results of that mammon-controlled board's insensitivity to the man of God's needs.

Another church was debt-free and had over $100,000 in the bank, just sitting there. The senior pastor asked the board to raise the pay of the youth pastor who was getting just $60 a week. One deacon said, "We can't afford to raise his pay. Let's just get him a gift certificate for a dinner at a local restaurant and call it a bonus." Did you hear the lie? "We can't afford to raise his pay." They could afford to have quadrupled his pay. Still the dynamic young pastor would have been underpaid for what he was doing. The spirit of mammon won. Eventually it cost them their youth pastor as God moved him on to another state. Many of the young people, sons and daughters of those board members, are no longer serving God. What a price to pay.

The spirit of mammon is a liar. He works for the devil, the father of all lies.

> **Ye are of *your* father the devil, and the lusts of your father ye will do. He was a murderer from the beginning, and abode not in the truth, because there is no truth in him. When he speaketh a lie, he speaketh of his own: for he is a liar, and the father of it.**
>
> **— John 8:44**

One of the biggest lies Mammon tells you is that you cannot afford to tithe or to bring offerings to God. Tithing and giving offerings are not the same. We'll talk more about that in the next chapter.

"When you release what you have to God's storehouse, God will release what He has to your storehouses. Nothing multiplies until you release it to God."

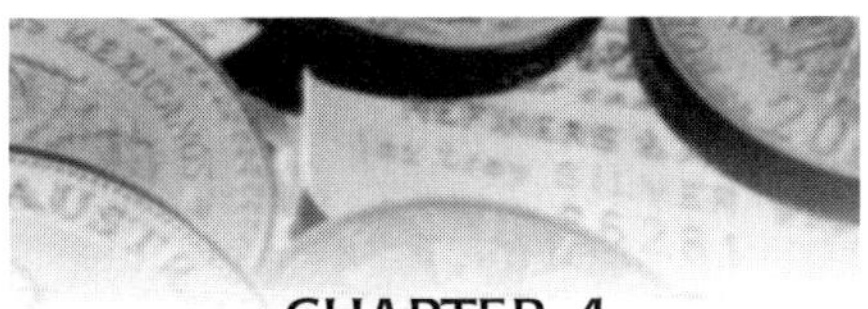

CHAPTER 4

Your Wealth Containers

Let's Talk About Tithing

When we say, "I gave my tithe," we are not exactly accurate. Tithing is not giving. The tithe (ten percent of our gross income) already belongs to the Lord. It's not "my tithe" it is the Lord's. We don't give it because it belongs to God. You can't give something that doesn't belong to you.

> **And all the tithe of the land, *whether* of the seed of the land, *or* of the fruit of the tree, [the tithe] *is* the LORD'S: *it is* holy unto the LORD.**
>
> **— Leviticus 27:30**

The Tithe Is A Test

God gives everybody at least ten percent more than they deserve. That ten percent extra that we all get is a test as to whether we will choose to honor

God, or choose to honor the malignant principality of mammon. Passing or failing this test may well determine your future wealth.

> **Will a man rob God? Yet ye have robbed me. But ye say, Wherein have we robbed thee? In tithes and offerings. Ye *are* cursed with a curse: for ye have robbed me, *even* this whole nation. Bring ye all the tithes into the storehouse, that there may be meat in mine house, and prove me now herewith, saith the LORD of hosts, if I will not open you the windows of heaven, and pour you out a blessing, that *there shall* not *be room* enough *to receive it*. And I will rebuke the devourer for your sakes, and he shall not destroy the fruits of your ground; neither shall your vine cast her fruit before the time in the field, saith the LORD of hosts. And all nations shall call you blessed: for ye shall be a delightsome land, saith the LORD of hosts.**
>
> **— Malachi 3:8-12**

God wants to be proved on this. In verse 10, He says, "Prove me . . .." Tithing opens the windows of Heaven to your life, but offerings (giving beyond the tithe) are what provide you with the container to catch all the blessings God pours through those windows. Remember tithing is not giving. Giving is when you go beyond the tithe.

Jesus, in talking about giving, said, "Whatever measure you use to give — large or small — will be used to measure what is given back to you," (Luke 6:38 TLB). In other words, tithing opens the windows of Heaven, but when you give beyond that in offerings, you will receive a spiritual container proportionate to your offerings. If you give big, you will get a big container to catch the blessings being poured out. If you give a tiny bit, you'll be given a tiny container for your blessings.

Those who are obeying the spirit of mammon will know nothing about the security of God's radical provisions. The foul spirit of mammon will tell you, "If you tithe and give offerings, you're a fool. You need that money. If you give so much, soon you'll be poor and have only crackers to eat."

The spirit of mammon will sometimes entice believers to tithe, but *not* where God has instructed them to. I've heard people say, "I tithe to my son who is using it to pay for his college tuition," or "I'm tithing to my daughter who is having a rough time since she lost her job." If that is the case, you are not tithing at all, and the blessing of prosperity is canceled over your life. God said to bring the tithes and offerings to the "storehouse" which is the temple treasury. Today it would be the church treasury.

A Generous Attitude

If you have a generous attitude, and are liberal in your giving, you'll get a huge spiritual truck to catch your blessings. If you have a stingy attitude in your giving, you may get a teaspoon to catch your blessings. It's all up to you. Even Paul made the statement in the New Testament concerning giving and receiving:

> **But remember this — if you give little, you will get little. A farmer who plants just a few seeds will get only a small crop, but if he plants much, he will reap much.**
>
> **— 2 Corinthians 9:6 (TLB)**

I have proven this over and over again in my own life. Back when I was living under the national poverty level, during my first couple years of ministry, I started speaking words of prosperity and abundance. I was making a grand total of $125 per week. My house payment was $189.10 a month. I had a wife and a child and another one on the way. I never told anybody but God when I had a need. Never.

My wife and I were tithing ($12.50 a week). Then we were giving offerings, too (another $12.50 a week). After taxes and offerings, our take home pay was $75. It took two pay periods, plus some, just to make our house payment. We had to pay our gas bill, phone bill, electric bill, and property taxes on top of that. We also needed gas money for the car and money for groceries.

I remember my wife and I sitting in a missions convention one Sunday night. We didn't have much, but we always were happy and acted like we were the most prosperous people alive. We knew that prosperity was God's will, so we acted like it, even though we weren't yet living in radical wealth. We prayed and made a faith promise of another $2 a week for missions. That was gigantic for us, but our wealth container for blessings and riches just got enlarged. Now we had $73 a week to live on, but we took God at His Word and proved Him, just as He asked us to do.

The more we gave, the more our wealth containers would grow. We didn't even know how we were making it, in the natural. But miracle after miracle seemed to be happening for us. We all stayed in great health. God Himself was rebuking the devourer for our sake, just like He promised. I found an old insurance policy with a cash value of $500, so I cashed it in. After tithing, I put the rest of the money into a mutual fund that brought 27 percent interest and growth that first year. The next year I received 21 percent. Then I switched mutual funds, just before the crash of 1987, and was spared from what would have been a major loss for me. While others were suffering the market's downturn, I was prospering.

Soon we discovered we had enough money to pay off the house, so we did. We now owned this little bungalow free and clear. No more house payments.

We started putting the money away for a down payment on a new house. By making wise investments, it wasn't long until that money grew to $15,000.

By this time our church was planning a massive multi-million dollar building program to expand our facilities. During the grand unveiling of the new project, God spoke to my heart and said, "Give $15,000." That's just what we had saved for a new house. But we gave it, and our wealth containers grew once again. Within a year after the new church was built, God provided us with a new, larger home to meet our needs. Our cars were all paid for. We always buy used cars and pay cash. I've never understood why people will buy new cars that depreciate 15 percent the first day they own them then make payments for three to five years and end up paying $20,000 for a $14,000 car. It doesn't make sense to me. That's why some don't prosper, let alone move into radical wealth. They aren't faithful with money.

By the end of 1987, after the market crashed, my family was doing quite well, so we decided to help some young African students get their ministerial education. That's when we began giving scholarships which eventually grew into our Strategic Global Missions Ministry today. We began to increase the size of our wealth containers once again.

We were learning to operate in radical giving and radical living. Often we would put our personal desires on "hold," so we could give more to missions.

What size containers do you have to receive the blessings from Heaven? Do you even have any wealth containers at all? The size of our wealth containers is determined by the size of our giving above and beyond the tithe.

Is Tithing Optional?

Tithing is not optional. In fact, the Lord said in Leviticus 27 that if someone is tempted to use the tithe for something else, they must replace it with a fifth, or 20 percent interest. In other words, if a person withholds his tithe for any reason, God charges 20 percent a week interest. I suppose that was to inspire people not to use the tithe for anything except bringing it to the storehouse (the temple treasury).

Giving, however, is optional. The tithe belongs to the Lord already. Everyone who loves and obeys God tithes. But the rest is yours to do with as you please. If you use some of what's left to give big, you'll receive big personal wealth containers for the blessings. If you give small, you'll get small wealth containers. If you don't give beyond the tithe, you'll get no wealth containers at all. You'll be on your own to try to catch the blessings the best you can some other way, only to be deeply disappointed.

I am so convinced that God wants us to prove Him in tithing and in giving offerings, that I have told my congregation this: "If you begin tithing and giving offerings, and you are not better off in one year from the time you begin, I'll give you every penny back if you'd like." Nobody — I mean nobody — has ever asked for the money back. Why? Because everyone who has dared to prove God in this financial realm has always been better off over time. Always.

I asked two thousand people for some volunteers one Sunday. I announced, "I want to conduct an experiment with two tithing families. I'd like for you to quit tithing for one year to see what happens. Any volunteers?" Nobody volunteered. They know the starting point to radical wealth is tithing, then making offerings, then going beyond what you think you can do by making radical faith promises … and keeping them.

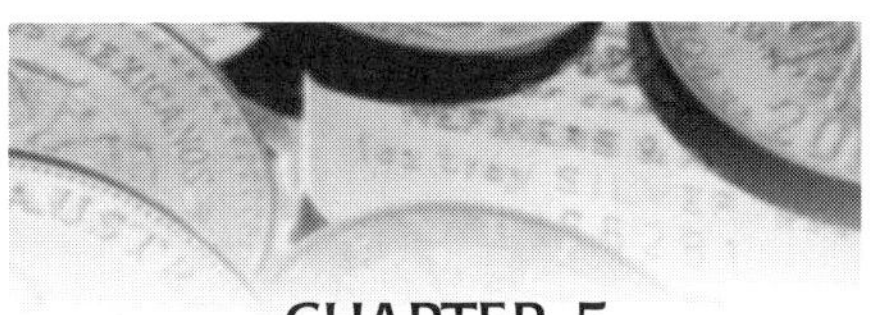

CHAPTER 5

The Malignant Principality Of Mammon

What a great contrast there is between God and Mammon.

The High Cost Of Submitting To Mammon

Ralph Mahoney, founder of World Map Organization, a global missions organization, tells a story about the wealth in a South American country where people make deals with the demon of mammon. Reverend Mahoney tells of a certain town where many people are very wealthy. At a young age, people learn to pledge their souls to a demon — Mammon — in exchange for wealth and riches.[2]

They make a pledge to the demon of mammon, "If you will give me riches, I will give you my soul." This is the power of Mammon to blind. Those who are under Mammon's delusion, typically see everything from a temporal point of view rather than eternal. Mammon prowls around your life, exploring a variety of strategies to push you into considering only the present, never the future. Mammon blinds people to the consequences of loving and living for money. It's sort of like Esau who traded his birthright for a bowl of food.

> **Lest there *be* any fornicator, or profane person, as Esau, who for one morsel of meat sold his birthright. For ye know how that afterward, when he would have inherited the blessing, he was rejected: for he found no place of repentance, though he sought it carefully with tears.**
>
> **— Hebrews 12:16-17**

Invariably each person in that city who made the vow to Mammon became wealthy by that country's standards. In an otherwise poor country, these Mammon devotees would drive their luxury cars, wear their gold chains, and arrogantly smile as they drove down the road, looking down upon those who had not made the wealth pledge to their god. This seemed wonderful for teenagers and those in their early twenties, but they were oblivious — blinded by Mammon — to what pitiful horrors lie just ahead.

Reverend Mahoney saw something dreadful and repulsive happen to every individual who made the soul-pact with Mammon. During mid-life, between the ages of 40 and 45, every one of them, without exception, would swell up in horrible pain. As their bodies bloated, they would start screaming and begging, "No, no! Please give me a little more time." They would plead for their lives. They begged Mammon not to take them now. Judging by their pitiful screams, the pain was excruciating. They shrieked in terror. It was worse than a Hollywood horror movie. These victims of Mammon, unsuccessfully pleaded with the demon, trying to negotiate for more time. But Mammon is merciless. Their voices faded, then their bodies exploded wide open. Then something gruesome and terrifying would follow. Slimy, disgusting little worms would actually begin crawling out of their dead bodies (see Acts 12:23).

They enjoyed their riches for about twenty years, then Satan, through the god of mammon, came to collect.

Whenever anyone serves Mammon, having no regard for God, the devil is going to come to collect. There is no use asking for more time, he won't negotiate.

God's Amazing Promises

Contrast the character of Mammon with the nature of the God of Heaven. God promises that when you bring tithes and offerings into the storehouse, He will personally stand up to the devourer when he comes to your life and will say, *"No!"* He has promised to stop the wicked thief in his tracks.

A great example of God rebuking the devourer for a faithful tither is found in the story of Alexander Kerr. You may recognize that name from your canning jars. Alexander Kerr was the founder of the Kerr Glass Company.[3]

At the age of fourteen, young Alexander was visiting a Presbyterian church in Philadelphia where a guest speaker by the name of D. L. Moody was ministering. Moody explained God's love and plan of salvation through faith in Jesus Christ alone. That night Alexander Kerr gave his life to Jesus and publicly confessed Him as Lord.

Immediately Kerr started reading the Bible and developed a hunger to learn more about God and His ways. He discovered a book by Bishop Allen and read how God had blessed Isaac one hundred-fold after tithing. At that point, young Alexander made a commitment to bring to God at least ten percent of everything God had entrusted to him. He refused to listen to the god of mammon. Many Scriptures concerning giving challenged him, including these:

> **Honour the LORD with thy substance, and with the firstfruits of all thine increase: So shall thy barns be filled with plenty, and thy presses shall burst out with new wine.**
>
> **— Proverbs 3:9-10**

> **And Abram *was* very rich in cattle, in silver, and in gold.**
>
> **— Genesis 13:2**

> **And blessed be the most high God, which hath delivered thine enemies into thy hand. And he gave him tithes of all.**
>
> **— Genesis 14:20**

I'm sure the spirit of mammon suggested that he start next week or when he could better afford it. That's exactly how this unruly spirit operates. But Kerr stood his ground against this demon.

"God said to prove him ***now***, so ***now*** I will begin," he determined.

He tithed. He gave. He saved. Before long he was able to open the Kerr Manufacturing Company, but it took every spare penny he could muster. He built his factory in San Francisco in the early 1900's.

While he was back in the East, something troubling happened. The San Francisco earthquake struck. Practically every penny to Kerr's name was wrapped up in that glass company, except for the investments he had been consistently making into God's Kingdom through tithes and offerings.

The fires raged as gas lines broke and tanks exploded. The city was in flames. Someone wired him saying, "Kerr, you are ruined." But he refused to believe it.

He stood solemnly on God's promise to rebuke the devourer and told everyone, "God will not go back on His promises."

Another telegram arrived: "Your factory is in the heart of the fire and undoubtedly destroyed. The heat is so intense we will be unable to find out anything for some days."

A Promise Only For Tithers

Kerr hung onto the Word of God. He boldly confessed the Scripture, "I will rebuke the devourer for your sakes, and he shall not destroy the fruit of your ground," (Malachi 3:11). Only a believer who has been tithing and giving offerings can have this kind of boldness. The promise is exclusively for generous tithers and givers.

A few days later, a third telegram arrived: "Everything for a mile and a half on all sides of the factory has burned, but your factory is miraculously saved."

Think of it. A two story wooden building surviving those ravaging fires when everything else in a one and a half mile radius was burned to the ground — nothing but ashes. For Kerr, the tither and giver, not even the wooden fence around his building was burned; not one glass jar was lost.

After that, Alexander Kerr wrote two little tracts. One was entitled, *God's Cure For Poverty,* and the other was *God's Loving Money Rule For Your Prosperity.* He printed these at his own expense and over the course of twelve years had freely distributed over five million copies.

He rose from near poverty to radical wealth by believing God would honor His promises. Kerr believed that one of God's highest wishes for His children was that they prosper and be in health even as their souls prosper (3 John 2). Even the negative preachers of his day who criticized the "gospel of prosperity" could not persuade Kerr to change his mind about God's Word and God's promises. Kerr had, as the Scriptures say, proved the Lord.

A young man named Robert Laidlaw started tithing and giving to God at the age of eighteen. He said that if money ever tried to get a grip on his heart, he would simply give more. I do this, too. If ever I feel that spirit of mammon approach me with enticements of greed or covetousness, I sit down and write a big check to some ministry. This is what Laidlaw did, and he became radically wealthy. He became one of the youngest, most successful businessmen in New Zealand.

Do you see the difference between the spirit of mammon and the Spirit of God? Mammon springs a terrible trap on its victims. God blesses, fights for, and opens the door to radical wealth for all who will serve him with gladness of heart in simple obedience.

> **If you will only let me help you, if you will only obey, then I will make you rich! But if you keep on turning your backs and refusing to listen to me, you will be killed by your enemies; I, the Lord, have spoken.**
>
> **— Isaiah 1:19-20 (TLB)**

In the next chapter, I will show you how following Mammon can bring all kinds of filth and wickedness into your life and home.

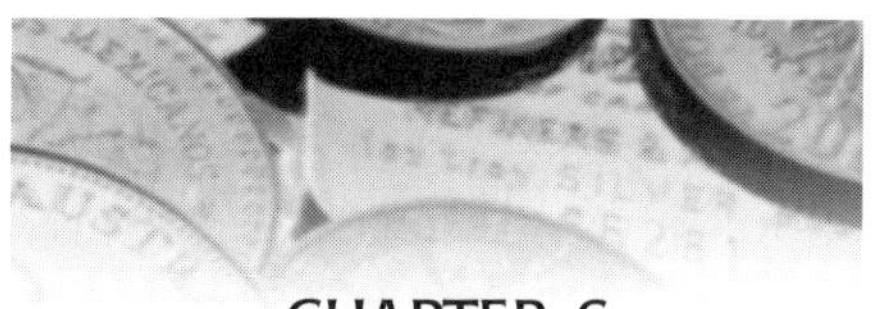

CHAPTER 6

The Tap Root

Now let's talk about the love of money. As a youngster, I used to hear the phrase, "Money is the root of all evil." It wasn't until I read the Bible for myself that I discovered that phrase is not true at all. Paul said it is the *love* of money that is the root of all evil.

> **For the love of money is the root of all evil: which while some coveted after, they have erred from the faith, and pierced themselves through with many sorrows.**
>
> **— 1 Timothy 6:10**

What Is "The Love Of Money?"

What does this mean? One way of looking at it would be to say that wherever there is evil, the love of money is somewhere at the root.

For example, I know a man who has been miserable all his life. He seems to delight in making others miserable too, especially preachers. You see, when he was a young man, God called him to the ministry but he was afraid it wouldn't pay enough money. As a result, he took a job rather than follow the will of God. That is evil. The fact is, if you are faithful to whatever God has called you to, He'll end up paying you more than you could ever get any other way. He'll even promote you to radical wealth if you meet the conditions. This miserable young man who followed the love of money grew old, stubborn, bitter, and poor. Oh, he thinks he has money. But the fact is, money has him. He serves it, but doesn't enjoy a penny of it.

War is often fought over money or things of value, like land, oil, or precious metals. It is the love of money that is at the root of many senseless wars. Robberies, thefts, and sometimes murder have their roots in the love of money.

Joel Kilpatrick toured the war-torn nation of Angola and wrote, "Angola could be one of Africa's richest countries."[4] They are a major oil-producing nation and once enjoyed the status of being the fourth largest diamond exporter in the world. By going after power and wealth, through civil war, the nation has sunk into wretched poverty. The spirit of mammon has come to collect.

It is easy to see the evil wrought by the love of money in these situations.

An Eye-opening Revelation

I had an eye-opening revelation that takes a little different approach and is harmonious with the original languages in which the Bible was written. Let me elaborate.

Have you ever had a mosquito bite? The mosquito sticks his straw-like stinger down into your flesh and begins to suck your blood into his own body. You've probably swatted a mosquito after it had "stung" some poor victim. The fat fellow was full of blood.

Well, the love of money is like that stinger. When the love of money is present in a person's life, it is like a root that burrows deep into a cesspool of evil. It goes down into the sewer of sin where all manner of evil exists and begins to suck all the corrupt sewage of vileness right up into your life. Covetousness, greed, and obeying the spirit of mammon will put a pipeline from your life right down into the gutter of filth.

Are You Having A Struggle?

If you are facing a certain struggle with sin, perhaps it's because you have a root going down into the evil cesspool of depravity, That began as the simple love of money.

Do you think about money all the time? Does money make your decisions for you? Do you get upset when a preacher talks about money? Do you buy lottery tickets, hoping to win the "big one?" If you answered "yes" to any of those questions, then chances are the spirit of mammon is present, and you have a pipeline into the septic tank of sin pumping up all manner of evil into your life.

Whenever a particular sin keeps surfacing in your life, you can almost be certain that the love of money is the invisible cause. You may be having a problem with lust, or temper, or appetite, or some other seemingly unrelated sin. Stop, and ask yourself the question: "Have I put the siphon down into the cesspool of evil because of my covetousness or greed?"

Think of it. The love of money is the root of (or into) all evil.

You may say, "I don't know why this sin keeps surfacing in my life over and over again." My first question to you is: Are you tithing? The love of money prevents people from bringing the tithe to God, and closes up their power to get wealth. My second question: Are you making offerings to the Lord beyond the tithe? Or, are you instead trying every get-rich-quick scheme that comes along? Are you feeling the pressure of money somewhere? Are you moonlighting to make ends meet?

In nearly one hundred percent of the cases I've studied where people had serious sin problems, the love of money was present first. People were prioritizing money matters instead of putting God first. In fact, in one hundred percent of the cases where we discovered moral failure, there was first financial failure, whether it was the failure to tithe and give offerings, or the failure to be honest in business or on taxes. Simply put, moral failure and all kinds of wickedness can actually begin by neglecting God's financial principles.

If only we would learn to love God and seek, as our top priority, His Kingdom, then all the things we ever wanted or dreamed about would be added to us. God Himself would command the blessings into our lives. We wouldn't have to go after them by using scheme after scheme. They would come to us.

> **But seek ye first the kingdom of God, and his righteousness; and all these things shall be added unto you.**
>
> **— Matthew 6:33**

When you go running after earthly treasures by direct pursuit, the spirit of mammon will spring his trap on you. You'll end up with no protection, no wealth, and you'll have just enough to get by in life. God is merciful and will give you the necessities of life, but you'll not experience the radical wealth that the true God-seekers will enjoy. But when you prioritize and pursue God, His Word, and His Kingdom, you will inherit the promise of protection, the guarantee of prosperity, and the wonderful confidence of experiencing the continuous blessings and security that only the faithful and generous tithers and givers can ever know.

> **Every man according as he purposeth in his heart, *so let him give*; not grudgingly, or of necessity: for God loveth a cheerful giver. And God *is* able to make all grace abound toward you; that ye, always having all sufficiency in all *things*, may abound to every good work:**
>
> **— 2 Corinthians 9:7-8**

Paul tells us that to give properly, we must do it purposefully and cheerfully. And what does He promise that God will do in return? Let's look at verse eight in the New Living Translation. It really explains it well:

> **And God will generously provide all you need. Then you will always have everything you need and plenty left over to share with others.**
>
> **— 2 Corinthians 9:8 (NLT)**

Look at that! God will give you everything you need ***and more***! Not only will you have enough for yourself, but also there will be ***plenty*** left over for you to give joyfully to others. Have you ever heard an evangelist pleading for help to feed the starving children in another country? Have you ever wanted to do something significant to help? You can do something great for others if you'll get into the radical wealth system of tithing and giving offerings in a radical way.

Opening The Door To Increase

Now here's something spectacular. The fruit of your righteousness will actually increase as a result of your giving. In other words, everything you do will have a greater impact. I saw this revelation and I began to rejoice as the concept unfolded to me. You will have more influence, increased power, and greater effectiveness when you give radically. See verse 10:

> **Now he that ministereth seed to the sower both minister bread for *your* food, and multiply your seed sown, and increase the fruits of your righteousness;**
>
> **— 2 Corinthians 9:10**

When I studied this verse, I suddenly realized that even when I have a struggle with a sin, habit, or emotional problem, I can actually get help in overcoming it by giving. Hoarding puts the siphon of my life into the cesspool of evil. Giving conquers the love of money and multiplies the fruits of my righteousness. God not only gives me the seed to sow, but when I sow it, He increases the fruits of my righteousness.

Someone will probably want to jump on me right now and say that we are only righteous by our faith in the Blood of Jesus. That is true. We have a right standing with God only through our faith in Jesus. But this Scripture is not talking about imputed righteousness. This Scripture is referring to "your righteousness." The right things you do will accelerate in fruit, productivity, or effectiveness. Think of it. If you are a preacher who is generous in giving, the fruit of your right preaching will be increased. If you are a businessperson, when you are generous in your giving, the effectiveness of the right things you do in your business will be amplified or increased. Now that's a deal.

You Cannot Buy The Blessings

Some will say, "Oh, you're teaching that you can buy God's blessings." Come on now! Let's get serious. You can't buy the blessings of God, but through obedient giving, you can get the blessings of God to chase you and overtake you. You won't have to run for blessings because they will be running to you.

> **And all these blessings shall come on thee, and overtake thee, if thou shalt hearken unto the voice of the LORD thy God.**
>
> **— Deuteronomy 28:2**

Money Seeds

When you plant seeds of money, God will not only multiply your seeds that are sown, He will multiply the fruits of your righteousness. And don't let anyone deceive you. Paul is talking about money in the eighth and ninth chapters of 2 Corinthians.

Do you want to know something interesting? I get prayer requests every week. Seventy percent of them relate to financial problems. Yet not once have I ever received a prayer request from the top one hundred ministry donors asking me to pray for their finances. They are prospering because of their generous giving. And many of them were poor when they first started attending Mount Hope Church. They learned, and are now practicing the principles I am teaching you here. Some of them have actually stepped into the arena of radical wealth. One of them had $43 million in sales last year. Twenty years ago, he was wondering how he was going to finish paying for his college education. But he tithed and started giving radically. And he did it consistently. Now he and his family are enjoying radical riches as God's blessings continue to chase them.

Another fellow, just ten years ago had very little. He started on God's financial system of tithing and giving offerings. Last year his tithe alone was over $50,000 from his personal income. He went from near poverty to radical wealth.

Some of the poorest people in our church end up giving the most. It's no wonder that two or three years later, they find themselves financially secure and on their way to radical wealth. God is not a liar. What He has promised, He will bring to pass.

> **God *is* not a man, that he should lie; neither the son of man, that he should repent: hath he said, and shall he not do *it*? or hath he spoken, and shall he not make it good?**
>
> **— Numbers 23:19**

> **That by two immutable things, in which *it was* impossible for God to lie, we might have a strong consolation, who have fled for refuge to lay hold upon the hope set before us:**
>
> **— Hebrews 6:18**

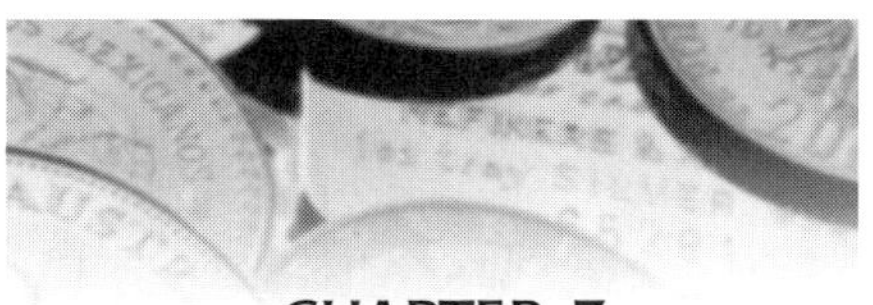

CHAPTER 7

Why The Man Of God Is A Key To Your Radical Wealth

One Saturday afternoon I received an urgent phone call from one of our church elders. He said that it was imperative for him to meet with me. Normally nobody disturbs me on Saturdays because they know it's the day I focus on praying for the Sunday services. So whatever the elder wanted, I knew it had to be important. Surprisingly, I had everything done early that day. I was almost finished studying, praying, and getting my sermon written for the next morning when he called. So I suggested we meet at the airport and take a little flight somewhere.

Duane, the elder who called, loves to fly with me, so I thought it would be a nice treat for us to hop in the plane, get above the clouds, and relax a little. He met me at the hanger, but didn't tell me what was so urgent. I guess he was trying to build up his courage first. We gave the plane a preflight check, got our clearance, and flew off to a little city southwest of Lansing. We enjoyed our time together.

We landed, parked the plane and went into the airport building for a Coke. After we purchased our colas, we went outside to sit on a bench.

"Okay, Duane," I asked, "What is so important that you would call me on a Saturday?"

"Well, Pastor Dave, we are going to do something tomorrow on Father's Day, and I wanted you to know about it. I never want to do anything behind your back or anything that would embarrass you. The elders and deacons met while you were away on a ministry trip, and we decided that we are going to honor you with a love offering on Father's Day."

"I know how you feel about that," Duane continued. "You haven't allowed us to have a Pastor Appreciation Day in more than 16 years, but Pastor Dave, we have heard from God. He has instructed us to take an offering for you tomorrow."

I couldn't believe my ears. I had never allowed any kind of pastor appreciation offering. I've always tried to keep our people focused on Jesus, not me. So my initial response was simply, "No way, Duane."

I Was Cheating My Flock

"But Pastor Dave," Duane reasoned, "You've served for twenty years and the people love you. You've helped many of them to step up from a miserable life to a joyous life in Christ. You are cheating them if you don't allow them to bless you."

When he said, "you are cheating them," it seemed that the Holy Spirit roared in my heart with a force like I hadn't experienced in a long time.

"You *are* cheating them."

I couldn't believe it, but it was true. It hit me like an asteroid. I had been cheating my flock out of many blessings by not allowing them to bless me in a visible, substantial way. I felt so foolish and ashamed.

The Holy Spirit began to show me how important it is for people to show their appreciation for the man of God in a tangible way. A slap on the back or a compliment is one thing, but unless there is something tangible attached to it, it can be meaningless and insincere. God showed me that people's wealth depends upon a proper relationship with their spiritual leader. Let me explain.

Opening The Door For Radical Miracles

When Elijah needed food, God commanded a widow woman to sustain him (1 Kings 17). When she released her meager substance to the prophet, a miracle happened. While famine raged through the land, and others were dying, this little widow woman was given a supernatural inexhaustible supply. She was miraculously able to feed her son, herself, and the prophet throughout the entire famine. By giving to the prophet first, she opened a door to radical miracles. Just look.

First, she experienced the miracle of never running out of the necessities of life. Second, when her son became sick and died, the power of God working through the prophet raised him back to life. How can you put a price on a child's life? Some say they cannot afford to tithe or to give offerings. But this widow woman experienced the radical riches of resurrection power when she needed it. All this because she took care of the prophet's needs first (1 Kings 17:8-24).

There are people who never do anything for the man who has watched over their souls, prayed for their families, fed them spiritually, and cared for them during the stressful and painful moments of their lives. They have an attitude that says, "We pay him well enough. We shouldn't be expected to do anything more for the pastor. After all, we don't want to make him rich, you know. We don't want him to get proud." This attitude blocks the miracle power to get wealth. What if the widow at Zarephath expressed that type of attitude? She never would have experienced the miracle of the supernatural supply of food, and never would have seen God's resurrection power when her son died.

On the other side of the coin, there are precious members who actually search for ways to bless their pastor. They are doing something that is close to God's heart — something that activates the power to get radical wealth. Every month I get $20 to buy a new tie, and a nice card from somebody who chooses to remain anonymous. I don't know who the thoughtful person is, but I know the door to miracles is opened in his or her life, just as it was for the widow woman who blessed the prophet first.

Another lady, who sees me working long hours, will walk into my office with a hot dinner plate, filled with vegetables, rice and a big T-bone steak. She does this regularly, and, oh, how it blesses me. It's not the cost or quality of the meal that blesses me so much. It's the time I've saved by not having to go out and find some food, especially when I'm heavily involved in a project with a critical deadline. This lady and her family are prospering more and more each year with miracle blessing-after-blessing. They have work while others are being laid off. They have good things happen to them financially, and they've seen great miracles in their children's lives.

Some people treat the man of God like he's nobody special. Listen, dear friend. The man of God is an important key to your radical riches.

After I read 1 Kings 17, the Holy Spirit began to show me how I had, in the past, cheated the people by not allowing them to give to me personally. The precious Spirit of Truth dealt with me as He brought to my attention another illustration of blessing the man of God and how it brings miracles into the giver's life.

Blessing The Man Of God

Let's talk about Elijah's successor, Elisha. The prophet traveled through a certain town regularly on his journeys and faced the weary task of finding a place to stay, eat, study, and pray. It probably became quite a strain on him.

A lady in the town was thinking about the prophet one day, and although she didn't know him very well, she invited him over for dinner. What a treat it was for Elisha. Each time he came through town she would provide him with a terrific meal. Being a thoughtful person, she figured this would ease his burden somewhat. And it did.

Later, she had a discussion with her husband about finding some special way to bless the man of God.

"Honey," she said, "This man is a holy prophet. Let's do something nice for him in a tangible way. We have lots of extra room here. Let's build an apartment onto our home and furnish it for him. That way, whenever he passes through town, he'll have a comfortable place to stay. He can pray here, study and get some rest too."

Some people are always thinking of ways to bless the man of God in some practical, tangible, meaningful way.

They built the apartment for Elisha. And oh, how he loved it. He deeply appreciated the kindness of this woman and her husband. One day, he wanted to do something nice for the woman and her husband, so he asked what she would really like. She told him she wanted nothing, that she was perfectly content. So Elisha started doing a little research about the lady.

A Miracle Harvest

While his assistant was digging around for information, he learned that the woman had been unable to have children. She always wanted to have a child but for some reason or another was unable to conceive. So Elisha marched downstairs and told the lady, "Next year about this time, you shall have a son!" The following year she had a baby boy, just as Elisha had prophesied. Talk about radical wealth. She was blessed because she thought enough of God's man to bless him.

But the story doesn't end there. One day her son developed a persistent headache and a fever. You can imagine the anguish of his mother. Then it happened — her worst nightmare. The boy stopped breathing and died. But the door to miracles was open to her family because of the way they had taken care of the prophet of God. Elisha laid himself over the boy's lifeless, cold body and commanded the breath of life to re-enter him. After a little while, the boy's cold flesh became warm, he sneezed, and woke up from death.

That's radical wealth. Helping the man of God was a small price for her to pay for having the supernatural power of God available when she needed it (2 Kings 4:8-37).

In studying these cases, it almost seems that God provides a special miracle-like benefit to the children of parents who honor the man of God. I never saw the connection until doing this particular study, but I've noticed it over the years and wondered why. Now I know.

Children of those who do not honor the pastor, evangelist, or church officials, seem to fall prey to the enemy. Some can't find jobs, others become undependable, and still others experience tragedy or heartache in one form or another, and some just go into flagrant wickedness and are lost. But the children of those who honor the man of God seem to flow in miracles, and have good things happen in their lives continually. They are vibrant, well balanced, respectful, and enjoy a great relationship with their parents and with God.

Bless Your Pastor In A Tangible Way

When I read these passages in 1 Kings 17 and 2 Kings 4 I began to understand how important it is for church members to do something tangible for their pastors. These men of God are often taken lightly. Carnal men who somehow get on their deacon boards often jerk them around and try to frustrate their vision. These shepherds are on duty 24 hours a day. They preach and teach and are more committed than most people will ever realize. They are usually good men. I did not say perfect men, but good men.

A precious pastor and soul-winner in Southfield, Michigan has helped lift countless lives from the sting of poverty. One day, the congregation decided to bless their pastor. They made him sit on the platform while people brought heaps of money and laid it at his feet. Before it was over, the pastor was almost buried in cash. Someone said, "All I could see was his head sticking out of the pile."

I'm sure that must have embarrassed this precious brother. But it opened the door to miracles for the people who participated.

Those with jealousy and covetousness will make excuses not to bless the man of God. "He gets a good salary as it is." "Well, we don't want to have another PTL situation on our hands." The list of excuses extends endlessly, but those who really desire to have an open door to radical miracles and radical wealth are the ones who cherish and bless the man of God financially.

The Pastor's Pay Has An Impact On General Church Income

A few years back, I thought I was being a good steward by not allowing the board to raise my pay for two solid years. We were in another building program and had some other important expenses, so I told the board there would be no pastoral salary increase. I did this two years in a row.

Something strange happened. For the two years I did not allow a pastoral pay raise, our church income stagnated. We had been growing in income by 15 to 20 percent each year. But those two years delivered only a two to three percent increase in the church income. During a meeting, one of our precious deacons suggested, "I think the problem with the church income is that we haven't given our pastor so much as a cost of living raise. There's some spiritual connection, I think." So they gave me a 10 percent pay increase. Immediately, the church income went back to growing by 15 to 20 percent. It's almost as if God blesses the church that blesses the pastor.[5]

Your Wealth Is Connected To Your Attitude Toward Anointed Leaders

Your radical wealth is connected with the man of God somehow. After church one Sunday, two ladies were excitedly rejoicing in the foyer about something. I asked them why they were so excited. They said they had heard about my blessing after I had made that $10,000 faith promise to the Kosovo project. "Pastor, we heard about your $80,000 harvest and we are so blessed. We pray every day for God to prosper you. We know that you are the head of this church and when the financial blessings hit the head, they will soon be dripping down to the rest of us!"

I understood what they were saying. I know Jesus Christ is the Head of His worldwide, universal

Church, but the pastor is the head of the local church. When the Old Testaments priests were anointed, oil was poured first over their heads. It then trickled down their bodies, right down to their toes. In the same way, if a pastor believes in and experiences radical wealth, it's only a matter of time before it starts trickling down to the flock.

> **The husbandman that laboureth must be first partaker of the fruits.**
>
> **— 2 Timothy 2:6**

While I was writing a chapter for this book, Cheryl Salem called me. Harry and Cheryl Salem are two of our most precious friends in all the world. Cheryl was Miss America 1980, and Harry served many years as the vice president of Oral Roberts Ministries. Today they minister with their family all around the country. We talked for about forty minutes, when suddenly she began to prophesy. She said that a fresh anointing for wealth and radical riches was upon me. She said, that as I accept it, this anointing would flow down to the rest of the people in my church.

She then quoted Psalm 133:2.

> ***It is* like the precious ointment upon the head, that ran down upon the beard, *even* Aaron's beard: that went down to the skirts of his garments;**
>
> **— Psalms 133:2**

To be frank, I never realized what an important key I was to people's wealth. But exactly two years ago from the time that I am writing this book, Mary Jo and I sat in a car with evangelists Dick and Betty Mills. We had just enjoyed a meal together and were saying good night, when Dick, under a sudden inspiration, began to make a prophecy over my wife and me. He said that in 24 months, God was going to open the floodgates to an anointing of wealth in our lives. He proceeded to say how this "wealth anointing" would flow out from us, into our entire church body and how God would give each believing member the keys to receiving it.

South Africans Grow In Wealth

Neville McDonald, a faith-filled pastor in Constantia, South Africa, proved that by honoring the man of God, people could break the spirit of poverty. He established a church, winning thousands of poor people to Christ. The church grew to several thousand members over the years. I have personally preached in many places and churches in South Africa, but never any place like Good Hope Christian Center, where Neville was pastoring.

In my many missionary trips to South Africa not one church ever received an offering for me, except Neville's church. I couldn't believe they would receive an offering for me. This was a new experience to me. I came to bless their church and didn't expect an honorarium or a love offering from them.

I told Neville, "Please, my dear brother, don't give me an offering. I came to bless you, not to receive a gift from you."

He turned around and pointed his finger at me, and I will never forget his words until the day I leave this earth. "Listen, Dave, many of these people are poor. The only way to get them out of poverty is to teach them to give their way out. You are a great man of God, and you *will* take this offering from our people. If you refuse, you will cheat them out of their own blessing of wealth."

That was enough of a lecture for me. I knew what he said was true, but I was trying to be "spiritual" by not wanting to receive their offering. I wasn't being spiritual. I was being stupid. I was actually setting the stage for keeping many of those precious people in poverty. Needless to say, I took the offering and thanked them from my heart as I prayed a miracle blessing over their lives.

Because the people who attend Neville's church have been taught to tithe, give offerings, and to honor the man of God, many of them are prospering and experiencing miracles in their lives.

In fact, one of the ladies from the church was approached one day by a dreaded gangster who was known to never leave a living witness. She knew her rights. In fact, she told God as she was being held at gun point, "Lord, I am a tither and I give offerings, and I have always shown honor to your servants. Therefore, the devourer is rebuked and no harm shall come to me." She started quoting Scriptures and the robber ended up running off waving his gun, but never harming her.

> **The LORD shall cause thine enemies that rise up against thee to be smitten before thy face: they shall come out against thee one way, and flee before thee seven ways.**
>
> **— Deuteronomy 28:7**

Cheating The Man Of God

Those who are constantly trying to figure out ways of cheating the man of God, keeping him poor and humble, or hurting him are the same people who will not have the faith they need in their time of trouble.

> **Touch not mine anointed, and do my prophets no harm.**
>
> **— 1 Chronicles 16:22**

It seems that there are those who always seek to hurt the man of God, with their endless gossip, contention, complaining, and jealousy. Others seek to bless their pastor with kind words, support, prayers, and tangible giving. Like everything else in life, it's a choice.

Always Bless The Man Of God

Pastors should not have to carry the unnecessary burden of personal financial pressures. They shouldn't have to supplement their income by selling Bibles or getting involved in multilevel marketing programs (1 Timothy 5:17, 18). Pastors need to focus on studying God's Word and praying for the people (Acts 6:4).

The Bible teaches us that we honor God by giving (Proverbs 3:9-10). We honor a pastor the same way — by giving, not only to the church, but also to him personally. This opens the door to radical miracles. Even Jesus had certain people who supported him with their substance.

> **And it came to pass afterward, that he went throughout every city and village, preaching and shewing the glad tidings of the kingdom of God: and the twelve *were* with him, And certain women, which had been healed of evil spirits and infirmities, Mary called Magdalene, out of whom went seven devils, And Joanna the wife of Chuza Herod's steward, and Susanna, and many others, which ministered unto him of their substance.**
>
> **— Luke 8:1-3**

A dear friend of mine went to the poverty-stricken people of Detroit to reach them for Christ. He could be pastor anywhere, but he chose to go to the poor. One-by-one, he led thousands to Jesus. In the process he was stabbed several times and almost gave his life trying to reach those people who are so dear to God's heart.

Well, he reached them all right. Not only did he lead them to salvation in Christ, he started teaching them the biblical principles of prosperity and abundance. When you listen to a man of faith, it's going to have an effect. Those people started prospering, just as the Bible declares. Oh yes, there are always critics and opponents to any biblical revelation. But those dear people in my friend's church listened to their pastor instead of the critics.

They tithed. They gave offerings. They honored their pastor with a good salary. But they didn't stop there. One night, after a particularly stressful time in their pastor's life, they decided to have a "Pastor Appreciation Day." They were grateful that their pastor had the courage to teach them the full counsel of God's Word and didn't fool around when it came to teaching them about tithing and prosperity. Many of them had been lifted up from poverty to prosperity because their pastor relentlessly taught them the keys to radical wealth. So they wanted to honor him.

The church gathered a love offering for their pastor. Now think of it. All these so-called "poor" people, the "down-and-outers," took an offering for the man who led them to Christ, prayed for them, and boldly taught them how to break the spirit of poverty. That love offering for their pastor was counted and ended up being a six-digit figure! That's right. Over $100,000 from people who once were known as Detroit's "poor." Imagine that. What a blessing for my pastor friend to be able to take a nice vacation with his wife, buy a new car, and give more money to his favorite missions project.

I don't need to tell you that the people of that church, are happy prosperous people who are on their way to radical wealth. Many of them knew nothing but poverty all their lives ... until the man of God told them the truth about money, tithing, giving and receiving.

The Man Of God Is One Of Your Keys To Radical Riches

You cannot serve two masters. You cannot serve both God and Mammon. Those who are racing toward radical wealth, refuse to give heed to the foul spirit of mammon. They listen only to the voice of God. Well, here from the Bible is the voice of God on how to bless the man of God. Never forget the fact, that he is an important key to your prosperity.

> **Those who are taught the Word of God should help their teachers by paying them. Don't be misled; remember that you can't ignore God and get away with it: a man will always reap just the kind of crop he sows!**
>
> **— Galatians 6:6-7 (TLB)**

> **Pastors who do their work well should be paid well and should be highly appreciated, especially those who work hard at both preaching and teaching. For the Scriptures say, "Never tie up the mouth of an ox when it is treading out the grain—let him eat as he goes along!" And in another place, "Those who work deserve their pay!"[25] In the same way, everyone knows how much good some pastors do, but sometimes their good deeds aren't known until long afterward.**
>
> **— 1 Timothy 5:17-18, 25 (TLB)**

> **Believe in the LORD your God, so shall ye be established; believe his prophets, so shall ye prosper.**
>
> **— 2 Chronicles 20:20b**

Now if you want to honor your pastor, please do it right. Don't let it be a slipshod, spur of the moment, sloppy surprise. I suppose that's better than nothing, but it would be really great if you would take the time to plan out a special day to show your appreciation.

First of all, during the service, before you take an offering, share with the congregation some of your pastor's achievements and accomplishments. Arrange to have a few short testimonies of how his or her ministry has impacted lives. Show a three-minute video of the more tender moments in your pastor's life, if possible. Make sure all the church leadership, deacons, and elders take part in this special tribute.

Someone in leadership should talk about the things you've read about in this chapter. Share with the congregation the principles used in the lives of those two women who blessed Elijah and Elisha, and what the miraculous results were. Assure the people that by honoring God's man, they are honoring God Himself. Make sure the offering is *specifically for the pastor.* If he wants to give it to missions that's his business. If he wants to buy a new car leave that up to him.

You could even enlarge some fun pictures of the pastor and his family and post them around the church building, announcing Pastor Appreciation Day. Receive a good, joyful, offering and really bless the man of God. He is an important key to the health and wealth of the church and its membership. Do it, but do it right.

Dr. LeRoy Thompson, in his excellent book, *Money, Thou Art Loosed,* talks about this important key of honoring the man of God. Here is what he says:

> In every church where I preach, I tell the people to see to it that their pastor and his wife are blessed. When you take care of God's things, He will take

care of yours. But not esteeming the office of the pastor is one thing that has been holding some people back concerning money.

You see, you have to put first things first. When you put God first, He will honor and bless you. In other words, when our church is blessed and your pastor has plenty of money in his pocket (without your being critical or concerned about it), then you are in a position for God to give you your increase.

Folks need to release the mentality that the preacher is supposed to be broke. They learned that through certain denominations, and they have the attitude, 'the preacher doesn't need very much.'

But the truth is, the higher your pastor goes in finances, the higher you can go too. But if you try to hold him back, the Lord is going to see to it that you are held back too! (Actually, you will be holding yourself back because you're not cooperating with God and His Word.)

So if you have ever had a bad attitude toward your pastor — if you have ever held your pastor back financially through your attitude and your lack of giving — you can make a little adjustment in your heart today. You can learn to say, and mean from your heart, 'Father, I don't care how high my pastor rises; in fact, I want him to prosper and be blessed. I don't care what kind of suit or shoes he wears. I don't care what kind of car he drives. Bless him, Lord. As a matter of fact, Lord, from this day forward, I'm going to get in on Your blessings by helping to make sure my pastor is taken care of.'

I would encourage you to order Pastor Thompson's book, *Money, Thou Art Loosed.* You may write to him at: **Ever Increasing Word Ministries, P.O. Box 7, Darrow, Louisiana 70725.**

Also, my book, *The Pastor's Pay* is available to you. In it you will discover some important scriptural, as well as practical principles for compensating your pastor fairly. Ask for it at your favorite Christian bookstore, or you may order it by calling 1-800-888-7284, or by writing to: **The Hope Store, 202 South Creyts Road, Lansing, MI 48917**.

The promise of Philippians 4:19, "But my God shall supply all your need, according to His riches in glory by Christ Jesus," is not merely a general promise to everyone who reads it. This promise of a ***rich supply***, was specifically given to those people who had blessed Paul, the man of God, by giving him more than enough money to achieve the call of God on his life, and for his personal needs. If you don't believe it, read the entire passage in context (Philippians 4:15-19).

Look for ways to bless the anointed man of God. He is a key to your radical wealth.

Zenas and Apollos were planning a missionary trip, being authorized and sent by the Church leadership. Paul endorsed them, and encouraged believers to help them financially. He instructed, "Do everything you can to help Zenas the lawyer and Apollos with their trip. *See that they are given everything they need,"* (Titus 3:13 NLT).

There are two key points I want to emphasize from this Scripture:

1. Do everything you can to help the man of God.
2. See to it that he has everything he needs. When you do this, Paul infers in the next verse that, as a result, ***you*** will become more productive in your own life.

The man of God is a key to your radical wealth.

"When you act on what you learn, you will be activating your power to get wealth."

CHAPTER 8

Getting Violent With The Spirit Of Poverty

The spirit of poverty is an insidious, treacherous demon that often convinces people they can never get ahead in life. This corrupt spirit produces an attitude of poverty in the minds of its victims. You can hear it in their words. "I can't afford it." "God can't bless me with the job I have." "Rich people are all evil." "I'm the wrong color to have wealth." "I have the wrong education to succeed." "Money doesn't grow on trees."

"Money Doesn't Grow On Trees"

While it is true that money does *not* grow on trees, it is the *attitude* behind this statement that reflects the spirit of poverty. Look at the first three words of this phrase and see the impression being made on the mind each time it is spoken. "Money doesn't grow." That's the lie that can condemn a good person to a life of lack instead of a life of abundance.

I know a pastor who never received more than $12,500 a year from his church. The small church was located in a rural, scarcely populated area. They did the best they could based upon the church's income, and tried to bless the pastor in other ways like bringing him vegetables and other "fruits" from their small farms. It wasn't much, but the pastor refused to look to the church as his source, or to allow the spirit of poverty to attach itself to his thinking. He stayed in his God-given assignment, looking only to God as his source. He set a good example by always planting generous money seeds into God's work, and was wise in handling the money that was entrusted to him.

He retired a millionaire.

Money Is A "Seed"

Paul likened money to a seed. When you plant it into God's work and into God's men, it will grow. Money *does* grow. Yet the spirit of poverty prevents people from seeing money as a seed, and keeps them chained to a condition of lack.

The spirit of poverty keeps people blinded to the fact that money is a fruit of your labor and wise investing. But it is more than a fruit. Money is also a seed.

A person with the spirit of poverty may write out a tithe check, but he will think, "There goes another fifty dollars." A person who has been released from the spirit of poverty, and is now exercising the power to get wealth, will be delighted to plant money as a seed, like a farmer, for his future harvest.

Pastor LeRoy Thompson had a powerful revelation at the grocery store one day while shopping. A man in the cashier's line just ahead of him paid for his groceries, looked back at Dr. Thompson with a frustrated look and sadly announced, "Money sure goes, doesn't it?" The pastor responded, "Yeah, money sure goes."[6]

As Pastor Thompson was walking out of the grocery store, the Holy Spirit spoke to him, "Money sure goes, does it? Why don't you start saying, 'Money cometh'?" That's when Pastor Thompson received the revelation of "money cometh." Now Pastor Thompson is teaching Christians everywhere how to get into a position where "money cometh."

It was the spirit of poverty behind the words, "Money sure goes, doesn't it?" So why agree with the devil? Why not agree with God who taught us unmistakably in His Word that money is a blessing from the Lord ... and it comes ... and it grows?

The spirit of poverty today traps many good people. One way this demon works is by giving them the feeling of hopelessness, like they can never prosper or experience any kind of wealth at all. But the devil is a liar (John 8:44). The spirit of poverty makes a person always think someone is trying to take from them. "The preacher is trying to get my money again," says the spirit of poverty.

There is a way to defeat the spirit of poverty and to get on the road to financial recovery and abundance.

First, as we have learned, we must put God first with our money. If we are not putting God first with our money, we are not putting God first ... period. Second, we must learn to make our financial decisions based upon God's Word and the prompting of the Holy Spirit, not the god of mammon, greed, or covetousness. Third, we need to get violent with the spirit of poverty. Let me show you what I mean.

Luke 21 provides what I believe to be a great example of casting out the spirit of poverty.

> **And he looked up, and saw the rich men casting their gifts into the treasury. And he saw also a certain poor widow casting in thither two mites. And he said, Of a truth I say unto you, that this**

> **poor widow hath cast in more than they all: For all these have of their abundance cast in unto the offerings of God: but she of her penury hath cast in all the living that she had.**
>
> **— Luke 21:2-4**

I want to look at this story in a little different light than perhaps you have ever considered. I want to focus on the phrase, "but she, out of her penury [poverty or lack] hath cast in all the living that she had."

Are You Tired Of Never Having Enough?

Here we find a poor little widow coming to the Temple and casting in everything she had! Everything! Others were giving some, but had much left-over for themselves. This women cast in all the money she had to live on. That's why Jesus said she gave more than all the rest.

It's almost as if she came to the end of her rope, finally tired of the poverty spirit that ruled her life, so she got violent and threw everything she had into the offering. It says she cast in all the living she had. The word "cast" is a violent word in the Greek language. It means to throw violently, as if you are fed up with something. I believe she was fed up with her lack, fed up with her poverty, fed up with barely getting by in life. She may have thought, "To cast out this spirit of poverty, I'm going to take a risk and cast in everything I have to my name." And she did.

She became violent with the spirit of poverty and cast that polluted demon out by casting in the best offering she could — everything!

She didn't know how she was going to get her next meal, how she was going to pay the rent, or how she would even survive. But she was wearied and exhausted with her poor life, so she took action. She gave. She gave violently and completely.

Now, we never read about the woman again, but based upon similar incidences in the Bible, we can be certain of a few things. First, she effectively got rid of the spirit of poverty. It was just like the widow woman of Zarephath who gave out of her poverty and stepped up to divine provision and miracle-working power. Second, she moved out of her poverty and into supernatural abundance. That's the pattern throughout God's Word. There's no doubt in my mind about this.

A Contemporary Success Story

I know a man whom I'll call George who was on the verge of bankruptcy. Everything was crashing all around him. The pressure on his young family was almost unbearable. His company downsized and George's job was terminated. With house payments, car payments, tax payments, and family needs, George didn't know what to do. He had been a nominal sort of Christian but not real serious about God, but now he needed help. He had a wife and a child to support.

This bewildered young man stumbled into a church in Colorado one Sunday evening to ask for God's help in overcoming his desperate situation. A missionary happened to be speaking that night, telling about the starving children in India that had been thrown on the garbage dumps outside the cities because their parents couldn't afford to feed or care for them. As the missionary spoke, George's heart was being moved into position for a miracle. He wanted so much to help the missionary save these throwaway children.

He looked at the balance in his checkbook. Sixty Eight dollars — that was all. He had nothing more. He had only $68 left to his name, and hundreds of thousands of dollars of debt and bills screaming to be paid.

George decided to get violent with the spirit of poverty that had descended upon his life. He wrote out one last check for $68 — everything he had — to give to the missionary's ministry to help the children. He took the check to the front of the church and cast it on the altar.

Like a miracle, peace poured into his soul, even though he didn't know what he was going to do about his debts, bills, or even feeding the family. The fear, anguish, worry, and stress all seemed to silently drain right out of George's heart as he cast that check on the altar at the front of the church.

God moved into George's financial affairs when he violently let go of *everything*.

The next week George received a phone call from a company in trouble. They had just fired their corporate head for taking the company into a financial mess. They invited George to become the new head of the company. This was a miracle in itself, but there was more.

George immediately began an inventory and started the process of pouring over the financial records of the company. It was worse than he had expected. He found the company to be two million dollars in the "red," so he told the officers and governing board of the corporation that they had to give something to God. They took one of their branch offices, sold it, and gave all the equipment to missionaries. Now he was getting God involved in the company.

Within just a few years, the corporation was in the black. Over the next ten years, they prospered so much they were able to contribute over $20 million to missions work around the world. George and his family were out of debt and living in radical wealth.

It all started with a check for $68.

The question is, would all this have happened if George hadn't first gotten violent with the spirit of poverty by violently and radically giving to God's work? I don't think it would have.

Money Is A Terrible Master

I tell you all this to save you the piercing pain of a miserable life into which I've seen so many others fall. Never allow money to be your boss. Money is a great servant, but it is a terrible master. Jesus is a wonderful master.

If you desire radical wealth in the days and years ahead, then right now, deal ruthlessly with the spirit of mammon and the spirit of poverty. When David cried, "Oh Lord, send prosperity now!" he did something. He brought his sacrifices (gifts) to the altar.

That's a great plan. Sometime during your church service, at an appropriate time (don't interrupt an altar call or the pastor's preaching) walk right up to the altar and throw your money down violently. Cast in the money you were going to use at the restaurant after church. Cast in the money you were going to use to go to the ball game. It may seem like a sacrifice, but a year from now, you will see it was no sacrifice at all. You'll discover it was a step toward the miracle that opened the door to your radical wealth.

The spirit of poverty makes people underachievers.

The spirit of poverty makes people focus on the cares of this life.

The spirit of poverty entices people to buy lottery tickets and to gamble in casinos.

Strangely, a person can have money, and still possess the spirit of poverty. They have money, but not the power of real wealth. A spirit of poverty makes people stingy, and keeps them from enjoying outrageous riches. Don't allow the spirit of poverty or the spirit of mammon to determine your financial future. Let's together make a bold commitment to get violent with the spirit of poverty and to allow God to release and catapult wealth into our homes.

Say out loud:

> *"Spirit of poverty, you have nothing in me. God wishes that I prosper and I shall prosper. Money shall not be my god. I will not bow my knee to the spirit of mammon or the spirit of poverty. In Jesus Name, I plant my best seed on your altar Lord. Now I know as I throw my seed on the altar, my future will be altered. I possess*

the power to get wealth according to Deuteronomy 8:18. I shall tithe, give offerings and make faith promises. I will be regular and consistent in my giving. Therefore I command money to come into my life, my work, and home! Thank you, Jesus! Amen!"

"God wants you to
have financial power,
not financial pressure."

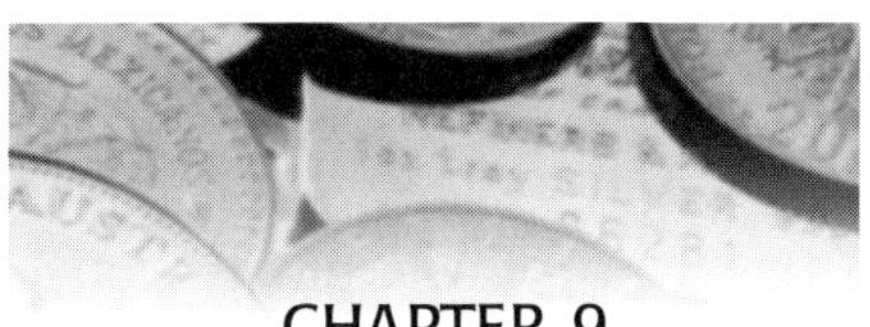

CHAPTER 9

Slaves To "Egypt"

I don't know why it is that some people think you should not talk about money in the church. They believe that money should be a subject off limits to the holy sanctuary. They seem to think that wealth is worldly. But you can be wealthy without being worldly just as easily as you can be worldly without being wealthy. The people that criticize the most are usually those who do the least. Remember, it was Judas Iscariot, the thief and betrayer, who criticized the woman for anointing Jesus with expensive ointment (John 12:4-6).

The Judas Attitude

I've found that it is usually those who possess the same spirit and attitude that Judas exhibited that do all the backbiting and criticizing about money. They think they are cute by calling this message the "gospel of prosperity," or the "hundred-fold heresy." They act as though they are superior because they give, expecting nothing in return. That's not being superior. That's being irresponsible, selfish and unbelieving.

If we believe the promises of God concerning eternal life, why then don't we believe the promises of God concerning wealth? Why do we find modern theologians and pastors changing the meaning of the word "wealth" to mean exclusively spiritual wealth? A promise is a promise. When we give our broken lives to Jesus Christ, He will save us just as He promised. We expect that. Likewise, we ought also to expect a financial harvest when we plant money seeds into God's work.

> **But remember this — if you give little, you will get little. A farmer who plants just a few seeds will get only a small crop, but if he plants much, he will reap much. Yes, God will give you much so that you can give away much, and when we take your gifts to those who need them they will break out into thanksgiving and praise to God for your help.**
>
> **— 2 Corinthians 9:6,11 (TLB)**

Does God Have A Problem With Talking About Money In Church?

God has absolutely no problem with money. And He has no problem with preachers who talk about money from a scriptural perspective. If He was going to gripe about somebody preaching on the subject of money, then He should not have put so much in the Bible about it. But it's there and He expects, and holds accountable, His servants to preach and teach the full counsel of His Word (Acts 20:27).

I heard about a $76 million dollar yacht that takes $70 thousand to fill up with fuel. One family owns the ship. That's right, not a corporation but a family. Think of the wealth that is out there and available to God's people. You could build a nice church for $76 million, wouldn't you say? You could print a lot of Bibles for $76 million, or send thousands of missionaries out to other lands. Most entire Christian denominations invest less than $76 million in world missions in any given year. Yet this $76 million boat is owned by one family.

Do you think God gets pleasure out of seeing the wicked possessing large resources while His own children go without? The Bible teaches us that,

> **The earth *is* the LORD'S, and the fulness thereof; the world, and they that dwell therein.**
>
> **— Psalm 24:1**

All the real estate belongs to God. Everything the devil is using on earth, he is using by illegal means. Whenever a church or gospel ministry is able to purchase property, the devil goes berserk. That's when, through carnal believers, he tears apart churches with strife and division hoping to get the property back that he was possessing. But the devil does not rightfully own any real estate. That's why when you, as a Christian, went to buy some property, you probably had a real struggle along the way in one area or another.

The devil hates to be evicted from the property he is occupying, so he resists.

God wants you to have financial power, not financial pressure.

Most Christians Are Still Operating On "Egypt's" Financial System

The fact is, most Christians are still functioning on the world's economic system rather than on God's wealth system. Egypt became a symbol of bondage for God's people. Today's "Egypt" is the bondage to this world's system of finances. Christians go to people out there in "Egypt," and beg to borrow money for their homes, their cars, their furniture, everything!

But the borrower is servant to the lender.

> **The rich ruleth over the poor, and the borrower is servant to the lender.**
>
> **— Proverbs 22:7**

When a believer borrows money on a consistent basis, through loans, credit cards, and time payment plans, he becomes a slave to the financial system of "Egypt." It's difficult to escape from this wealth-draining system. That's the way the "Egyptians" like it. They want you to believe that borrowing from them is a normal way of life. But it's ***not*** normal for people of faith. God told His people that if they would hearken to His voice, they would be the lenders and not the borrowers.

> **The LORD shall open unto thee his good treasure, the heaven to give the rain unto thy land in his season, and to bless all the work of thine hand: and thou shalt lend unto many nations, and thou shalt not borrow.**
>
> **— Deuteronomy 28:12**

The System Is Leveled Against You

This world's system of finance is leveled against you. It's almost like a conspiracy.

Suppose you earn, on the average, say $50,000 a year. Over forty working years, that's $2,000,000. Yes, you are a millionaire. Now you buy a $200,000 home on a thirty-year loan. Because of interest you will pay $600,000 for your $200,000 home. So "Egypt" took

$400,000 of your two million right there. Can you think of anything that $400,000 could be used for if Egypt hadn't taken it?

That's only if you buy one house and stay there. Most Americans change residences on the average of every seven years. That means that over the course of forty years, most people will have five or six different homes. You may think you have a "low interest loan," but there is something else to consider. Most of the interest you pay on any home loan will be paid in the first seven to ten years. You don't believe me? Just look at your first set of payment coupons. You'll find that if your payment is, let's say $1,000 a month, $900 or more of your loan payment is going toward interest. That's money paid to "Egypt" that you will never be able to spend or invest for yourself or your family. Then over time, as you get the loan balance (principle) down, the interest payments are reduced, until toward the end of your loan, you are paying more on the principle than the interest.

That means if you buy a new house, in the first seven years of your loan, you are paying mostly interest and very little on the principle. The principle is what you owe on the house. The interest is what you pay for the privilege of using the bank or lending institution's money to purchase your house. If you repeat this process every seven years, you are paying the maximum amount of interest five or six times in a forty-year period. That interest is money that goes into the whirling black hole, down into an invisible pit, never to be seen again. At least you'll never see it again.

It is conceivable that out of your $2,000,000 dollars of lifetime earnings, "Egypt" could get not just $400,000 from the interest on just one home, but upwards of $1,000,000 if you borrow on a new home every seven years and then pay only the minimum payment each month. Remember, most of the interest you will pay on a loan is due the first seven to ten years of the loan pay-off period. That means you could be paying $150,000 to $200,000 in interest alone during the first seven years of house payments, depending on the amount borrowed and the current interest rate. That translates into $750,000 to $1,000,000 of money you have earned that *you will never be able to use for God, yourself, or your family.*

"Egypt" Never Seems Satisfied

But "Egypt" is not yet satisfied getting almost half of your earned income over a forty-year stretch. It wants more from you, so it offers to loan you money for a new car. What a great deal! I'll have a new car and pay only $436 a month for five years. The new car had a sticker price of $19,900, but you are paying $26,160 for the car because you borrowed the money. "Egypt" just got another $6,260 from you. Multiply that by the number of times you buy a new car and it will probably come to over $75,000, over a forty year period that you paid in interest alone. What could that $75,000 buy for you if "Egypt" hadn't gotten it from you?

I overhead a fellow say, "That Cadillac was the best investment I ever made. I bought it for $35,000 brand new and sold it for $25,000 two years later." I thought, I'd hate to have this guy managing my money if that was the best investment he had ever made. First, he probably paid $10,000 in interest for his loan over two years. Next, the car dropped $10,000 in value. So he lost $20,000 on his $35,000 "investment." He paid $35,000 and got back $15,000, not $25,000. Does that sound like a good investment to you? Whenever you borrow money to purchase a new car, you are going to lose.

Still "Egypt" is not satisfied yet! It wants to bring you into deeper slavery, so it offers you a wonderful convenience — a credit card. Did you know that most people do not pay off their credit card balance every month? "Egypt" knows this and they like it that way. In fact if your credit card has reached its limit, and you make just the minimum payment on it each month, it will take 20 to 28 years, depending on the interest, to pay it off, even if you never have another charge on it. You've just paid ten to twenty times more for the things you charged than if you had paid cash. Let's say your credit limit is $10,000 and you charged your card to the limit. By making the minimum payment on the credit card each month, it's conceivable that you could end up paying $38,000 to $56,000 for your $10,000 charges. That's $28,000 to $46,000 paid to "Egypt" for the privilege of using their $10,000.

And of course the Internal Revenue Service of "Egypt" wants its share also. So you can figure on at least one third or more of your income going to the various taxes, income tax, property tax, gas tax, sales tax, state tax, local tax, rain tax, sewer tax, highway tax, school tax and so forth.

You earned $2,000,000 during your working years. Let's see how much "Egypt" took and how much it left for you. First, you paid at least $600,000 in taxes, leaving you with $1,400,000. Then you probably gave "Egypt" an additional $750,000 in interest to buy your five homes over the forty years, leaving you with $650,000. Now subtract the interest you will pay for using credit cards over the course of forty years, and you are left with only $622,000. Subtract the car interest you've paid to Egypt over forty years and now you have $547,000 left of your total earnings.

You are earning $50,000 a year, but on "Egypt's" financial system you have only $13,675 a year left for God, groceries, bills, clothing, education, vacations, and general living expenses.

It's no wonder some people say "money sure goes, doesn't it?" It's because they are operating on "Egypt's" financial system of constant borrowing. They are enslaved and losing nearly 75% of the wealth they have earned. Ninety-six percent of the American people are set up for financial failure because they continually have interest working against them (by borrowing) instead of having interest working for them (by investing). Yet God said that His people were supposed to be the lenders (those who profit from interest) not the borrowers (those who suffer from interest).

"Play Now … Pay Until You Die"

But it seems that most folks don't want to delay any gratification. They don't want to wait until they have the cash for a decent car. They want a house that is a stretch beyond their means. And they are sucked right into "Egypt." The jail door slams closed, keeping them in financial bondage all of their lives.

And they wonder why they can't seem to make ends meet.

Think about this. If you make a few commitments *now,* you could be a multimillionaire in the future. Here they are:

Spend Less Than You Earn

Make extra payments on your home loan every month. Get those interest payments down and get the house paid off.

Never borrow for an automobile. Drive a "junker" if you have to. Pay the price now for a wonderful future. The day will come when you will be able to buy *with cash* any car you want.

Never borrow for any depreciating asset like furniture, appliances, stereos, etc.

Develop a plan to get out of debt.

Open an investment account, and put in a set amount each payday. You'll be tempted to skip a week or two, but if you do, you will get into a dangerously costly habit.

Keep your bookwork with Heaven right. Always bring the tithes and your offerings to God's storehouse first. Make sure the first check you write each week (or pay period) is written to God's work. It's a symbol of putting Him first.

If you do these simple things, you could easily have between $5 million and $18 million over the course of the forty years. Wouldn't you rather have $5,000,000 from interest and gains than barely scraping by and throwing all your money into the whirling black abyss of interest payments? Some people will learn this, prosper, and step into radical wealth. Others will pooh-pooh it and keep living in bondage to "Egypt."

Does God Condemn You For Borrowing?

Am I saying God condemns all borrowing? No, of course not. God does not condemn short-term borrowing on appreciating assets. But borrowing for cars, stereos, furniture and other depreciating items is certainly a violation of God's high desire for us, which is to "owe no man anything, but to love one another," (Romans 13:8).

People are bowing down to "Egypt" and wonder why they feel like slaves. They wonder why they never have enough to take a nice vacation or buy a nice wardrobe. Then they accuse their employer of not paying them enough, when the fact is they sold themselves into "Egyptian" slavery by tenaciously clinging to the "debt is normal" attitude. God does not condemn those trapped in "Egypt's" bondage. He shows them a better way.

I always tell people that if they can't live on $500 a week, they'll never be able to live on $5,000 a week. If they aren't faithful over a little, they won't be faithful over much.

Say "No" To Constant Debt

If you want to be an individual who gets radical wealth, you are going to have to determine to say *"No"* to "Egypt." If you need to borrow on an appreciating asset like property or a home, make double payments and determine to pay it off *within seven years.* That's considered a short-term loan.

By living under "Egypt's" rules, you will always have financial pressures.

Will you say something out loud with me right now as you read this? Say this with me:

> *"I was **not** created for poverty. I was **not** created for just enough. I was **not** created to be a slave to Egypt's financial system. I **was** created to walk in God's overflow of blessings. I was created for **wealth**. Right now, I decide to cast off the shackles of Egypt and begin to follow God's financial principles. God has given me the power to get wealth. I will seek first His Kingdom. Things will be added unto me. Money will come into*

my life because I know God's will is for me to prosper. In the Name of Jesus, I declare it and decree it. Amen!"

CHAPTER 10

The Land Of Abundance And Wealth

A bright young man was wondering how some people became so wealthy. He decided to ask a man who appeared to possess great riches.

"Sir," the young man asked, "Will you share with me the secret of your great wealth? How did you become rich?"

"Well, young man," the old fellow replied as he stuck his thumbs under the lapels of his suit, "It happened this way. It was the height of the Great Depression in 1932, and I was down to my last nickel. I took that nickel and bought an apple. I spent all day polishing and shining that apple, and at the end of the day I sold it for a dime. The next day I bought two apples and did the same. I sold them for a dime each. This continued for an entire month, by which time I had saved a total of $26. Then my wife's grandfather died and left us $14,000,000!"

For most of us, wealth won't come that way.

Your journey into radical wealth will be much like the journey of the children of Israel into the Promised Land. God promised them a prosperous land, flowing with milk and honey. Milk and honey symbolizes abundance. But they had to go to it, conquer their enemies, and possess the wealth of this marvelous land.

As you recall, Egypt had enslaved the children of Israel, similar to the way "Egypt" (the world's system) enslaves God's people today. They were poor, broke, and frustrated, so they cried out to God for help. God answered by raising up Moses to deliver them.

The High Price Of Complaining

Moses led them out of Egypt and started marching them toward the land of abundance. But because of their complaining, negativity, and bad attitudes, they were forced to go through the wilderness for many years. God met their needs, but they certainly were not prospering. They needed to be taught many things and have their attitudes changed. They still thought like slaves.

The Land Of "Just Enough"

Finally they arrived at the Jordan River, the gateway to the Promised Land. It was time to cross the river and enter the prosperity God had promised. But some were content to stay where they were, in the "land of just enough." They possessed no motivation to go for the abundant land, even though it was clearly promised to them by God. So they camped at the Jordan, satisfied with just enough. This is like those Christians who are satisfied with "just enough for me."

But the rest of the people, led by a man of faith, Joshua, decided to take the plunge and cross the river. It looked like a real risk, but they wanted more in life than what they had. They wanted all God had promised.

Are You Happy With Your Financial Condition Today?

Are you content being a slave to finances? If not, come out of Egypt!

Are you content with having your needs met, but still living poorly? If not, come out of the wilderness!

Are you content with having just enough? If not, come over to the other side of the river and into the land of abundance! You can expect a battle with the enemy, but the Lord will give you instructions and He will fight for you. You can't lose.

Joshua led the Israelites across the Jordan River and into the Promised Land. Now they needed to start possessing the cities. The first city to conquer was Jericho. God gave them the plan and some clear instructions on how to successfully take the city. In the process, He wanted to teach them an important principle about wealth. God told them how to conquer the city. He told them that the city belonged to them,

> **But all the silver, and gold, and vessels of brass and iron, *are* consecrated unto the LORD: they shall come into the treasury of the LORD.**
>
> **— Joshua 6:19**

God's Lesson On High Finance

God wanted the ***first*** of all the wealth. After they conquered the city by God's prescribed strategy, they destroyed every possession of the enemies of God, except for the wealth. They put it ***all*** into the Lord's treasury, just as He had commanded.

> **And they burnt the city with fire, and all that *was* therein: only the silver, and the gold, and the vessels of brass and of iron, they put into the treasury of the house of the LORD.**
>
> **— Joshua 6:24**

Because they obeyed in giving God the firstfruits of the wealth they had taken, God then started allowing them to share the wealth of the next conquest. God said the spoil and cattle from the next conquest would be theirs to keep.

> **And thou shalt do to Ai and her king as thou didst unto Jericho and her king: only the spoil thereof, and the cattle thereof, shall ye take for a prey unto yourselves:**
>
> **— Joshua 8:2**

The point is, when we trust God by giving to Him in a radical way *first,* He then trusts us and begins releasing into our lives more power for radical riches. The children of Israel went from slavery, to having their needs met, to having enough, to enjoying a prosperous land of their own, with real estate and other wealth of all kinds. As long as they listened to God, and put Him *first,* their wealth was secure.

Years ago my family was planning a trip to Tulsa, Oklahoma. I was going to attend a conference at Oral Roberts University and my family was going to enjoy a little vacation time. I heard about a fine men's clothier in Tulsa that catered to all the great evangelists, so I saved some money to buy a new suit during our visit. I had never paid more than $160 for a suit, so I figured $300 would be plenty. I was excited. I could hardly wait to be fitted for my new suit, just like the television evangelists. I sacrificed and saved hard for nearly four months so I could get that new outfit.

We arrived in Tulsa a couple days before the conference, so we set out to find this wonderful men's clothing store I had heard so much about. We found it, walked in, and were greeted by a friendly man who had the appearance of a young gangster. He showed us around the store and made several suggestions for suits that would look just "awesome" on me. The only problem was, I couldn't find one for less than $900 and most of them were $1,200 and above. They didn't look all that special to me, and besides, I only had $300, so I left the store very disappointed.

My wife and I went to a few other stores in the mall, only to discover that the suits were $500 or $600. It seemed that my dream for a nice new suit started to unravel. We searched for two days to find a decent suit within my budget, but had no success.

One evening while I was attending the conference and my family was enjoying the swimming pool back at the hotel, God spoke to me. I was just sitting there in the audience, minding my own business, when the Lord spoke to my heart, saying, "Give $100 to ORU."

"But, Lord, I saved only $300 for a new suit. I haven't been able to find one for $300, and surely it will be even more difficult with just $200."

"Give $100 to ORU." The Lord seemed unreasonable to me, nonetheless, when I finally determined that it was really the Lord speaking to my heart, I cheerfully put into the offering $100 of my $300 suit money.

The conference ended, and we loaded up our little station wagon and headed back to Michigan. I was blessed by the conference, but disappointed that I didn't get a new suit. But this experience was meant to teach me the important lesson that God never asks for something unless He has something better just ahead for you.

As we were driving near St. Louis, I noticed a sign that read, "Men's Slack Outlet — Next Exit." My wife encouraged me to check it out, so we pulled off the exit and began to search for the outlet store. It was not very visible, but we finally found the pole barn type building on an old access road. What happened next just about sent me down "Hallelujah Lane."

We walked into the store and saw thousands upon thousands of men's suits and sports jackets for sale. These were brand names, but the labels were cut. And the selection of sizes was better than I had ever seen in any men's clothing store. Usually suits will come in sizes like 42, 44, 46, etc. But this outlet store had them in 41, 42, 43, 44 and so on, which was perfect for me because I took one of those in-between sizes. They even had custom tailoring right there in the store and would do it while you waited.

It just happened that they were having a big sale that day, trying to move inventory out, so they could bring in more. Now, listen to this. I walked out of that men's store with not one suit, not two suits, but *five* beautiful, perfect-fitting new suits, complete with the pants hemmed, and it all cost me less than $200!

I couldn't find one nice suit for $300 in Tulsa, but after I gave God $100, He saw to it that I got *five* suits for less than $200. I was just a young preacher at that time, but God was teaching me that obedience is a key to radical blessings. He never asks you to give something beyond your normal tithes and offerings, unless He is planning on blessing you with some kind of miracle supply.

Don't settle for less than God's best. Don't stop short of the "Promised Land."

Now back to the children of Israel. What happened to those who never crossed the Jordan, the ones who were satisfied in the land of "just enough?" Tragically, their enemies conquered them and they lost everything — even what they thought was secure.

God wants you to move ahead in prosperity and never look to anything, or anyone, for security except Him. He wants the ***first*** part of all your increase. And He wants you to obey His gentle nudging concerning your finances.

You may think it's a sacrifice at the time. I know I did when the Lord impressed me to give that $100 from my suit money. But when you get over to the other side, you'll see that it was no sacrifice at all compared to the rich reward He has prepared for you. Your obedience provides an open door for the Lord to bring you into radical wealth.

"God never requires us to give anything without Him planning to give us something far better."

CHAPTER 11

Solomon's Plan For Plenty

> **Honour the LORD with thy substance, and with the firstfruits of all thine increase: So shall thy barns be filled with plenty, and thy presses shall burst out with new wine.**
>
> **— Proverbs 3:9-10**

Everything in life that people could ever want is found in Proverbs chapter three. Read the entire chapter and count the blessings promised to you for gaining wisdom and obeying God.

- Long life
- Peace
- Favor
- Good reputation
- Divine direction
- Good health
- Overflowing wealth

- Happiness
- Riches
- Honor
- Good life
- Pleasure
- Energy
- Safety
- No disaster
- Protection
- Promotion

One Of The Wisest Things You Can Ever Do

In verse 9, we are told one of the wisest things you can ever do. Here it is. Honor the Lord with your substance (that's your "stuff") and with the *firstfruits* of all your increase. The promises that follow are astonishing. After you have given to God *first,* He promises, "So shall thy barns (storehouses) be filled with plenty, and thy presses shall burst out with new wine." Let me explain exactly what this means by defining some of the terms with which you may not be familiar.

Substance. This simply means everything you have. We show honor to God when we understand that He really owns everything. All that we have is on loan from God. Thus, He gets honor when we use all that we have to bless Him. Open your house to a Bible study or fellowship group. Use your car to bring people to church. Give some of your clothes to the poor. In so doing, you are honoring God.

Firstfruits. We also honor God by giving to Him the first of all our income and increase, just as Joshua and the children of Israel did after capturing the first city in the Promised Land. First means ***first***. Someone asks, "Should I tithe on my net or my gross income?" The answer is simple. If you tithe on your net income, you are not tithing to God ***first***. You are giving to the Internal Revenue Service first. God requires a tithe not only on your income (your salary or pay), but on your increase (that which is in your accounts). It's not because He needs it or He's trying to make you miserable. It's just that He's trying to get you to operate on His system of finances so He can bring you into the place of radical wealth.

When I realized this, I started tithing not only on my income as I had always done, but also on my increase. This included all my accounts including my tax-deferred retirement accounts. You may think I'm extreme, but I don't care. You have to be extreme about giving if you want to be extreme about receiving. I discovered that my retirement account had gained $30,000 in value over the course of a few years just because of good investments. So I quickly wrote out a check for the firstfruits.

I tithe on everything. I tithe on any tax return money I get back, even though technically I've already tithed on it because I tithe on my gross income and increase. But I am radically blessed. Blessings seem to chase me. I'm like a blessing magnet. If you want to experience radical riches, you have to get radical about your giving.

Increase. As I've already said, this includes everything that comes to you whether it's income from a job or interest from a bank account. Everything. Now I need to explain something here. If you are running a business, the firstfruits will be on the profit, not the total income. The reason is this: If you have a store, for example, and someone buys a candy bar for $1, you don't tithe on the dollar. The dollar is not the increase. You had to pay fifty cents for that candy bar, so your increase is only fifty cents, thus the tithe would be a nickel.

Your Barns. What is a barn? In the Hebrew language it is "Acam," or storehouses. Notice it is plural. God expects you to have several storehouses. The storehouse is used for heaping up valuable things, whether grain, gold, or other possessions. In modern vernacular it could even be called an "account."

You bring the firstfruits to God's storehouse and He'll see to it that your storehouses are filled and overflowing.

> **The LORD shall command the blessing upon thee in thy storehouses, and in all that thou settest thine hand unto; and he shall bless thee in the land which the LORD thy God giveth thee.**
>
> **— Deuteronomy 28:8**

Filled. Oh, I love this. We are coming into the mighty promise of God to fill our storehouses with plenty. "Filled" is a Hebrew word, "Mala," which has a three-pronged meaning. The first meaning is "to draw." The picture is that God Himself will draw wealth to your storehouses. In other words, He'll make you a wealth magnet. Second is "to flow." Wealth will flow to your storehouses in a steady stream. Third is "to replenish." Whatever you give will be restocked, restored, and you'll have to add more barns, storehouses, or accounts to hold it all.

Plenty. This comes from the Hebrew word "Saba" which means abundance, riches, luxury, affluence, and an inexhaustible supply. This concept is no doubt what the Psalmist had in mind when he wrote "my cup runneth over." In other words, I have much more than I need and my containers — storehouses — are running over.

> **Thou preparest a table before me in the presence of mine enemies: thou anointest my head with oil; my cup runneth over.**
>
> **— Psalm 23:5**

Presses. God tells us in this Proverb that our presses are going to burst forth with new wine. The winepress had two cycles, the upper press and the lower press. The upper press was designed to crush the grapes and the lower press was the part into which the juice drained. The picture Solomon is trying to paint for us is that of supernatural productivity. It means you will get more juice than what the grapes were "rated for."

For many years Fred and Arlene Kortryk have been faithful tithers and givers. Fred told me that, just like the presses get more juice than the grapes are rated for, he and Arlene always get more mileage out of everything they have. For example, they enjoyed the same carpeting in their home for over 32 years now, and still it has no worn spots. They are still using a bedroom suite and living room couch they purchased 41 years ago. They always put more miles on a set of tires than what they are rated for, and get many more. And the list goes on and on. You get the point, I'm sure.

Whatever your life's work, when you honor the Lord with your substance and your firstfruits, He is going to give you supernatural productivity. The picture is magnificent. Your presses are bursting and running over. God is making you a super achiever, a peak performer, a high performance wealth magnet!

You Can Be A Super-Achiever

Joe Gandolfo, who lives and works in Lakeland, Florida, is a great example. He's a money magnet. Practically everyone in sales, especially insurance, has heard about the famous Sicilian boy who made a fortune in the insurance business. He is a legend.[7]

Joe, born in 1936, grew up in the hills of Kentucky with his sister and two brothers. His parents had come to America from Sicily, the "old country." All four children slept in one bed. Then when Joe was 11 years old, tragedy struck. He watched as his mother wasted away with ovarian cancer. She died at the age of 39.

Joe's dad was left to raise the children, but tragedy once again hit the Gandolfo home. Dad suddenly died of a heart attack, leaving all the children orphans. Joe's uncle declined to be guardian to the children, saying in essence, "The heck with those kids." He took all of Joe's dad's belongings and left the children with virtually nothing. The children were separated and Joe never saw his sister or brothers again.

He didn't get any breaks in life. He could have felt sorry for himself and taken on a bitter spirit. Nobody could have faulted him for doing so. But he didn't. Instead Joe found that faith in God would carry him through life. He learned that many of the nation's greatest success stories, men like J.C. Penney, H.J. Heinz, and William Colgate were tithing Christians, so Joe set out to make his mark on this world by serving people, putting God first, and giving generously to the Lord.

My wife and I spent an entire morning with Joe. He has authored several books for salespeople, and has appeared on *The 700 Club* and other television programs to talk about investments. Today he works advising thousands of clients on investments and estate planning.

Joe is a devout Christian who understands and practices the principle of putting God first in everything. Even today, Joe goes to church every morning. He built a beautiful chapel in his office building to pray during the day. Joe is always giving. I recall one time he heard about a poor widow in town who needed a new roof, so he contracted a professional roofer to go over and put a new roof on her house, and he paid for it all. The widow never knew who provided this blessing, so she could only give glory and thanks to God. Joe does this kind of thing all the time.

Today, Joe Gandolfo gives 50% of his income and increase to the Lord in tithes and offerings.

And God has blessed him by making him a super-achiever, a peak performer, a real producer. He's a multi-millionaire who honors God with his firstfruits. Over the years Joe never forgot God's warning in Deuteronomy chapter eight.

> **But thou shalt remember the LORD thy God: for *it is* he that giveth thee power to get wealth, that he may establish his covenant which he sware unto thy fathers, as *it is* this day.**
>
> **— Deuteronomy 8:18**

Joe says, "Many people think they can get by on earth by lying, cheating, stealing, hurting other people, being arrogant or indulging in sexual satisfaction. But God will get their attention ... If you disobey God, you'll run into disaster, financial or otherwise."

When you realize that it is only God who can give you the power to get wealth, it's easy to seek Him first. Without Him, you have no power.

> **Except the LORD build the house, they labour in vain that build it: except the LORD keep the city, the watchman waketh *but* in vain.**
>
> **— Psalm 127:1**

> **. . . for without me ye can do nothing.**
>
> **— John 15:5**

Joe has never forgotten that, and even though he enjoys wealth beyond most people's fondest wishes, he still daily seeks the Lord and His Kingdom as the top priority of his life. And best of all, he is a beautiful, wise, insightful person who is fun to be with. God has shown him favor because his priorities are right.

Here is the key. When you release what you have to God's storehouse, God will release what He has to your storehouses. Let me repeat that. When you release what you have to God's storehouse, God will release what He has to your storehouses. Nothing multiplies until you release it to God.

At Mount Hope Church, we practice honoring the Lord with our firstfruits, even corporately. When we were entering our first multi-million dollar building program, we realized we had no possible hope of doing it ourselves. We had to release what was in our storehouse so God would release what was in His storehouse. So we gave our entire building fund to other ministries. We bought a church building for a pioneer pastor. We provided a down payment for a new building for another church in our city. We gave the rest to the poor through Dr. Mark and Huldah Buntain's ministry. Now we had no building fund. We had given it all away.

But within six months we had $2 million dollars in cash and securities, commitments for another $4 million, and a buyer for our old building. So we started construction on our new 3,000 seat worship center and never had to depend upon the bank for construction loans. We did issue some bonds, but paid them off quickly. Since then, we have had two major building programs, and have always given ***first*** to other ministries before we began. That way, we knew God would be involved in our financial matters and we could trust Him to finance everything He had directed us to do.

We currently have over $20,000,000 in assets and are operating totally debt-free. We have never borrowed for operational expenses, and it takes nearly $200,000 a week to operate this ministry. God has been, and continues to be very faithful.

Each year we give away nearly a third of the entire church income to missions and ministries around the world. We are blessing the nations of the world, and God is pouring His supply of plenty into our storehouses here in Lansing.

I figure Solomon must have really known how to get God involved in his finances. After all, he built that *$87 **billion*** temple totally debt-free.[8] I guess he practiced what he preached in Proverbs 3:9 and 10.

When we give what we have to God's storehouse, God gives what He has to our storehouses.

> **Let them shout for joy, and be glad, that favour my righteous cause: yea, let them say continually, Let the LORD be magnified, which hath pleasure in the prosperity of his servant.**
>
> **— Psalms 35:27**

I will talk more about storehouses in a later chapter when we get down to the practical matters of finance. But let's move on and talk about some more of God's principles for radical wealth.

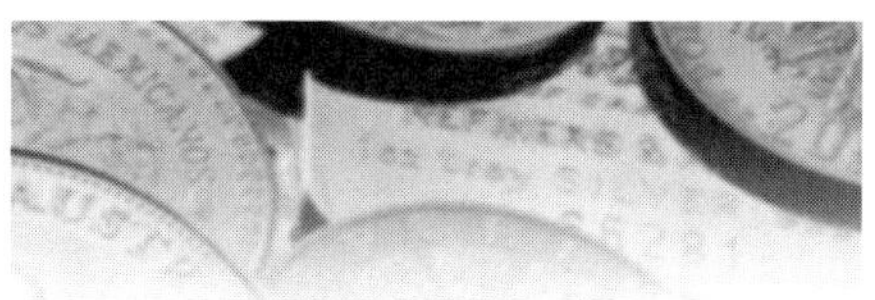

CHAPTER 12

How I Know God Wants You Wealthy

Whenever we are dealing with a subject like wealth, there are many that question its importance. They will say something like "soul-winning is more important" and suggest that we spend our time on something more valuable than mere financial prosperity. They have a point. Yet I think it's a misguided point.

Leading someone to a saving faith in Jesus Christ is certainly more important than guiding them into temporal wealth. Nonetheless, God has spoken volumes in His Word concerning wealth, so we cannot just ignore the subject. I could ask the question, "Why is that preacher talking about joy, when eternal life is more important?" Or "Why does he waste his time talking about sanctification, when getting people saved is more important?" The list could go on indefinitely, but you get the point.

If God plainly announced the fact that He gave us the power to get wealth (Deuteronomy 8:18), then we should take the time to learn about that power.

I'd like to enumerate for you several reasons why I know God wants you to be wealthy. To me, it is very clear. Let's take a look.

1. God wants you wealthy so you can return His tithe (Leviticus 27:30-32; Malachi 3:8-11). We discussed the tithe in a previous chapter so I won't belabor the point here. As I have mentioned previously, God gives everyone ten percent more than they deserve. As a test, He commanded us to return that ten percent to Him by bringing it to His storehouse (the church treasury). When we pass the test, we are ready for the next stage in our journey on the road to radical wealth.

2. God wants you wealthy so you can send missionaries to others who have not heard the gospel.

> **And how shall they preach, except they be sent? as it is written, How beautiful are the feet of them that preach the gospel of peace, and bring glad tidings of good things!**
>
> **— Romans 10:15**

Think of it. If none of God's people had any money, how could we send missionaries and preachers to other lands to share the gospel? If God's will was for His people to always be barely scraping along, there would be nobody to finance His evangelistic causes.

3. God wants you wealthy in order to establish His covenant.

> **But thou shalt remember the LORD thy God: for *it is* he that giveth thee power to get wealth, that he may establish his covenant which he sware unto thy fathers, as *it is* this day.**
>
> **— Deuteronomy 8:18**

It takes money to print Bibles and good gospel literature. It takes money to establish God's wonderful covenant over television and in Bible training centers throughout the world. God gives us the power to get wealth for a very specific, concrete purpose: to establish His covenant. If we refuse to use this power God has graciously given us, our enemies will triumph and, as a result, millions will perish in their sins, never knowing about God's merciful agreement to save them through faith in Jesus Christ.

Our archenemy, the devil, will raise up more zealous cult leaders and false prophets that millions will follow, like sheep being led to the slaughter, if we do not use our wealth to establish God's true covenant. Prosperity is both an Old Covenant and New Covenant privilege and blessing.

4. God wants you to be wealthy so you can provide for your loved ones.

> **But if any provide not for his own, and specially for those of his own house, he hath denied the faith, and is worse than an infidel.**
>
> **— 1 Timothy 5:8**

The Lord, through the Apostle Paul, makes some fairly serious statements here. He says that if you don't take care of your family properly, you are worse than an infidel [unbeliever, sinner, wicked person]. Your family needs food, shelter, transportation, insurance, and other necessities. Your children need an education. If you don't develop the power to get wealth, you are cheating your family.

Sometimes when people realize they have ignored their God-given power to get wealth, they will seek to justify themselves by belittling the prosperity promises. When they realize their families have been robbed of many blessings over the years and they don't want to accept the responsibility for ignoring God's principles of prosperity, they may even begin to lash out at preachers who teach that prosperity is within the divine will of God. You'll find them criticizing the man of God who is trying to lift them from lack and put them on the path to abundance. They will call these ministers "health and wealth" pastors or "name it and claim it" preachers. But it's these very preachers who can put them on the right track to financial wealth.

If you have neglected the power to get wealth and your family has suffered as a consequence, don't condemn yourself. Worse yet, don't condemn the preachers who teach God's plan for prosperity. Instead, just get yourself up, ask God to help you, meditate on the promises of prosperity and start moving forward. You've been moving sideways long enough. Unbelief is always a thief. Start believing, confessing, and receiving the promises of God for your advancement into abundance.

It's not too late. Even if you are past mid-life, or even in your eighties or beyond, it's not too late to start now.

Michael Cardone, a Philadelphia entrepreneur and very committed Christian, developed God's power to get wealth and became radically wealthy. I was present when the superintendent of the Assemblies of God awarded him the "General Superintendent's Medal of Honor" for his generous financing of missions work throughout the world.

Cardone wrote a book entitled, *It's Never Too Late.*

It isn't too late for you. If you have cheated your family over the years because of your laziness, carelessness, or lackadaisical attitude toward finances, you can begin today to recover what has been lost. Ask God to put your financial life on "fast forward," and begin to make up for lost time (Joel 2:25). You can do it by God's mercy and grace. But you have to begin by changing your attitude about wealth and by nurturing a willingness to give everything you have to God if necessary.

5. God wants you to have wealth so the church can pay its spiritual leaders a good salary.

> **Let the elders that rule well be counted worthy of double honour, especially they who labour in the word and doctrine. For the scripture saith, Thou shalt not muzzle the ox that treadeth out the corn. And, The labourer *is* worthy of his reward. Likewise also the good works *of some* are manifest beforehand; and they that are otherwise cannot be hid.**
>
> **— 1 Timothy 5:17, 18, 25**

> **And in the same house remain, eating and drinking such things as they give: for the labourer is worthy of his hire. Go not from house to house.**
>
> **— Luke 10:7**

We already covered this in a previous chapter and in my book, *The Pastor's Pay*, so we will move on.

6. God wants you wealthy so you can pay your taxes and other obligations.

> **They say unto him, Caesar's. Then saith he unto them, Render therefore unto Caesar the things which are Caesar's; and unto God the things that are God's.**
>
> **— Matthew 22:21b**

> **For this cause pay ye tribute also: for they are God's ministers, attending continually upon this very thing.**
>
> **— Romans 13:6**

Taxes may be unfair. But it could be worse! Jesus didn't have a bad attitude about paying taxes. He didn't lead a revolt in the nation over high taxes. He simply told His followers how to get a supernatural supply to pay their taxes.

> **And when they were come to Capernaum, they that received tribute *money* came to Peter, and said, Doth not your master pay tribute? He saith, Yes. And when he was come into the house, Jesus prevented him, saying, What thinkest thou, Simon? of whom do the kings of the earth take custom or tribute? of their own children, or of strangers? Peter saith unto him, Of strangers. Jesus saith unto him, Then are the children free. Notwithstanding, lest we should offend them, go thou to the sea, and cast an hook, and take up the fish that first cometh up; and when thou hast opened his mouth, thou shalt find a piece of money: that take, and give unto them for me and thee.**
>
> **— Matthew 17:24-27**

Nobody should pay more in taxes than they have to. Unless you plan properly, you'll end up paying more in taxes than necessary. There are plenty of tax breaks and tax deferred investments available if you'd only take advantage of them. However unfair taxes may be, God still expects you to pay them. You can never get away with cheating. Not even on your taxes. God sees and rewards your honesty.

When we are living in radical wealth, and keeping our heavenly accounts balanced, God will be glad to show us a supernatural means of paying our taxes.

7. God wants you wealthy so you can give good gifts unto your children.

> **If ye then, being evil, know how to give good gifts unto your children, how much more shall your Father which is in heaven give good things to them that ask him?**
>
> **— Matthew 7:11**

> **Every good gift and every perfect gift is from above, and cometh down from the Father of lights, with whom is no variableness, neither shadow of turning.**
>
> **— James 1:17**

God loves it when earthly parents reflect His nature in their dealings with their children. At the time of this writing my son is attending Oral Roberts University and has discovered what it's like to be a student away from home. It can be lonely, and money can be tight. So, as a dad, I delight in putting together boxes of "goodies" and shipping them to his dorm. He always calls me when a package arrives to thank me.

Last week, I sent him a little letter with $200 tucked into it. He was so surprised and so happy. He called me at my office right away to thank me. He had just given $2 above and beyond his tithes and offerings during a chapel service, and then the letter arrived. He is so grateful he learned the principles of sowing and reaping. It seems that the more he appreciates me, the more I want to do for him. God is that way, too. The more gratitude we express to Him, the more He seems to give to us.

Our Scripture texts for this point show us quite clearly that God is delighted whenever earthly parents have enough wealth to give good things unto their children. When you are poor, or barely getting along, it's impossible to give good things, other than intangibles, to your children. I'm not saying the intangible things are not important. They are the most important. But they won't pay tuition or buy books for your child wanting to attend college.

God is not poor and He doesn't want you to be poor either.

> **The silver *is* mine, and the gold *is* mine, saith the LORD of hosts.**
>
> **— Haggai 2:8**

> **For every beast of the forest *is* mine, *and* the cattle upon a thousand hills.**
>
> **— Psalm 50:10**

> **The earth *is* the LORD'S, and the fulness thereof; the world, and they that dwell therein.**
>
> **— Psalm 24:1**

8. God wants you to be wealthy so you can easily help the poor.

> **When you help the poor you are lending to the Lord — and he pays wonderful interest on your loan!**
>
> **— Proverbs 19:17 (TLB)**

> **He that giveth unto the poor shall not lack: but he that hideth his eyes shall have many a curse.**
>
> **— Proverbs 28:27**

Only people with money can help the poor. The poor have no means to help the poor. Only an employer can help the unemployed. Only the healthy can help the sick. It only makes sense. If God made such an emphasis on helping the poor, it must be that He expects His people to have the means to help them.

It takes money to help the poor. Every year our church gives 4,000 coats to poor children around our city. God's people provide the money to buy the coats. We couldn't do that if we were all poor.

We minister to a thousand children weekly who come to us from the city housing developments. Many of them have no fathers. Their mothers are doing the best they can with what they have, but they don't have much. So we help them week after week with rides, snacks, blankets, and solid gospel ministry. God's people must learn how to tap into the power to get wealth if we want to reach the poor.

God made some radical promises in Isaiah 58 for those who would help the poor, especially those who would help the poor while fasting. He promised to give advancement, success, supply, productivity, and prosperity to those who remember the poor.

Jesus said, "the poor you have with you always," (John 12:8). Notice what he *didn't* say. He didn't say it had to be you!

9. God wants you to be wealthy in order to bring pleasure to His heart.

> **Let them shout for joy, and be glad, that favour my righteous cause: yea, let them say continually, Let the LORD be magnified, which hath pleasure in the prosperity of his servant.**
>
> **— Psalms 35:27**

We were created to bring pleasure to God (Revelation 4:11). That is our purpose in life. Here in Psalm 35 we are told that the Lord has pleasure in the prosperity of His servant. In other words, it brings pleasure to God when His servants prosper. God knows that wealth will cause you to rejoice and that you will use it for His righteous cause.

10. God wants you to be wealthy to reward you for your productiveness and faithfulness over money matters.

> **His lord said unto him, Well done, *thou* good and faithful servant: thou hast been faithful over a few things, I will make thee ruler over many things: enter thou into the joy of thy lord.**
>
> **— Matthew 25:21**

Yes, God is a wonderful Father who rewards us for our faithfulness. There is a story in the Bible about three fellows who were each given a certain amount of money by their master. The two productive men that doubled the money were rewarded. The unproductive man who buried the money to keep it safe, refusing to take a risk, was punished. The master told him that he should have at least put it in the bank to gain some interest. God loves rewarding those who are faithful and productive.

> **But without faith *it is* impossible to please *him*: for he that cometh to God must believe that he**

> **is, and *that* he is a rewarder of them that diligently seek him.**
>
> **— Hebrews 11:6**

11. God wants you to be wealthy so you can leave an inheritance.

> **A good *man* leaveth an inheritance to his children's children: and the wealth of the sinner *is* laid up for the just.**
>
> **— Proverbs 13:22**

It's no picnic when someone you love dies and leaves you with a pile of bills. God said it is the good man that leaves an inheritance that is big enough to even share with his grandchildren.

This is probably a good place to talk about estate planning. Do you have a will and a trust in place? Without both documents, your family can go through a nightmare in probate court when you leave this life. It may take years to settle it all. Make an appointment with a respected estate planner, regardless of your age, and get your house in order. Learn not only the spiritual principles of tapping into the power to get wealth, but discover the practical things necessary to do now so you can leave a nice inheritance to your family, church, and favorite ministries.

12. God wants you to be wealthy in order to work His perfect will in your life.

> **Beloved, I wish above all things that thou mayest prosper and be in health, even as thy soul prospereth.**
>
> **— 3 John 2**

One of God's highest wishes for your life is that you prosper and be in health, just as your soul prospers. God's desire for your life is not only spiritual and intellectual prosperity, but physical and financial prosperity as well. Jesus became poor so that you could become rich.

> **For ye know the grace of our Lord Jesus Christ, that, though he was rich, yet for your sakes he became poor, that ye through his poverty might be rich.**
>
> **— 2 Corinthians 8:9**

I know that some teach this is only talking about spiritual riches. But to say that, you'd have to be consistent and say also that Jesus became poor spiritually. I don't think anyone would be so naive as to think that the Son of God ever accepted any kind of spiritual poverty. He became poor compared to Heaven's normal standards of outrageous opulence, so we can become rich compared to earth's normal standards.

It's interesting to note that everywhere the gospel of Jesus Christ has been received, the standard of living has increased. Some wonder why nations like India are so poor and people are starving, and even throwing away their children. It is easy to understand. They are not in covenant with God. They worship false gods who take them into abject poverty the same way the spirit of mammon takes greedy people into inevitable chaos and final destruction.

Jesus came to give you an abundant life not a life of lack (John 10:10). When Jesus becomes your Shepherd you will lack no beneficial thing (Psalm 23:1).

God cares about your needs, your dreams, and your desires. You will begin to prosper and step onto the road to radical riches when you first begin to believe it is God's will for you.

These twelve reasons demonstrate God's will for you to have wealth.

God not only wants you to survive. He wants you to thrive!

"No matter how much good you do for people in this world, criticism is going to occur, and it will be continual over your lifetime."

CHAPTER 13

Handling The Criticism Of Wealth

Some of you will remember the Christian ministry scandals of the 1980's. The secular press was so intrigued with these disgraceful reports they coined the phrases "Holy Wars" and "Pearly Gate Scandals." The multi-million dollar a year PTL ministry came crashing down amidst sex scandals and allegations of financial mismanagement.

In August of 2000 an article appeared in the EP News that told of the founder and host of an infamous Christian talk show and popular theme park, returning to his childhood church after spending four years in a federal prison. The article said that the preacher addressed the congregation, asking forgiveness if he had caused them any hurt. He then went on to blame his downfall and the ruin of his ministry on the "message of prosperity."

The fact is, it was *not* the message of prosperity that brought down this preacher and his ministry. The message of prosperity is a message from God. How can a God-given biblical concept cause a ministry to collapse? It can't. The truth is, it was *not* the message of prosperity that caused the ministry giant to crumble. It was sin and greed. Greed is not the same as prosperity. In fact, Larry Martz wrote an entire book entitled *The Ministry of Greed.*[9]

The preacher is a good man. I'm happy that he is back in the ministry. I think he took the rap for a whole lot more than he deserved. But because he lost everything, and went through a season of poverty, he sees through a different lens now. If I sincerely believed the message of prosperity had the power to crumble God's work, I would criticize it too.

Critics abound.

A Drop Out Becomes Radically Wealthy

Peter J. Daniels came from a broken home, failed every grade in school, and was a third generation welfare recipient. In 1959 he attended a Billy Graham crusade and gave his life to Jesus Christ. Peter began to study the Bible and developed a remarkable understanding of God's principles of radical wealth. Using only God's biblical principles he became a multi-million dollar land developer and one of Australia's most sought after motivational speakers.

In his book, *How to Be Happy Though Rich,* Peter writes, "Wealth means criticism."[10]

You would think everyone would esteem this man as a hero. He had nothing going for him in a natural sense, yet he went on to become one of the wealthiest men in Australia, simply by applying God's principles for abundance. He learned also that with the increase of wealth comes the increase of unjust, and sometimes cruel, criticism. "For the person of wealth," writes Daniels, "criticism is as certain as death and taxes."

It's strange how some young people think it is quite okay for the rock star or the film star to be outfitted in all types of jewelry, ride in limousines, and live in mansions but as soon as a Christian exhibits any such riches, he is labeled a "rip-off artist," a "Mafia member," or a "money grubber." The wealthy Christian will hear whispers behind his back like, "Why doesn't he give his money to the poor?" You may be giving 95% of your wealth to the church and to the poor, but still people filled with jealousy and envy will criticize you.

Peter J. Daniels at first submitted to his critics' remarks but learned that the more he listened to them the heavier his personal burden was becoming. Finally he accepted the fact that no matter how much good you do for people in this world, criticism is going to occur, and it will be continual over your lifetime.

The Nature Of A Critic

Critics complain the most and do the least.

Critics point out problems but do nothing toward solutions.

Critics see themselves as the judge, jury, and executioner.

Critics seek to dehumanize the one they are speaking abusively about.

Critics think they reinforce their power and ego through attacking others.

Unjust critics are losers.

Wealth Attracts Persecution

St. Mark tells us of an amazing story in the life of our Lord. It's about a wealthy young man who wants eternal life, but is unwilling to give up everything. If you want to follow Jesus, you must be willing to give everything. Let's read the account.

> **And when he was gone forth into the way, there came one running, and kneeled to him, and asked him, Good Master, what shall I do that I may inherit eternal life? And Jesus said unto him, Why callest thou me good? *there is* none good but one, *that is,* God. Thou knowest the commandments, Do not commit adultery, Do not kill, Do not steal, Do not bear false witness, Defraud not, Honour thy father and mother. And he answered and said unto him, Master, all these have I observed from my youth. Then Jesus beholding him loved him, and said unto him, One thing thou lackest: go thy way, sell whatsoever thou hast, and give to the poor, and thou shalt have treasure in heaven: and come, take up the cross, and follow me. And he was sad at that saying, and went away grieved: for he had great possessions.**
>
> **— Mark10:17-22**

The young man lost out on eternal life because he wasn't willing to listen and obey. But that's not all he lost. Let's read on.

> **And Jesus looked round about, and saith unto his disciples, How hardly shall they that have riches enter into the kingdom of God! And the disciples were astonished at his words. But Jesus answereth again, and saith unto them, Children, how hard is it for them that trust in riches to enter into the kingdom of God!**
>
> **— Mark 10:23-24**

Jesus explained that it's difficult for those who have riches to enter the Kingdom of God because God requires access to everything, including their wealth. When a person comes to Christ, rich or poor, he must be willing to relinquish his right to any material possessions, and submit them all to Christ's Lordship. In other words, when a person desires to be saved, he must be willing to give everything he possesses if God requires it. The rich young man was not willing and he became the loser.

Then Jesus went on to explain that it is *not* riches that keep people out of the Kingdom, but trusting in those riches rather than trusting in God. That is what prevents them from entering the Kingdom of God.

Let me ask you a couple of questions. Could you, right now, give all your material possessions for the gospel if God required it? If God spoke to your heart about giving your car, your home, your money or anything else that is important to you, could you do it? Your answers to these questions serve as a good indicator of where your heart is today. If you can walk away from your money and possessions at the command of God, then Jesus, not money, is certainly your Lord. Do you have an attitude of ownership or an attitude of stewardship? Wherever your treasure is, there your heart will be also (Matthew 6:21).

> **It is easier for a camel to go through the eye of a needle, than for a rich man to enter into the kingdom of God. And they were astonished out of measure, saying among themselves, Who then can be saved? And Jesus looking upon them**

saith, With men *it is* impossible, but not with God: for with God all things are possible.

— Mark 10:25-27

Now Jesus makes a statement that has been misused by minimalist corrupters and anti-wealth preachers for many years. They say that riches will keep you out of Heaven and, since it's impossible to get a camel through the eye of a needle, it's impossible to get to Heaven if you are rich. That's *not* what Jesus said.

He said it's hard (not impossible) for a rich man to enter into the Kingdom of God. Of course it's hard because it's hard to give Jesus access to all the riches he's earned over the years. It's easier for a person who has nothing to come to Christ. He's not worried that God is going to ask him for all his money. But for someone with great wealth, it's harder because he has come to depend upon, or trust in that wealth.

Then in verse 27, he assures us that with men it's impossible, *but with God all things are possible.* Yes, it is possible for a rich person to come to Jesus Christ as Savior and Lord.

Another observation I'd like you to see is that Jesus did not say that it is hard for a wealthy person to stay in the Kingdom of God. I've heard preachers that have constantly scorned men and women of wealth, blaming them for everything from inflation, to recession, to a conspiracy, and everything all the way to the most recent war. What nonsense that is! If God made so many promises of prosperity, increase, and abundance to His people, why would he suggest that their wealth would put them on shaky ground in His Kingdom? The answer is simple. He wouldn't, and he didn't.

> **Then Peter began to say unto him, Lo, we have left all, and have followed thee. And Jesus answered and said, Verily I say unto you, There is no man that hath left house, or brethren, or sisters, or father, or mother, or wife, or children, or lands, for my sake, and the gospel's, But he shall receive an hundredfold now in this time, houses, and brethren, and sisters, and mothers, and children, and lands, with persecutions; and in the world to come eternal life.**
>
> **— Mark 10:28-30**

Let's look at the astounding promise that came right from the lips of the Son of God, Deity Incarnate, God Himself in the flesh. He said in a nutshell, "Nobody has given up anything for my sake, and the gospel's, but he shall receive . . .."

He shall receive. God never requires us to give anything without Him planning to give us something far better. When we give, we are supposed to expect to receive. Just like when a farmer plants his seeds, he expects a crop. But what did Jesus say we would receive?

A Hundred Times More

"A hundred fold." That's 100 times more than you gave. If the rich young man had been willing to give Jesus all that he had, he would have become one hundred times richer. He missed the greatest opportunity of his life.

When can we expect to receive from God? In the sweet by and by? When we all get to Heaven? Sometime when we arrive in the heavenly Jerusalem? During the Millennium? No, Jesus said clearly, "Now, in this time." That means while we are still on earth we can fully expect to receive back from God many times more than we ever gave to Him. Because we are trusting in Jesus, instead of trusting in our riches, we will "in the world to come" receive "eternal life." What a phenomenal deal!

But notice two little words Jesus interjected. He said all this wealth will be "with persecutions." Ah, there it is. Criticism. Persecution. When God begins to bless you financially and with real estate, possessions, and true friends, you can expect the critics to raise their voices against you. They envy you.

> **Then Isaac sowed in that land, and received in the same year an hundredfold: and the LORD blessed him. And the man waxed great [rich], and went forward, and grew until he became very great: For he had possession of flocks, and**

> **possession of herds, and great store of servants: and the Philistines envied him.**
>
> **— Genesis 26:12-14**

My First Encounter With The Hundred-fold Return

After my wife and I were married for a couple of weeks, we received a surprise bill for $800 for something to do with our wedding. We had no idea how we were going to pay that bill. I was reading God's Word and stumbled upon Mark 10:30. I got excited and told Mary Jo that we can get a hundred fold return if we'll give to God. We were, of course, already tithing and making offerings, but now we had a serious need. So we searched through the chairs, the couch, car seats and every place we thought maybe we could find some money. We came up with $8. That's it. We couldn't scrape up one penny more.

We gave the $8 to God's work and asked Him to provide a hundred fold return on our investment into His Kingdom based upon Mark 10:30. We prayed together and believed together.

We were excited. But the next day we received a newsletter from one of those anti-prosperity preachers. The lead article was entitled *"The Hundred-fold Heresy!"* I read it and wished I hadn't. It was sarcastic and critical of Oral Roberts, Kenneth Copeland, Dr.

Yonggi Cho, and others who were helping people to get out of debt and step up to divine abundance. Our hearts sank. Confusion descended upon us like an airplane out of control, spiraling downward.

We were fairly young Christians at that time. All we wanted to do was to please the Lord, but now we wondered if maybe we had misinterpreted that Scripture. We decided to pray until we heard from God on the matter. We prayed. We praised God and sang songs of worship to Jesus. It wasn't long before something started happening. Bubbling up on the inside of me, it was as if words were trying to come out, so I spoke them out with my mouth. The words were right from the Bible (2 Timothy 3:16).

"My children, all Scripture is given by My inspiration and is profitable for doctrine, for reproof, for correction, for instruction in righteousness: that the man of God may be thoroughly furnished unto all good works."

Now we were excited again. Mark 10:30 is part of the Scriptures, thus it is profitable. I didn't need a negative evangelist to reprove me or correct me; God's Word was capable of doing that all by itself. I did, however, need to be thoroughly furnished with $800 for the good works of paying my bill! Oh, we were happy.

The next day I received a telephone call from the electric company where I worked at the time. "Dave, we were wondering if you could come in and work overtime for a few days. Something strange happened at our new power plant and we can't figure it out. We need your help."

So I worked a week or so at the new power plant in a very nice atmosphere. It was no burden at all. When I received my paycheck, I noticed over $800 extra than normal. I had enough to tithe, give an offering, plus pay my bill for $800! I had just experienced the hundred-fold return spoken of by Jesus Himself. I told everyone. And I received a lot of persecution too. Critics were jealous that I was selected for the overtime and not them.

The "hundred-fold return" seems to be reserved for those who have the faith to give everything they have at the moment just as Jesus instructed the rich young man to give everything he had.

Ministry Persecution

In 1981, when I became pastor of Mount Hope Church, our attendance was less than 230. I preached a series entitled, "Genuine Prosperity — A Biblical Perspective." You should have seen the nasty notes that came to me. Persecution and criticism became common. But in just a few short years, our members were beginning to prosper nicely. The attendance grew to over 1,200, then 2,000, then 3,000 and up. To this day, our church continues to grow.

Within four years of that "prosperity series" we found ourselves establishing new churches around the state. People were being saved and delivered from all kinds of sins every week. I thought the older ministers in town would be happy that so many people were coming to Jesus Christ. But I was wrong.

I Became The Talk Of The Town

I learned that I had become the subject of countless negative sermons in town. It seemed that a profuse number of preachers were no longer talking about Jesus in their sermons, they were now talking about Dave Williams, even on the radio. When I'd see other pastors around town they seemed semi-cordial, but I could feel a coldness toward me for some reason.

One couple came to visit our church. What they told me really shocked me.

"Pastor Williams, we came to visit your church so we could see all the Cadillac cars in your parking lot."

"What?" I responded.

"Yes, we were attending such-and-such a church, and the pastor told us that to be a member of your church, it was required that you drive at least a Cadillac. So we came over to see it for ourselves. After seeing your parking lot, we now know that our pastor lied to us. We don't want to be in a church where the pastor lies, so we are requesting that our membership be transferred over to your church."

We all had a good laugh. That was twenty years ago and those precious people are still with our church. When you prosper, you will be persecuted, misunderstood, and lied about.

One pastor told his congregation that he had enjoyed a very comfortable ministry "until Dave Williams came to town." Isn't that ridiculous?

All of the preachers that made a strong effort in those early days to criticize me and turn people against me are out of the ministry today. I never once responded to them with counter criticism. That is the way of the loser, not the way of the person who wants radical wealth.

Years ago, Rex Humbard, one of the great soulwinners of the twentieth century, came to my office and knelt down on the floor with me. Sensing that I was struggling with massive criticism, he placed his hand over my heart and began to pray for me. He asked God to give me a sweet spirit toward my critics and persecutors, and to never allow them to hinder me from fulfilling the anointing on my life. Peace flooded my heart as Rex prayed, and after that, I've never allowed any criticism to burden me. Now I can laugh it off, knowing that the same thing happened to the prophets of old.

Jesus promised that you could have wealth, but you'd also be required to deal properly with the resultant persecution that comes with it.

Why Do People Criticize?

Why do people criticize? I've found that people criticize and persecute in order to project their own feelings of failure and misery. They criticize often because they are jealous, like the Philistines when they envied Isaac's great wealth from God. Critics think their criticism will cause them to be elevated in the eyes of their listeners, but it does just the opposite.

When you face persecution because God is blessing you with wealth (and wealth is a blessing), don't retaliate. Don't grow worried or feel that you have to explain your position. Don't overreact and don't allow bitterness to creep into your heart. It will destroy your faith (Hebrews 12:14, 15). Refuse to fight back! We are not fighting with people, but with demons which are inspiring carnal Christians and motivating those who don't know God (Ephesians 6:12).

The Lord will fight for you. You don't even have to defend yourself.

> **Moses answered the people, "Do not be afraid. Stand firm and you will see the deliverance the Lord will bring you today. The Egyptians you see today you will never see again. The Lord will fight for you; you need only to be still."**
>
> **— Exodus 14:13-14 (NIV)**

> **Behold, I give unto you power to tread on serpents and scorpions, and over all the power of the enemy: and nothing shall by any means hurt you.**
>
> **— Luke 10:19**

> **No weapon that is formed against thee shall prosper; and every tongue *that* shall rise against thee in judgment thou shalt condemn. This *is* the heritage of the servants of the LORD, and their righteousness *is* of me, saith the LORD.**
>
> **— Isaiah 54:17**

The bigger you grow, the more prosperous you become, the more critics you will attract. Opposition will help you grow; just like a muscle grows through resistance training. Whatever people mean for your harm, God will turn around for your good. Whenever you handle persecution properly, God will not only vindicate you, He will multiply the number of your supporters.[11]

Let's get on the road to radical wealth, regardless of the persecution and criticism it may attract. Let's follow the example of Jesus:

> **He did not retaliate when he was insulted. When he suffered, he did not threaten to get even. He left his case in the hands of God, who always judges fairly.**
>
> **— 1 Peter 2:23 (NLT)**

"When God tells you to give, JUST DO IT!"

CHAPTER 14

If God Owns It, God Can Give It

Kevin and Renee Berry, youth pastors, were conducting a youth missions convention, encouraging the young people to be involved in world evangelism. It came time to ask the young people to make their faith promises. Kevin and Renee invited the young people to pray and ask the Lord what He would like for them to give over the course of the next year to help missionaries around the world.

Make A Faith Promise

Suddenly, the Holy Spirit spoke to both Kevin and Renee's hearts and said, "Make a faith promise of $10,000."

$10,000 on a youth pastor's salary is significant. But God wanted to make them a channel of blessing for the nations of the world and to bless them back in the process. So in obedience to the voice of the Holy Spirit, they signed their faith promise card stating that they would trust God to supply $10,000 to world missions through them within the next year. They had no idea how it would happen, but were determined to obey God, and give more than they could possibly give in one year from a human standpoint.

That's why it's called a faith promise. You take a leap of faith when you act upon the voice of the Holy Spirit. You commit yourself to do whatever the Holy Spirit says to do, even though you can't see any possible way of making it happen. The beauty of a faith promise is that ***you don't have to make it happen***. God will make it happen if you have the faith to make an "impossible" commitment, then trust Him to use you as an instrument of finance for a particular gospel project or mission.

St. Paul told us that the Macedonians gave more than they could give when the Jerusalem church fell on hard times.

> **For I can testify that they gave not only what they could afford but far more. And they did it of their own free will.**
>
> **— 2 Corinthians 8:3 (NLT)**

They gave not only what they could afford, but far more. How do you give more than you can give? Here's how. By listening to God and making a faith promise to your church, or some other ministry that God has laid on your heart. The supernatural part of all this is, when you obey the voice of God and commit yourself in faith to supply a certain amount of money, God will use you as a channel through which that money will come. Then when you give it, He counts it as seed for your personal harvest of wealth.

Did you catch that? It's one of those "wow" statements. When you plant the money God has provided through you, He counts it as seed for ***your*** financial harvest.

Kevin and Renee gave what they could the first six months and trusted God to provide the rest. Six months after making that faith promise to missions, they received a $10,000 check in the mail from a distant relative's estate that needed to be partially liquidated for some reason. You can imagine their excitement and faith level when they saw how God provided. They planted that money in God's work, just as they had promised. Now they have a $10,000 seed in the ground that will produce a great harvest for them personally. They are on the road to radical wealth.

Just Do It!

When God tells you to give, just do it! If you don't have the money right now, write out a faith promise and send it to the ministry where God told you to give. That will open you up for a financial miracle.

The power to get wealth is based upon a covenant with God. The covenant has two sides, God's side and your side. Your side is to "hearken diligently unto the voice of the Lord your God, and to observe, and to do all His commandments."[12] In other words, God *will* command the blessing upon your storehouses. He *will* give you the power to get wealth. Your part is listening and obeying even when you can't understand. Kevin and Renee didn't understand how they would come up with $10,000 for missions, but that isn't the point. The point is, they listened, obeyed, and made a promise to do exactly what God said, even though they had no idea how.

> **Trust in the LORD with all thine heart; and lean not unto thine own understanding. In all thy ways acknowledge him, and he shall direct thy paths. Be not wise in thine own eyes: fear the LORD, and depart from evil.**
>
> **— Proverbs 3:5-7**

A pastor was driving through town one day and noticed another local pastor driving a new Mercedes. He knew that pastor was also building a new home and seemed to be very well off financially. But the Spirit of God spoke and said, "Give him $500."[13]

Now the wealthy pastor certainly didn't need that $500, but it's not a matter of need, it's a matter of obeying God. The pastor called his wife, asking her to write out a check for this other pastor and to send it over to him. It was a check for the pastor himself, not for his church. That's what God spoke to him, so he didn't try to finagle a tax deduction on his gift by giving it through the church. Within about three weeks of giving that $500 where God had told him to give it, he came into possession of an extra $11,500. The seed he planted into that other minister's life is where that $11,500 harvest came from that he received. He obeyed God, and his harvest came in quickly.

Our big problem is first, we don't listen to God's voice enough, and second, we don't obey when the Holy Spirit puts an impression upon our hearts. Even so the Scriptures tell us that if we are willing and obedient, we will become rich.

> **If you will only let me help you, if you will only obey, then I will make you rich!**
>
> **— Isaiah 1:19,20 (TLB)**

Christian Tither Wins $500,000

It was a Christian tither, Mike Mentz, who won $500,000 on a television game show recently. He said he felt the presence of God while competing on the program. He knew God had helped him with the correct answers to the questions, and he walked away a half-million dollars richer. What do you think was the first thing he did with his winnings? The first thing he did was to present the tithe to the Lord and provided a bus for a youth ministry and a senior citizen's ministry.[14]

Can the Lord trust you with wealth? Will you do with money as the Holy Spirit instructs?

God Owns It All

God owns it all (Psalm 24:1). If He owns it all, He can distribute it where He chooses. If you were to distribute a million dollars, would you distribute it to people who don't respect or honor you? Would you give your wealth to everyone except your own children? The answer is, of course not. You want your wealth to go to your children, not the children of your enemies.

God is the same way. He owns all the wealth in Heaven and earth, but Satan has unlawfully confiscated much of it and distributed it among those who can do the most damage to other people's lives. And Satan hopes to keep God's covenant children from knowing about God's promises for their wealth.

"Light Purse – Heavy Curse"

The devil has used the "poverty gospel" to keep many believers from their rightful inheritance. Of course the poverty gospel is a misnomer. There is never any good news about poverty. Benjamin Franklin said, "A light purse is a heavy curse." He was right. Poverty is a curse, not a blessing.

In fact, did you know that God never blessed poverty anywhere? God never commanded blessings upon anybody's lack? He commands blessings on His children's ***increase***, not on their lack. He commands blessings on their storehouses, not their empty pockets. Poverty is ***not*** a virtue or a blessing, but the devil works hard to convince Christians that it is.

Who Gets The Key To Radical Riches?

God gives the key to radical riches to His covenant children, not to His covetous children.

> **For the LORD God *is* a sun and shield: the LORD will give grace and glory: no good *thing* will he withhold from them that walk uprightly.**
>
> **— Psalm 84:11**

> **If ye then, being evil, know how to give good gifts unto your children, how much more shall your Father which is in heaven give good things to them that ask him?**
>
> **— Matthew 7:11**

God desires to give you the power for radical wealth.

> **Riches and honour *are* with me; *yea,* durable riches and righteousness. That I may cause those**

> **that love me to inherit substance; and I will fill their treasures.**
>
> **— Proverbs 8:18, 21**

Think about it. God's best friend, Abraham, was a millionaire (Genesis 13:2; 26:12-14). Jesus calls you His friend if you obey Him (John 15:14, 15). If you obey, God promises that wealth will be chasing you. The problem is that so many of God's children are running from wealth instead of letting it overtake them.

> **The LORD shall command the blessing upon thee in thy storehouses, and in all that thou settest thine hand unto; and he shall bless thee in the land which the LORD thy God giveth thee. The LORD shall establish thee an holy people unto himself, as he hath sworn unto thee, if thou shalt keep the commandments of the LORD thy God, and walk in his ways. And all people of the earth shall see that thou art called by the name of the LORD; and they shall be afraid of thee. And the LORD shall make thee plenteous in goods, in the fruit of thy body, and in the fruit of thy cattle, and in the fruit of thy ground, in the land which the LORD sware unto thy fathers to give thee. The LORD shall open unto thee his good treasure, the heaven to give the rain unto thy land in his season, and to bless all the work of thine hand: and thou shalt lend unto many nations, and thou shalt not borrow. And the LORD shall make thee the head, and not the tail; and thou shalt be above only, and thou shalt not be beneath; if that thou hearken unto the commandments of the LORD thy God, which I command thee this day, to observe and to do *them*:**
>
> **— Deuteronomy 28: 8-13**

When you increase your wisdom, you will increase your wealth.

> **Length of days *is* in her right hand; *and* in her left hand riches and honour.**
>
> **— Proverbs 3:16**

> **Blessed *is* the man *that* feareth the LORD, *that* delighteth greatly in his commandments.**
>
> **Wealth and riches *shall be* in his house:**
>
> **— Psalm 112: 1b, 3a**

> **I love them that love me; and those that seek me early shall find me. Riches and honour *are* with me; *yea,* durable riches and righteousness. My fruit *is* better than gold, yea, than fine gold; and my revenue than choice silver. I lead in the way of righteousness, in the midst of the paths of judgment: That I may cause those that love me to inherit substance; and I will fill their treasures.**
>
> **— Proverbs 8:17-21**

Let me ask you a question. Are your treasuries filled? Would you like your treasuries (your accounts) to be filled? Of course you would. By gaining wisdom, God promises, ***"I will fill their treasures."*** Treasures mean treasuries, or storehouses, in the Hebrew language. In other words, wherever you keep your money and wealth, God will fill it if you qualify for it through wisdom.

Three Wise Practices

I want to talk to you about some wise things that will speed you along on the road to radical riches.

1. Ask. People tell me they need more money. I ask them how much more they need, but usually, they can't tell me specifically how much more. They don't know how much they owe or how much they'll need for the next year. I tell them if they can't be specific about the amount they need or how much they desire, they will likely receive nothing.

Some folks will never have more in life because they haven't asked for more or they haven't been specific about what they want. Jesus taught us to ask. Have you asked the Lord for the salary or income you desire for the year? Have you asked the Lord specifically for the amount necessary to pay off your debts and bills? If you are like most of the people I have dealt with over the years, you haven't even asked God for what you really need and want.

> **Therefore I say unto you, What things soever ye desire, when ye pray, believe that ye receive *them*, and ye shall have *them*.**
>
> **— Mark 11:24**

> **Ask, and it shall be given you; seek, and ye shall find; knock, and it shall be opened unto you:**
>
> **— Matthew 7:7-8**

Ye have not, because ye ask not.

— James 4:2

If you are wise, you will sit down ***right now*** and figure out everything you owe and precisely what it is you desire as an income for next year, and ***ask*** God for it. You have the right to ask if you are tithing, giving offerings, and meeting your faith promises. Don't ask your employer. He is not your source. Ask God.

2. Get a storehouse. How can God command blessings on your storehouse if you don't have a storehouse? How can God fill your storehouse to overflowing, if you don't have a storehouse? How can He fill your treasuries if you don't have some kind of savings or investment account? If you really believe that God wants to bless your storehouses, then you'd take a step of faith and open up some bank accounts or brokerage accounts.

Start by opening a savings account at your local bank or credit union and make it your "Do Not Touch" account. Set a goal to let it grow to $5,000 or $10,000. Ask God to bless this account. Every time you get paid, put 10% of your income into this account, after you have given to God first. Remember the principle: nothing happens until you give something in faith. Furthermore, nothing spectacular will probably happen in your accounts until you first give to God in a spectacular way.

After the money has grown in your bank account, you may want to consider getting a brokerage account. I like Charles Schwab Company, personally. They are flexible and easy to deal with. You can buy stocks, bonds, mutual funds, money market funds, and other investment vehicles all from the same account. God will command blessings on your accounts after you have given to Him in a radical way.

One year the Lord spoke to my wife and me during a missions convention to double our faith promise from what we had given the previous year. We had given $25,000 to missions the previous year, so we wrote out a faith promise to missions for $50,000 for the coming year. I couldn't believe it. Just sixteen years ago we were scraping through our furniture to find enough money to plant an $8 seed into God's work, and here we are now making a $50,000 faith commitment. We were going to give more to God in the next twelve months than we were going to keep.

I knew we could give $25,000. After all, we had done it the previous year. But $50,000! I had no clue how we could do it. Thank God, though, it was He who put it on our hearts, therefore it was He who would have to provide it through us somehow. I don't have to know how. When I make a faith promise, I only need to know what. $50,000 was the *what*. The *how* was up to God.

After making that radical faith promise, at least radical for us up until that point, I started doing a little research on my computer. I happened to find a technology company selling for 25 cents a share. So I called my broker (Charles Schwab) and took $2,500 out of my "treasury" and bought 10,000 shares in this technology company. I felt like God was speaking to me about buying these shares, so I simply was obeying.

Two weeks later I was checking on how the company was doing and got a great and wonderful surprise. The stock had gone up to $3.00 a share in just two weeks. I asked the Lord what to do. In my heart, I heard a gentle voice say, "Sell now." So I called my broker and told him to sell my 10,000 shares of this company. By the time he sold them, the price advanced to $3.50 a share, giving me $35,000 minus the original $2,500 investment. That meant my profit was $32,500 for two weeks. I tithed on the increase, paid my capital gains tax (by a miracle like the disciples had when they caught the fish with the tax money in its mouth), and I gave $25,000 to missions. After I sold the stock at $3.50 a share, before the day was over it had dropped to $1.00 a share, so I sold it at precisely the highest point, at just the right moment.

Things like this are always happening to the faithful people who will ask big, dream big, believe big, and give big. God commands blessings upon them in their storehouses; their accounts. Set up an account. It is a wise thing to do.

It's also wise to let your accounts grow. Don't be tempted by a bowl of beans, like Esau was. Don't be dipping into your storehouse just yet. Don't take out money for the sake of some instant gratification like buying a new wardrobe or something else. There will be a time for that, but let God bless those storehouses. Don't eat up all the grain. Let it grow, always remembering the Lord, for it is He who gives you the power to get wealth.

May I offer you a million-dollar suggestion here? Make sure that you have an IRA (Individual Retirement Account) storehouse, as well as a 401(k) or 403(b), if your employer offers them. Fund your 401(k) first, especially if your employer offers some kind of matching funds. Next, fund your IRA account, setting a goal to deposit the maximum allowed by law each year. These accounts will grow tax-deferred, which means less money will go to "Egypt" for income tax, and the money in these accounts will grow much faster. After you have set up an IRA storehouse and a 401(k) storehouse, consider a variable annuity storehouse. That should be your last tax-deferred investment vehicle.

In order of priority:

A. Get a bank storehouse.

B. Open a brokerage account with Charles Schwab or some other discount brokerage company. Or you can invest in a good family of mutual funds, like Fidelity, Vanguard, Invesco, or Janus (see Chapter 26 for telephone numbers).

C. Open and fully fund your 401(k) or 403(b) each year, if you have this option.

D. Open and fully fund your IRA each year.

E. Open and fund a tax-sheltered variable annuity each year. Put in as much as the law permits (based on your adjusted gross income).

Make November Your Planning Month

Now, figure out how much you will need to fund these storehouses each year. I'd suggest that you sit down in November to figure your total needs for the next year.

Write everything out on paper so you will have a record to review throughout the year and especially the next November.

Then ***ask*** God to bless your storehouses and ***ask*** specifically for the amounts. And remember the Lord. When you see the blessings coming upon your accounts, don't quit tithing, giving offerings and making radical faith promises. You want to keep the door to your radical wealth wide open.

3. Keep a right attitude about money and a right attitude toward others who are being blessed financially. This is one of the most overlooked keys to radical wealth. The beloved Apostle said that God wishes above all things that His people prosper and be in health, even as their souls prosper. Soul prosperity involves the area of your mind and attitude. If you want radical wealth, you're going to need to have a radically good attitude toward others who are farther down the road to wealth than you are.

Your attitude toward money will largely determine your level of future wealth. If you say things like, "Oh, money is not important," or "I don't want to talk about money," or "I'm happy without much money," then that's exactly how you will be treated financially.

"Money will never make you happy," is a statement I've heard for years. Why don't people change their thinking around and start saying, "Poverty will never make you happy?" Or "Lack of money will never make you happy?"

Some will never get on the road to radical wealth due to their lousy attitudes. They will ridicule, sneer and make belittling remarks while the preacher is receiving an offering. They will criticize others who are being blessed financially. They will make statements like "He preaches a money gospel," or "That won't work in third-world countries."

One day a lady walked up to me after church and said:

"My husband left me eight years ago. I was so hurt and devastated over it that I quit coming to church. Today was my first day back in church in over eight years. It really bugged me when you talked about money at the offering time. I don't think you should talk about money. It really bugged me."

I don't know what she expected me to do. Here was a lady who had a bad experience in life, so, instead of standing in faith and turning to a deeper relationship with the Lord, she turned her back on God altogether for eight years. Now she comes strolling back into church, and her first day back, wants to dictate what I should say and what I shouldn't say from the pulpit. No way!

Her attitude, unless changed, will keep this lady off the road to radical wealth.

What do you think when you see a preacher driving a nice car? What is your attitude? Do you rejoice that he has a comfortable, nice vehicle, or do you show jealousy and envy by making belittling remarks behind his back? I just have a difficult time respecting anybody who doesn't rejoice in other people's blessings.

It's easy to be critical of someone who has been blessed by God in an amazing way financially. But if you are critical, you are cutting your own supply line. God wants us to rejoice with others in their blessings, even when their blessings are financial in nature. He doesn't want us to be making "cute" or cutting remarks about their prosperity.

Rejoice when others are blessed. Believe the best when you see a minister driving a nice car. An automobile dealer may have given him that car to drive. I know a minister's wife who drives a nice Mercedes. A Mercedes dealer gave it to her because God told him to give it to her as a blessing from the Lord. If you criticize her, you are criticizing the One who blessed her with it. And that's not a good thing for you.

One night I drove up to the grocery store to buy some snack food for my family. We had rented a movie we were going to watch, so I ran up to buy some potato chips, pretzels, and dip. A lady spotted me. I didn't recognize her, but she walked right over to me without so much as a greeting, looked into my shopping cart and said, "So that's what you spend our tithe money on?" Then she walked away.

Well, I wasn't spending anybody's tithe money. I was spending money from my paycheck. She seemed irritated that I would be buying snack foods for an evening of fellowship and a movie with my family.

What is your attitude toward money and those who have money? God owns it all. He can give it, take it, or withhold it. We become recipients of radical wealth when we qualify.

Think about this. Our planet, the earth, is only one planet. It is known that there are over one trillion bodies in space, including stars, planets, and the sun. That's just in our galaxy, the Milky Way. Our galaxy alone measures 100,000 light years from edge to edge. That means if you could travel at a speed of 186,000 miles per second, you'd have to travel for 100,000 years just to get from one side of our galaxy to the other.

That's not all. Scientists now know there are at least one billion other galaxies out there in space. The telescope at the Mount Palomar Observatory allows a viewer to see two billion light years into space, yet nobody has ever found the end of space. God is still creating. He does it at a velocity of at least the speed of light. He is the Creator.

He owns all the wealth in all of creation, not just the wealth of the world. He loves sharing His wealth with those who meet the qualifications.

CHAPTER 15

The Inexhaustible Supply

Sometimes you need radical breakthroughs. In this chapter, I will give you seven principles for your radical breakthrough. They are the foundational keys to a radical breakthrough when your life is up against the wall.

This true story found in 1 Kings 17 is so important to your breakthrough, Jesus Himself commented on it (Luke 4:24-26).

> **And Elijah the Tishbite, *who was* of the inhabitants of Gilead, said unto Ahab, *As* the LORD God of Israel liveth, before whom I stand, there shall not be dew nor rain these years, but according to my word. And the word of the LORD came unto him, saying, Get thee hence, and turn thee eastward, and hide thyself by the brook Cherith, that *is* before Jordan. And it shall be, *that* thou shalt drink of the brook; and I have commanded the ravens to feed thee there. So he went and did according unto the word of the**

> **LORD: for he went and dwelt by the brook Cherith, that *is* before Jordan. And the ravens brought him bread and flesh in the morning, and bread and flesh in the evening; and he drank of the brook.**
>
> **— 1 Kings 17:1-6**

God provided for Elijah by sending him to camp beside a brook. God commanded birds to bring him bread and flesh. Today we would call that a sandwich. Elijah looked to God as his source of supply, and God didn't let him down. How many people do you know today that have birds deliver their breakfast and dinner? God knows how to get a supply to you in ways you never dreamed about. But, you have to look only to Him as your source.

Principle Number 1 — Make God your source. Some are always looking for a source of more income, more wealth, and more abundance. When Jesus taught us to refer to God as our Father, He was painting a picture of a provider, protector, nurturer, and supplier. He taught us to seek the Father and His Kingdom first, then all the things in life we need and want would be propelled into our lives from Heaven's resources (Matthew 6:33). We wouldn't be forced or under pressure to always be searching for a fresh resource for more income.

When you have really made God your source, you won't drag out of bed in the morning and complain about going to work. You may work at a gas station, but because you work for the Kingdom of God, and have God as your employer, you hop out of bed and get to your Kingdom job. You do your work, not as eye pleasers to men, but as unto the Lord, your true employer — your source. You are not just "working for a living." You are putting the Kingdom first and doing your work happily as unto the Lord, your source. You know He's going to eventually show you how to own that gas station, if that's what you desire, so your work is no burden at all.

You see, when you are seeking first God's Kingdom, your job is not your source. God is your source. As you are faithful to that "small" job, God is going to promote you to rulership over great things (Matthew 25:21). Perhaps He will show you how to own that business, instead of just working there. It depends upon who your source is.

Elijah was not looking to the brook as his source. He was not looking to the ravens as his source. He was looking only to God as his source of supply. So when his current provisions came to an end, God showed him where to find his next supply.

> **And it came to pass after a while, that the brook dried up, because there had been no rain in the land. And the word of the LORD came unto him, saying, Arise, get thee to Zarephath, which** ***belongeth*** **to Zidon, and dwell there: behold, I**

> **have commanded a widow woman there to sustain thee.**
>
> **— 1 Kings 17:7-9**

Elijah's resource had dried up. That's no problem when you have God as your source. God is omniscient. He knows where the money is, He knows which stock is the next to soar, He knows how to point you in the direction of your next miracle provision. In this case, He told Elijah about a widow woman who was commanded to sustain him throughout the famine that had resulted from no rain.

Elijah needed only to listen to and obey his source.

> **So he arose and went to Zarephath. And when he came to the gate of the city, behold, the widow woman *was* there gathering of sticks: and he called to her, and said, Fetch me, I pray thee, a little water in a vessel, that I may drink. And as she was going to fetch *it*, he called to her, and said, Bring me, I pray thee, a morsel of bread in thine hand.**
>
> **— 1 Kings 17:10-11**

The prophet found the woman about whom the Lord had spoken and asked her for some water and a little food. This brings us to the second principle for your breakthrough.

Principle Number 2 — Ask. This is a humbling experience. Whenever the Lord instructs me to ask for a special offering, it is uncomfortable for me, but

I obey. Later I hear about all the miracles that happened in the people's lives that responded to my appeal, and I'm glad I asked.

Notice Elijah didn't ask randomly. He asked a very specific person a very specific request on very specific instructions from the Lord. You can spend months asking the wrong questions of the wrong people when you are facing a need. God knows whom you can ask and who will give you the right answers.

If you have lost a job, the Lord, if He is your source, can point you to a perfect employer to ask for a new job. Elijah asked for something and his request was very specific.

"Give me some water and food."

Let's look at the widow's response.

> **And she said, *As* the LORD thy God liveth, I have not a cake, but an handful of meal in a barrel, and a little oil in a cruse: and, behold, I *am* gathering two sticks, that I may go in and dress it for me and my son, that we may eat it, and die.**
>
> **— 1 Kings 17:12**

This seems like the worst possible time for a preacher to be asking for something. Here was this little woman and her son that had only one meal left, then they were going to starve to death. It seems like the last thing the preacher would ask for is something from a person who is on the edge of dying. Elijah asked, and she responded with resistance, explaining her grave situation to the prophet. But she didn't condemn or criticize the man of God for asking.

> **And Elijah said unto her, Fear not; go *and* do as thou hast said: but make me thereof a little cake first, and bring *it* unto me, and after make for thee and for thy son.**
>
> **— 1 Kings 17:13**

Principle Number 3 — No condemnation. The widow did not condemn the prophet for asking. Neither did the prophet condemn the woman for her initial negative response. Sometimes the relentless pressures of life weigh on people and they momentarily step out of the faith realm.

It is not a sin to have a need or to be facing a critical moment in life. Elijah did not criticize her for her lack of faith.

It seems like whenever someone is facing a difficult time in life and needs a breakthrough, some overly spiritual, insensitive know-it-all will come along to condemn them. Job had some friends like that. When Job was facing a severe trial in his life, his spiritual buddies "knew" Job's problem was because of his sin and lack of spiritual insight. Thankfully God rebuked those friends and their unkind, misguided insights into Job's problem.

One summer our church was having a particularly difficult time financially. The county roads were torn up from repair work, and it was difficult for cars to get into our parking lot. Businesses also were suffering during that time. It was only a "season" like Elijah faced when the brook dried up. I needed to make a special appeal to our congregation for some necessary finances. We have never borrowed money for any operational expenses for this ministry and I refused to even consider it as an option.

After I told the congregation that we needed a little boost, a fellow set up an appointment with my chief of staff to give him some "insight."

"There's sin in the camp somewhere," he ranted. "That's why you're having a financial challenge this month. When finances dry up, it's always a sign of sin in the camp somewhere."

Oh, please! There are always those who think they know more than you do. They are standing by to bring condemnation and criticism. Ignore them.

Principle Number 4 — Fear not! The first spirit that will try to strike you when you are facing a crisis is the spirit of fear.

> **For God hath not given us the spirit of fear; but of power, and of love, and of a sound mind.**
>
> **— 2 Timothy 1:7**

The spirit of fear is not from God. Fear paralyzes. Fear tries to force you to make decisions independent from God's counsel. Fear will stop faith, the one thing you desperately need when facing a serious setback or crisis of some kind. Elijah told the woman not to fear. He could see that the spirit of fear was gripping at the heart of this precious mother, and it's no wonder. After all, she and her son were facing certain death unless a miracle arrived . . . and soon!

Well, the miracle was about to appear. Elijah was there to show her how to receive it. But first he had to get her out of her fear and into active faith.

"It's okay," he told the woman, "Go and do as you planned. Make a meal for you and your son, but I have one alteration for you to make in your plan. Give some food to me ***first!***"

That sounds like the ultimate in selfishness. Some preachers are accused of this, but it wasn't selfishness at all. He knew that the quickest way for this woman to get something from God was by helping someone else to get it. In other words, Elijah was trying to get her to "plant a seed" for a miracle harvest. Then he motivated her by changing her picture of the future.

> **For thus saith the LORD God of Israel, The barrel of meal shall not waste, neither shall the**

> **cruse of oil fail, until the day *that* the LORD sendeth rain upon the earth.**
>
> **— 1 Kings 17:14**

Fear will give you all kinds of tragic imaginations concerning the future. Faith will give you a movie of success, prosperity, abundance and miracles.

> **What is faith? It is the confident assurance that what we hope for is going to happen. It is the evidence of things we cannot yet see.**
>
> **— Hebrews 11:1 (NLT)**

Principle Number 5 — Motivation. Elijah offered an incredible motivation for her to give to him first. He promised, in the Name of the Lord, that if she met his need ***first,*** God would see to it that her needs would be supernaturally met throughout the famine years. She needed to move into the arena of miracles. She and her son needed a miracle supply. If they didn't get some food they were going to die.

Nothing multiplies until it is placed into God's hands.

Elijah did not try to motivate this woman by reminding her of her love for God. He did not say, "If you really love God, you'll give to His prophet and expect nothing in return." I hear that kind of talk so much I just want to scream. People think they sound spiritual, and it's not really their fault. They heard it from some preacher or some older Christian, so they just repeat, like a parrot, what they've heard. They say things like "Oh, I don't expect anything in return when I give to God." " I give because I love God, not because I expect something in return." "Oh, brother, I never give to receive."

Talk like this is simply and clearly unbelief. God motivates us to give by promising us a harvest, a supply, a need fulfilled.

Elijah did not ask her to make a sacrifice. He didn't say, "You know you're going to die soon, and it's the will of God. If you give your food to me sacrificially, when you and your son get to Heaven, you have eternal rewards waiting for you." No, he didn't say that.

He motivated her to give by giving her the promise of perpetual supply. He said, "If you do this — give to the man of God *first* — then God will give you a miracle supply, and you and your son will live with plenty."

Someone said to me that it's wrong to motivate people to give by promising something in return. But that's exactly the way God motivates. He always — ***always*** — promises something in return for our obedient giving. Go through the Bible and try to find sowing without reaping, giving without receiving, seed time without harvest. The only time you'll ever find God's people sowing without reaping is when their finances came under a curse for their disobedience.

Elijah changed the widow's faith movie from a tragedy to an adventure. He replaced her picture of lack and starvation with a picture of life, and supply, and miracles. But she had to do something to get into the stream of miracle supply. She had to give to the man of God *first*. This type of giving sounds risky, but the rewards are life changing.

> **"For I know the plans I have for you," declares the Lord, "Plans to prosper you and not harm you, plans to give you hope and a future."**
>
> **— Jeremiah 29:11 (NIV)**

Now let's see what happened next.

> **And she went and did according to the saying of Elijah: and she, and he, and her house, did eat *many* days.**
>
> **—1 Kings 17:15**

This brings us to the next powerful principle for your breakthrough.

Principle Number 6 — Don't criticize the man of God. Can you get this picture in your mind? Here comes this prophet to a poor woman who is about to die with her son, and he asks her to give him some food *first*. Now, Elijah would be a great target for criticism if he had done this in our generation. Can you imagine the nerve of him? She could have responded differently than she did. She could have used the famous lines we hear today.

"All you preachers want is money."

"Why don't you go ask the rich instead of the poor?"

"You preachers waste money on fancy buildings, and then go to people trying to live on social security and pressure them to get all their money to pay for it."

Sins of the tongue stop the flow of miracles. And when you need a breakthrough from Heaven, you better not criticize the man of God who is bringing you the solution to your problem.

> **Thou art snared with the words of thy mouth, thou art taken with the words of thy mouth.**
>
> **— Proverbs 6:2**

> **For by thy words thou shalt be justified, and by thy words thou shalt be condemned.**
>
> **— Matthew 12:37**

> **Death and life *are* in the power of the tongue: and they that love it shall eat the fruit thereof.**
>
> **— Proverbs 18:21**

> **Whoso keepeth his mouth and his tongue keepeth his soul from troubles.**
>
> **— Proverbs 21:23**

This little woman did not criticize the man of God for asking. Instead she saw a faith picture of supply and ***obeyed*** the man of God. When you have a true man of God come to you, even though he has imperfections, you better not criticize him. Criticizing the man of God will stop your flow of miracles and will bump you off the road to radical riches.

This is what Jesus was referring to when he mentioned this woman in the gospels. He was talking about her respect for the man of God. Read it.

> **And he said, Verily I say unto you, No prophet is accepted in his own country. But I tell you of a truth, many widows were in Israel in the days of Elias, when the heaven was shut up three years and six months, when great famine was throughout all the land; But unto none of them was Elias sent, save unto Sarepta, *a city* of Sidon, unto a woman *that was* a widow.**
>
> **— Luke 4:24-26**

Jesus said there were many other widows during this famine. He told how Elijah was sent to none of them, except this widow in 1 Kings 17. In its context, Jesus was saying that this particular widow received the miracle because she respected the man of God.

Apparently all the others had little or no respect for the prophet of God, so they didn't get any miracles. But the woman in Zarephath did! Your relationship to the man of God is a key to your wealth.

> **Believe in the LORD your God, so shall ye be established; believe his prophets, so shall ye prosper.**
>
> **— 2 Chronicles 20:20**

Principle Number 7 — Act upon the prophet's words. In other words, obey! Elijah was a man of like passions, just like you and me (James 5:17, 18). He had his faults and idiosyncrasies but he was a man sent by God to bring a series of miracles to this woman's life. Her future and her son's future depended upon what she did the moment she received the instructions from the prophet.

Her future was in her hands not somebody else's. People with poverty mentalities are always blaming something or someone else for their lack. "Well if my boss would pay me what I need, I could make a good living." "If the people at the bank weren't so stingy, my loan would go through. Then, I'd be able to get ahead in life." "If the government was better . . ." and the list goes on and on. The fact is this: Your future is in *your hands* right now. If you let go of what you have in your hands, God will let go of what He has in His hands. Your future supply depends upon *you* and what you do with your seed right now.

> **And she went and did according to the saying of Elijah: and she, and he, and her house, did eat *many* days. *And* the barrel of meal wasted not, neither did the cruse of oil fail, according to the word of the LORD, which he spake by Elijah.**
>
> **— 1 Kings 17:15-16**

The widow's obedience led to a miraculous adventure. She became a recipient of God's inexhaustible supply. Her food never ran out. She, her son, and Elijah enjoyed meals as long as they wanted. And miracles became common for this widow woman who gave to the prophet of God *first* (1 Kings 17:16-24). She got her breakthrough.

Do you need a breakthrough today? Go back over these seven principles several times a day. Ask God to send you a word like He sent a word to the widow through Elijah. Do something radical. Let go of what's in your hand expecting God to let go of what's in His hand. When you do, you'll see the breakthrough you desire, and move along the road to radical miracles and radical riches.

"Those who remember the Lord their God will be given the key to the door leading into the wealthy place."

CHAPTER 16

Coming Into The Wealthy Place

Picture yourself in a room with one door. You don't know how you got into that room — you've just always been there. We'll call it "the room of your life." All your needs are met in that room, but somehow you never seem to have more than just enough. Beyond that door is another room known as "the place of wealth." There is massive wealth just beyond the door. You want in the worst way to get what is in that other room, so you devise all kinds of schemes.

You try to break the door down without success. You stick your fingers under the door hoping to grasp onto some of the wealth stored in that room so you can slide it over to your room. But your fingers are just too fat. Next, you bend some coat hangers to slide under the door and every once in awhile you're able to pull a little bit of wealth over to your room. That makes you happy and your cleverness makes you proud.

Every day you are thinking of ways to get the wealth from that other room over to yours. "If only I could get some of the treasure that's in that other room," you think, "then I'd be happy." You don't know how much of the treasure you want, you just know you want some. So you keep trying.

You find an advertisement that reads, "I made $12,000 a month in my spare time. You can do it, too!" So you investigate the opportunity. You read the literature promising you a fortune. So you try it. You start licking envelopes for a company in your spare time. Then you sign up fifteen others to lick envelopes. Soon you're not only getting the money for your licked envelopes, but you are profiting from all those you signed up to lick envelopes under you.

You start watching the envelope-licking videos and tapes. Oh, you are motivated now. You fly off to the envelope-licking motivational rallies on the weekends. You are excited. Soon the money starts rolling in. You receive a check for $300! And all you had to do is lick 15,000 envelopes and sign up fifteen people under you to do the same.

After a few months, you realize you've spent more money on traveling to the rallies and buying the videotapes, plus, you've added forty hours a week to your schedule licking envelopes in your spare time. Now you begin to come to your senses and realize this is not the way to get into the wealthy place.

So one day you see a television infomercial that tells you that can make millions of dollars by buying into this "once-in-a-lifetime" opportunity. "Maybe this will bring me some of that wealth," you think. So you start moonlighting in a business that shows great promise. But you find that, after investing countless hours on the business, you still don't accumulate any outrageous wealth. So you try another scheme, hoping to somehow tap into the treasures sitting in that other room. All through life you find yourself frustrated. You can never seem to wiggle enough treasure out of the wealth room. What is the problem?

It is so simple. God seems pleased to use the simple things to confound those who think they are wise. Very few discover the secret. But I'm going to unveil the secret now. If you are ready for it, something will leap in your heart telling you it's true. If you're not ready for it, then the concept will go right over your head and you'll need to come back again and again to read this book and meditate once again on the truth it reveals. You need to get your spiritual heart into a position to receive the truth I am about to share.

The truth is this. You will never be able to pull enough wealth into your life ***unless you change rooms.***

You are trying to pull wealth from the "room of wealth" instead of going in and living in the "room of wealth." You cannot come into one place without coming out of another place. If I am in Sacramento, there is no way I can come into San Francisco without leaving Sacramento first. I can watch television shows and read brochures about San Francisco, but I can't actually come *into* San Francisco without leaving Sacramento, and getting on the road to San Francisco.

Likewise, you can never enter the "room of wealth," until you are ready and willing to come out of the other room.

> **Thou hast caused men to ride over our heads; we went through fire and through water: but thou broughtest us out into a wealthy *place*.**
>
> **— Psalm 66:12**

Notice the two words "out" and "into." You can't get into one place without coming out of another place first.

Fire And Water Financially

Here is the room in which many people live today. It's the "fire and water room." It's the room in which they exist. Most people live in the "fire and water room" all their lives. And even as the Scripture here declares, men are riding over their heads.

To me, it's interesting how we use terms relating to fire and water to describe our financial conditions. For example, "Money sure burns a hole in my pocket." Fire. "It looks like I'm going under financially." Water. "I'm over my head in debt." I think you get the idea.

The Wealthy Place

But ... (we need to focus on the right side of the "but,") "But thou broughtest us out into a wealthy place." God brought His people out of the room of fire and water, and into the room of wealth. It is something they could not do for themselves, no matter how hard they schemed, stayed motivated, or wrestled to get the door opened.

Not much wealth can flow to the "fire and water room." It just gets burned up or drowns. If you want to come into the wealthy place, you have to come out of the place you are today.

God's people had men riding over their heads. These men had enticed them to go into debt over their heads. When you decide to come out of that old room, and come into the new room, no longer will men be able to ride over your life. No longer will money burn a hole in your pocket. Never again will you say, "I'm drowning financially," for you have chosen to come out of the old and into the new.

You'll never get into the wealthy place on your own, though most try. But God doesn't want any "self-made millionaires." It was "Thou" that brought us out, the Psalmist declares. Who is "Thou?" "Thou" is God ... and God alone!

> **Some *trust* in chariots, and some in horses: but we will remember the name of the LORD our God.**
>
> **— Psalm 20:7**

Some trust in human instruments to open the door to the wealthy place. They are unsuccessful or at best experience bitter disappointment. Those who ***remember*** the Lord their God will be given the key to the door leading into the wealthy place.

> **But thou shalt remember the LORD thy God: for *it is* he that giveth thee power to get wealth, that he may establish his covenant which he sware unto thy fathers, as *it is* this day.**
>
> **— Deuteronomy 8:18**

There it is again. ***Remember*** the Lord, your God. It is ***He*** that giveth ***thee*** the power to get wealth. He doesn't automatically give you wealth. He gives you the power, or the key, to get wealth. God gives you the power to get wealth. That is the key that unlocks the door to the room of treasures.

The Power Is In You

This is so difficult for some to understand that they miss it all their lives. It brings pleasure to God when He can prosper you. He gives you power to get wealth. Many are trying hard to get that door open with self-efforts, when all along the power to open that door is in them. Many are asking God to send them wealth. God has answered by sending them the key to wealth, but they ignore it.

> **Now unto him that is able to do exceeding abundantly above all that we ask or think, according to the power that worketh in us,**
>
> **— Ephesians 3:20**

The power is ***in you***. You already have the key for anything you can think, ask, or imagine. As an obedient, covenant child of God, you have everything you need to come out of lack and into abundance.

Remembering the Lord and obeying the Lord is the key to unleashing that power. Remember the Lord's tithe. Remember the Lord in offerings. Remember the Lord's house. Remember the Lord's Day.

Even in Holy Communion, Jesus said, "This do in remembrance of me." How often do you come to the Lord's table to remember Him?

It all is summed up in Matthew 6:33. When we seek first the Lord and His Kingdom, all the things that others are struggling for will be added to us. We gain, not lose, by putting God's Kingdom matters first place.

Do you wake up in the morning saying, "Thank you, Lord! This is the day You have made. It's another beautiful day to be about your Kingdom business?" You should. Because no matter where you may work, you are on assignment from the King. There is no authorization from the King to complain, only that you walk in love, perform with excellence, and look forward to the promotion He is going to bring you as you serve His Kingdom faithfully.

After twenty some years in the ministry, I've seen plenty of people end up on the spiritual scrap heap by pursuing wealth their own way instead of God's way. They start out with good intentions, attend motivational rallies, sign people up, act enthusiastic, confess the right things, and away they go … beating on the door to the "wealthy place" with their puny human energies. No wonder they burn out, stress out, and finally fizzle out.

To come into the land of plenty you must be willing and obedient.

> **If ye be willing and obedient, ye shall eat the good of the land: But if ye refuse and rebel, ye shall be devoured with the sword: for the mouth of the LORD hath spoken *it*.**
>
> **— Isaiah 1:19, 20 (TLB)**

I know I am repeating Scriptures throughout this book. I'm doing this purposely. I want the Word of God to be planted in you deeply. This Scripture says you must be willing and obedient. Let me ask you a few questions. Are you willing to come out of debt in order to come into wealth? Are you willing to wait in the Lord's presence in prayer until He speaks to you concerning wealth, or would you rather swing into action on your own? Are you willing to delay some things you want now in order to have a brighter future?

I Did It My Way

It's sad, but some Christians will come to the end of their lives without ever experiencing the full financial blessings of God. It won't be God's fault. The theme song for these self-styled, always scheming, believers will be Frank Sinatra's *"I Did It My Way."* Only too late will they discover that God's way, not "my way," was the way into the wealthy place.

The good news is this. God wants you to begin *now* to come out of the fire and water room, and to start stepping into the wealthy place.

> **This is the LORD'S doing; it *is* marvellous in our eyes. This *is* the day *which* the LORD hath made; we will rejoice and be glad in it. Save now, I beseech thee, O LORD: O LORD, I beseech thee, send now prosperity.**
>
> **— Psalm 118:23-25**

When the Lord does this marvelous thing, it won't take forever. When the Lord brings you into the wealthy place, it can happen in one month or one year. It all begins with you and where you are going to place your trust. Will you trust in human ideas or in God's power? Will you trust in carnal skills or in God's gift? He gives you the power to get wealth. It does not say that He gives you the skill or the ability to get wealth. He gives you the power.

God is delighted to give this power to all that will favor His righteous cause and establish His covenant in the lives of other people. He does it. We let Him do it.

> **For the LORD thy God bringeth thee into a good land, a land of brooks of water, of fountains and depths that spring out of valleys and hills; A land of wheat, and barley, and vines, and fig trees, and pomegranates; a land of oil olive, and honey; A land wherein thou shalt eat bread without scarceness, thou shalt not lack any *thing* in it; a land whose stones *are* iron, and out of whose**

> **hills thou mayest dig brass. When thou hast eaten and art full, then thou shalt bless the LORD thy God for the good land which he hath given thee.**
>
> **— Deuteronomy 8:7-10**

God has given us His covenant of increase. This wonderful covenant will cause our children to be mighty and will bring wealth and riches to our homes. We need to make sure we are building our homes in the "wealthy place," and not in the "place of fire and water."

> **Praise ye the LORD. Blessed *is* the man *that* feareth the LORD, *that* delighteth greatly in his commandments. His seed shall be mighty upon earth: the generation of the upright shall be blessed. Wealth and riches *shall be* in his house: and his righteousness endureth for ever.**
>
> **— Psalm 112:1-3**

How The Lord Is Magnified

Is the Lord magnified in your bills? Does the Lord receive glory from your debts? Is the Lord blessed by seeing poverty and lack in the lives of His children? Will unbelievers see the Lord as the Great El Shaddai (the God who is Sufficient; the God who is more than enough) when they see that His children are just as bad off as others are? No, the Lord is magnified (promoted) when we allow Him to prosper us.

> **Let them shout for joy, and be glad, that favour my righteous cause: yea, let them say continually, Let the LORD be magnified, which hath pleasure in the prosperity of his servant.**
>
> **— Psalm 35:27**

Why Some Don't Come Out ... Into The Wealthy Place

There are reasons why some refuse to come out into the wealthy place.

1. ***They are satisfied.*** Like the children of Israel that camped on the wrong side of the Jordan, they are content with just enough. As long as they can make their monthly payments to "Egypt," go to McDonalds a couple times a week, and give a little to God, they are happy. They desire no more in life.

2. ***They are unwilling to make the decision to come out now.*** Faith is always ***now*** (Hebrews 11:1). God said to "prove me ***now***" (Malachi 3:10). Caleb, one of the spies who later became very wealthy, said, "Let us go up at once." The others who hung back, vacillating, ended up losing everything.

3. ***Some step out of their God-given calling.*** This is a major lack of wisdom. Some will actually leave the place God has called them to for the sake of money. Then they wonder why miracles have ceased in their lives.

Pat and Mary Jo Fox have been faithful members of Mount Hope Church for many years. In 1983 when I preached on the subject of getting out of debt, they listened. They set a goal to get out of debt and they did it. They decided to ***come out***, so they could ***come into*** the wealthy place.

Many times employers offered them new positions that would have taken them away from Lansing, and offered to pay them up to twice as much as they were currently earning. But they knew their assignment from God. They were destined by God to stay here at Mount Hope Church, even if it meant renouncing some short-term benefit. They stayed in their assignment from God.

Mary Jo and Pat medically could not have children, but when they came into the wealthy place, God gave them two astounding miracles. First Mary Jo gave birth to a little girl, then a little boy. Their dreams have come true. They now have a beautiful, growing family, they are free from "Egypt," and they both have jobs they love. They serve on my staff now. Pat is our property manager, perfectly suited for the job. Mary Jo is working successfully with our Bible Training Institute, loving every minute of it. Their lives have been a series of miracles because they stayed in their assignment, even when it looked more profitable to move on. They are living in the wealthy place.

4. They refuse to see wealth as a blessing. The Bible tells us that Abraham was blessed with wealth. God blessed Job with wealth. Read Proverbs 8:18-21. Wealth is a blessing. Poverty is a curse.

Giving Up Too Soon

> **So don't get tired of doing what is good. Don't get discouraged and give up, for we will reap a harvest of blessing at the appropriate time.**
>
> **— Galatians 6:9 (NLT)**

Many years ago, an old pastor told me the story about a fellow who sold everything he possessed to buy an oil rig. He was sure there was oil on this little piece of property he bought in Texas. So he set up his rig and hired a team to begin drilling. They drilled every day without any success. The money was running out and still they hadn't struck oil. The owner decided he had better sell the property and equipment quickly before he went bankrupt. A large oil company bought him out for pennies on the dollar. They drilled just three feet deeper and struck one of the biggest oil veins in the history of that part of Texas. The original owner lost out on multiple millions of dollars because he stopped three feet short of a miracle.

Many give up just before the miracle was scheduled to arrive. They quit tithing. They quit sowing, or they become sporadic about their planting. Paul tells us to keep sowing, keep doing good, because if we don't give up, we'll reap a great harvest.

Are you ready to come into the wealthy place? Make sure you count the cost. It may mean that you have to put something off now so that you can have a better future. It's up to you. God loves you regardless of whether or not you are living in the wealthy place spoken of by the Psalmist. It's just that it's more fun in the wealthy place.

"You need a plan of attack. And that's exactly what I am giving you."

CHAPTER 17

Practical Wealth Concepts

Jake and Carlene lead a fairly normal life. They work, attend church, give regularly, and are doing their best to raise three beautiful children. They have a mortgage on their house, make monthly payments on their two cars, try to save a little when they can, but it always seems to be the same old story: "Too much month left at the end of the money." They keep waiting for some miracle to change things, but it never seems to happen.

Their life is okay. They aren't complaining. They just wish they could somehow change things for the better financially. They'd like to be able to afford nice vacations, send their children to a private school, put more money away for their golden years, remodel their house, and work less so they could have more family time. But every year, it's more of the same.

Jake and Carlene are good people. Like many couples, however, they are frustrated financially. They don't understand how to reach their financial dreams, but they are waiting for that big miracle to arrive.

Are they wrong to be waiting for their miracle? Not at all. But what Jake and Carlene must come to understand is that *they* hold the key to their financial future. It won't come to them by chance. Wealth is a choice, not a chance. A choice will change your destiny. That's why God said, "Choose this day. . .."

> **I call heaven and earth to record this day against you, *that* I have set before you life and death, blessing and cursing: therefore choose life, that both thou and thy seed may live:**
>
> **— Deuteronomy 30:19**

> **Choose you this day whom you will serve.**
>
> **— Joshua 24:15**

Will you serve money? Or will you serve the Living God? Will you choose life? Will you choose wealth?

Many people choose poverty by default. It's because they have never consciously chosen wealth. Wealth doesn't just happen. It has to be chosen. You can choose to find all the reasons why wealth is evil, or you can choose to find all the reasons why God wants you to have wealth. The choice is yours and will determine your financial destiny.

It's up to you. You can ***decide today*** to change your future. Once you make the decision for wealth, the rest will fall into place. You'll seek a vision. You'll find the right knowledge for wealth. Then you'll begin to take the right actions toward your financial vision.

These are the three important keys to your wealth: vision, knowledge, and action. Let's look at these three keys.

Vision

There are thousands of reasons for ***not*** coming into the wealthy place. But it only takes one good reason for you to come into the wealthy place. That one reason will be your motivating springboard. Can you think of one good reason to come into the wealthy place?

To bring pleasure to God?

To finance a particular mission?

To have personal financial freedom?

Perhaps you'd like to list more than one reason. That's up to you. But all it takes is one good reason. I'd suggest that you stop reading for a moment, take out a piece of paper and a pen and list all the reasons why you want to experience radical wealth. This will help you develop vision. Spelling out your financial vision on paper is always an important step toward turning it into a reality. The moment you start clearly listing your dreams and desires on paper, you're forced to get down to specifics and faith will be activated.

Faith cannot go after nebulous, obscure wishes. Faith is the substance of things (specific things) hoped for (Hebrews 11:1). When you know specifically your vision, dreams, and desires when it comes to wealth, and you are convinced that it is within the framework of God's will, then faith can be activated to pursue whatever it is you hope for (envision).

Many people are like Jake and Carlene. They live good Christian lives, daydreaming that someday their wealth ship will come in. But that's like a hunter shooting aimlessly all over the forest hoping to hit a deer. No, you need focus; a vision.

> **Where *there is* no vision, the people perish: but he that keepeth the law, happy *is* he.**
>
> **— Proverbs 29:18**

With vision, you'll be able to see things others don't see.

> **While we look not at the things which are seen, but at the things which are not seen: for the things which are seen *are* temporal; but the things which are not seen *are* eternal.**
>
> **— 2 Corinthians 4:18**

What would you do if you had $5,000,000 right now? What would you do for your church? What would you do for your family? What would you do to leave your mark on this generation? What would you own? What schools would you send your children or grandchildren to? Write these things down on paper. If the vision is valuable to you, it's worth writing down on paper.

> **And the LORD answered me, and said, Write the vision, and make *it* plain upon tables, that he may run that readeth it.**
>
> **— Habakkuk 2:2-3**

A Wealth Notebook

Get a wealth notebook. It doesn't have to be anything fancy, just a book full of blank pages. Booksellers sometimes have in stock those 8 ½ by 11 journals that have 200 blank pages. These are perfect. You will use this wealth book ***only*** to write out your financial vision, your financial goals, your giving records, and everything relating to your finances.

Write in your book:

1. *Your vision for wealth* and the reason(s) you want to have radical wealth.

2. *A list of 50 things you really want* (education, giving goals, ministry or business goals, ministry or business dreams, etc.). When you do this, you'll be surprised how difficult it is, especially if you've let your mind grow musty over the years you've been living in the room of "just enough."

3. *Pictures that motivate you* from magazines. Paste them into your wealth book. This will help your vision.

Most people need a vision stretching exercise, so don't be afraid to go wild in this. Cut out pictures of missionaries you'd like to support, vacation spots you'd like to see, and material things you'd like to own. Stretch your vision. This is pleasing to God.

Knowledge

That brings us to the next step in our walk to the wealthy place: knowledge. Nobody is born with the knowledge required for radical wealth, it has to be learned. Knowing the truth will set you free from financial bondage. Yet one thing you have to remember and hold onto tenaciously is the fact that God gives you the *power* to get wealth. It is a gift. But He expects you to get the practical know-how.

There are two kinds of knowledge you need: (1) Spiritual, and (2) Practical. Spiritual knowledge, of course, is found in God's Word. Jesus said, "The words that I speak unto you are spirit and they are life," (John 6:63). Spiritual knowledge can bring you amazing prosperity and success.

> **This book of the law shall not depart out of thy mouth; but thou shalt meditate therein day and night, that thou mayest observe to do according to all that is written therein: for then thou shalt make thy way prosperous, and then thou shalt have good success.**
>
> **— Joshua 1:8**

> **Blessed *is* the man that walketh not in the counsel of the ungodly, nor standeth in the way of sinners, nor sitteth in the seat of the scornful. But his delight *is* in the law of the LORD; and in his law doth he meditate day and night. And he shall be like a tree planted by the rivers of water, that bringeth forth his fruit in his season; his leaf also shall not wither; and whatsoever he doeth shall prosper.**
>
> **— Psalm 1:1-3**

We have discussed what God's Word declares about wealth already. You already have received the spiritual knowledge about tithing, giving, and making supernatural faith promises. You know about God's laws of sowing and reaping. You are committed to doing these things. Now I want to look at some practical matters that will help you. I want to give you some practical knowledge to help you come out of the room of "just enough" and move into the room of "more than enough."

1. *Step 1 — Itemize all your assets and liabilities to find out where you are financially.* Make a "T-chart" in your wealth book. On the left side, list all your assets. On the right side list all your liabilities. In other words, on the left side, write "What God has entrusted to me." On the right side, write, "What I owe."

WHAT GOD HAS ENTRUSTED TO ME:

"My Assets"

Be sure to list on the left side:

- Cash on hand
- Savings account balance
- Checking account balance
- Money Market account balance
- Whole Life Insurance policy cash value
- Stocks
- Bonds
- Government Securities
- Mutual Funds
- Precious Metals
- Certificates of Deposit (C.D.'s)
- Automobiles
- Furniture

- Collectibles
- Clothing
- Jewelry
- House equity (Value minus what you owe)
- Other properties
- IRA account
- Pension Fund
- 401(k) or 403(b)
- Tax-sheltered annuity
- Anything else of any value you have

WHAT I OWE:

"My Liabilities"

On the right side of the paper, list:

- Monthly rent (times 12)
- Utilities (times 12)
- Charge Account balances
- Credit Card balances
- Insurance premiums (annual)
- Other expenses (phone, cable, etc.)
- Federal Income Tax (annual)
- State Income Tax (annual)
- City Income Tax (annual)
- Property Tax (annual)
- FICA (social security, annual)
- Home (balance owed)

- Other taxes
- Other property (balance owed)
- Auto payments (balance owed)
- Education (loan balance, tuition, etc.)
- Home improvements
- Other

Now add up the left column. Then add up the right column. If your liabilities (right column) are more than your assets (left column), then you are in debt. You now have the knowledge of your net worth. You can put this knowledge to use by praying specifically for what you need to get out of debt and start coming through the door to the wealthy place.

2. *Step 2 — List your financial goals in your wealth book.* You know how much you need to pay off your debts. This should be one of your financial goals. Get out of debt as rapidly as you possibly can. If you owe $140,000 on a house, your payments will be approximately $1,200 a month. Out of that $1,200, over $1,100 will go to pay interest in the early years of the loan. That's over $250 a week going into the whirling black hole, never to be seen again — at least by you.

3. *Step 3 — List the price you are willing to pay to come out of debt (the room of your life that is "just*

enough.") Jesus taught us to count the cost before embarking on a project like this (Luke 14:28).

Ask yourself these tough questions and answer them by writing them in your wealth book:

❒ Am I willing to avoid credit card purchases for a season, until I come into the wealthy place and can pay the balance in full every month?

❒ Am I willing to make extra payments on my house every month in order to pay it off speedily and avoid those interest payments?

❒ Am I willing to drive a "junker" until I can afford to pay cash for the car I really want?

❒ Am I willing to invest in newsletters, magazines, and books that will give me more knowledge about investments and financial planning?

❒ Am I willing to turn off the television and listen to audiocassettes or watch videocassettes that will improve my knowledge in the area of finances?

❒ Am I willing to stop buying on my emotions in response to slick advertising?

These are some tough questions, but you have to ask them and be brutally honest with yourself. God doesn't want you to put your brain on the shelf when it comes to wealth.

You need a plan of attack. And that's exactly what I am giving you, a plan of attack.

Knowledge Arrives When You Are Ready For It

I'll always remember the day I decided that wealth was within the will and purpose of God for His children. By "chance," I stumbled upon a cassette tape by Venita Van Caspel, entitled "Money Dynamics." She taught about stocks, bonds, mutual funds, and other investment options. She said that she always set a goal of 20% growth in her investments each year. At that rate, money doubles every three and a half years.

Then I went to the bookstore and purchased all kinds of books about investing. I studied them until I had a basic understanding of the various types of investment vehicles available. I wanted to have some storehouses God could command blessings into, so I set up some accounts. I started with practically nothing except a wealth book, some goals, and a few books. I found an old whole life insurance policy that had a cash value of $500, so I cashed it in, bought term life insurance, and started a storehouse account.

I was walking with my wife through Mount Dora, Florida one day, going through all the antique shops. We walked into an old used bookstore, and there was a $29 book by Venita Van Caspel selling for just $2. So I bought it and studied more. Knowledge was coming to me, even though it seemed like a huge maze at first. Once you make the commitment to radical wealth, determine the reason why you want radical wealth, lay out a vision, and commit everything to God, the right knowledge will begin to come your way for activating that power to get wealth. That's what happened with me.

Maybe this book is an answer to your prayer. Perhaps you have committed to radical wealth, and so God brought this book to you. It's not an exhaustive study, but it's enough to whet your appetite for more.

Ignorance is not bliss. Ignorance is not blessed. Ignorance is inexcusable, because it means you are ignoring something that is available. Ignorance is ignoring knowledge that is available. Ignorance carries a high price tag. This is why many folks don't know how to prevent money problems and can never figure out how to solve money problems. Ignorance.

Do you know the definition of a fool? It's a person who does the same thing over and over again, hoping to get different results. I know people who would love to have some extra wealth to do some wonderful things, but they never bother reading a book like this. It may challenge them to do things differently. So, they remain in their rut of doing the same things over and over and getting the same financial results over and over.

Some are always complaining about not having enough money. Yet they have not even once visited the library to research any books that may be able to help them. Hundreds are available. But they reject knowledge. Consequently, they are rejected from the wealthy place.

Get spiritual knowledge. Get practical knowledge. But don't stop there. Put your knowledge into action!

Action

If you are not yet enjoying "the wealthy place," then it's only because you haven't taken enough actions in the right direction yet. I'm going to share with you some simple wealth actions that you can begin right away.

Action 1 — Get out of debt. Deuteronomy 28:12-13 tells us that we are to lend to many nations and not borrow. This is one of the ways God promised to make His people the head and not the tail. List all your debts and come up with a plan for paying them off rapidly. John Avanzini has a complete course you can study. You may write for information: John Avanzini, P.O. Box 1057, Hurst, Texas 76053.

I bought both my son and my daughter a course entitled Debt Free and Prosperous Living by John Cummuta. It wasn't cheap, but worth every penny. John teaches why it's important to get back to the Biblical principle of living debt free. He believes you should pay off your home mortgage within seven years. I agree with him wholeheartedly. You may write for information to: Debt Free & Prosperous Living, Inc., 310 Second St., Boscobel, WI 53805

Action 2 — Open a storehouse account. It's alright to have a bank savings account, but don't expect much increase there. They will loan you money for a high percentage, but when you loan them money (by keeping your money in a savings account) they will pay you hardly any interest at all. It's better to get the "One Account" from Charles Schwab and Company. You will get check-writing privileges, a Visa debit card, and you can buy virtually any kind of investment through your "One Account." You may call (800) 435-4000 for information.

Another company I like is Fidelity Investments. Call them at (800) 544-8888. They have something similar to the "One Account." You can purchase stocks and mutual funds right through your account. It's easy once you do it a few times. It's a little scary at first, like anything, but before you know it, you'll be acting like a pro, buying and selling.

Action 3 — Use legal tax shelters. Some people are afraid of tax shelters, but Congress created them to meet specific needs in the country. When the need is no longer there, they will create some different tax shelters. The IRS isn't out to "get you." They want you to take every legitimate deduction and deferral within the framework of the law. But they want you to comply with the laws. That's their job.

I know a Christian man who is a high ranking official in the IRS. I spent an hour or so one afternoon chatting with him on the phone about taxes, deductions, and the IRS. What a precious man he is. You don't have to be afraid of the IRS. They don't want you to pay more taxes than you are required to under the law. Under our law we can utilize tax deferred investment vehicles such as Individual Retirement Accounts, Keoghs 401(k)'s, and tax-sheltered variable annuities. Make it your goal to fund these to the maximum every year.

Start with a 401(k) or 403(b) with your employer if it is offered. If there is a matching funds program, put in as much as you possibly can. That's 100% increase each time your employer will match your contribution.

Next, establish a simple IRA or Roth IRA. Put the maximum in every year. Make it one of your financial goals and write it in your wealth book.

Years ago, I helped an associate minister set up an individual retirement account. The first year he received 12% interest on his tax-deferred investment. Then, after reading The Mutual Fund Forecaster[15], I suggested he switch to another fund. Within less than two years he had gained 123% interest and growth on his investment.[16]

The law of compounding interest is amazing. It works against you when you borrow. It works for you when you invest regularly. Benjamin Franklin said, "Compound interest is the eighth wonder of the world." Albert Einstein stated that, "Compound interest is the world's greatest discovery." With the miracle of compound interest, everyone can attain wealth.

It's not how much money you earn that makes a difference. It's what you do with the money you earn that will determine whether or not you are destined for wealth. Theodore Johnson, who never made more than $14,000 a year working for United Parcel Service is a great example. He plowed every cent of savings he had back into UPS stock and let the law of compound interest work for him. Last year, his net worth was a cool $70,000,000!

Let's say your parents had put $1,000 into a good mutual fund for you back in 1950. Today that single $1,000 investment would be worth a whopping

$217,630. How does that work? It's the law of compound interest. You don't have to understand it to benefit from it. Essentially, after the first year of your investment, you start getting interest not only on your principle (original amount deposited), but also on the interest it has earned. Your investment will eventually move into exponential growth. It's amazing.

If your grandparents had put just $100 into a trust fund for you back in 1926,today, at an average rate of return, it would be worth $266,139. That's how compound interest works.

If today, you put $1,000 into a good IRA investment like a growth mutual fund, in 30 years, because of compound interest, you could easily have $636,372.

Many don't have the discipline to say "no" to the things they want now. So they sacrifice their future, their children's future, and their grandchildren's future. It's not too late to start now. Every unnecessary dollar you spend now, that could have been invested, will actually cost you $636! That item you bought at the dollar store — that thing you really didn't need — costs you $636 in future money. Think about that! Every ninety-nine cent special you buy on impulse is costing you over $600! The power of compound interest is astonishing.

Set up an IRA today. Don't wait. The clock is ticking and it will stop for nobody. Every moment you waste could cost you thousands of dollars.

After you have your 401(k) and IRA set up, establish a tax-sheltered annuity. Make it a faith goal to put as much as you possibly can into this investment vehicle. It all grows tax-deferred, which means you can make a fortune in interest if you keep it long enough. I like Vanguard Company for annuities, because of their low expense ratio. You can get information at (800) 462-2391.

Study the tax laws and use them to your benefit. There is a publication I like that you can order called *Tax Hotline*. You can write to the subscription service center at P.O. Box 58454, Boulder, CO 80323-8454. Call (800) 288-1051.

There are more tax advantages you can enjoy on certain select investments, but they change so often, it's best for you to check this out for yourself, rather than take a chance on getting some outdated information from me.

Action 4 — Make small corrections along the way. The best pilots have something in common. They have a firm fix on their destination and they make small corrections along the way. You can do that in your investments, also. Sometimes you'll want to own domestic stocks, sometimes you'll want international stocks, and sometimes you'll want both. But you'll always be making small corrections here and there along the way to the "wealthy place."

Doug Fabian writes a newsletter called the *Maverick Investor* that tells you, according to his research, the best times to buy and sell. I have used Fabian services for a number of years. His goal is to provide advice that will help you gain between 17% and 20% growth per year in your investments. He helps you to make those small corrections along the way. You can call (800) 950-8765 for information. Fabian advises the use of mutual funds exclusively.

With the advent of the Internet, you can check your investments virtually any time you want. You may have the computer savvy to use an Internet brokerage company. Schwab, Fidelity, e-Trade, Ameri-Trade and others offer Internet trading services, making it easy for you to make little corrections along the way.

Action 5 — Don't count on Social Security. The Social Security System was not designed to be a retirement plan, but a supplement. The maximum annual benefit to recipients in the year 2000 was $12,663. Can you live on that? Don't even try. Plan ahead by funding your storehouses and letting God bless them.

If an 18 year-old saves just $1 a day at an easy 15% return, he will have a little over $2,646,156 by the time he retires. If he saves $2 a day, it will come to over $5,000,000. Most people are currently putting all their money into interest payments, so they will suffer in the years ahead. You be smart.

If you invest in just eight of America's Finest Companies, your money will double every five years. $100,000 will go to $200,000 in five years. Bill Staton, "America's Money Coach," has an excellent audio cassette series on America's Finest Companies. Bill became a millionaire investor by the age of 35. You can contact the Staton Institute, 5955 Carnegie Blvd. #100, Charlotte, NC 28209.

Also, you need to read the best-selling book by David Chilton entitled, *The Wealthy Barber.* He has a video series available as well. Check with your local book store.

Action 6 — Protect your assets. Don't go "hog wild" with insurance, but you do need to protect your family. You probably don't need a whole life or universal policy. You probably need to buy only some cheap term insurance. Forget the mortgage insurance. It's a waste of money. Use your term life insurance to cover everything in the event of your death. But make sure you have at least enough life insurance to carry your family through five years. If your annual income is $50,000, get $250,000 in life insurance for your family.

Make sure you have a will and a trust set up properly. This in invaluable in protecting your assets after you've gone to Heaven. You'll need to invest in a good attorney who handles things like this.

*Action 7 — **Warning! Don't throw money into speculations on commodities, precious metals or options, unless you have a clear word from the Lord and you know what you're doing.*** Many people lose their proverbial shirts on these investments.

Don't buy investments on "hot tips." You will usually find a bankrupt brother-in-law who knows everything about the next big winner. Right! Never buy on "hot tips." And don't buy because of a phone pitch from some broker or dealer. Investigate all your investments yourself. Buy when they are low and sell when they are high.

*Action 8 — **Don't even think about robbing from God to begin your storehouse accounts, or to add to them.*** Bring your tithes to God's house. Give your radical offerings and keep making those supernatural faith promises. God will make it all up to you and more by commanding blessings on your storehouses. You don't want your finances under a curse, so be sure to make your principle investments into God's Kingdom.

If you, like Jake and Carlene, have now decided to change your future, you are ready for the adventure of coming into the wealthy place. You have chosen wealth. You have written out your vision and committed yourself to getting knowledge, both spiritual and practical. Now it's time to take action! So get busy with your wealth book. Do it ***right now***.

Here's your action plan:

A. Start a wealth notebook.

B. List all your financial goals: Tithing, giving, sharing, debt-reduction, investments, etc.

C. Carefully think about and list the price you are willing to pay to come into the wealthy place.

D. Write out your wealth vision.

E. Get knowledge (purchase books, tapes, newsletters, etc.) Go to a certified financial planner if necessary.

F. Take action ***now****. Find out whether or not your employer offers a 401(k) or has a stock purchase plan. Get into it. Establish an IRA and a Tax Sheltered Annuity. Also, set up an investment account like Charles Schwab's One Account.*

G. Keep your accounting with Heaven right by tithing, giving offerings, and making radical, supernatural faith promises.

CHAPTER 18

Roadblocks to Radical Wealth – Part 1

I am a pilot. I love to fly. I am sometimes asked, "What is the most important part of any flight?" My answer is always the same. "The most important part of any flight is the pre-flight inspection." If there is something wrong with the aircraft, you want to find it during the pre-flight inspection while you are still on the ground. Pilots have checklists to assist them in the various inspections and operations of an airplane.

That's what I'm going to give you in the next two chapters — a checklist. I'm going to show you the potential roadblocks on the road to radical wealth. There are thirty in all. I don't claim to have an exhaustive listing, but these are the most common pitfalls, or roadblocks, to avoid.

1. Failing to apply the law of synergy. Synergism is the simultaneous action of separate agencies, which, together, have a greater total effect than the sum of their individual effects. In other words, normally 2 + 2 = 4. But with synergy 2 + 2 could equal 10, or even 20!

For example, if you take Vitamin E by itself, it will have a certain effect. And if you take Selenium by itself, it also will have a certain effect. But if you take the two together, the total potency of both substances more than quadruples. That's synergy. The Bible speaks of synergy when it says, one can put a thousand to flight, but two can put ten thousand to flight. Two working harmoniously together can achieve ten times more than one working alone, and five times more than two working separately.[17]

The law of synergy says that when we engage all the principles simultaneously, our success will be greater than if we engage the principles one at a time.

For example, tithing is a great practice. Yet it is more productive when offerings are added at the same time. More success will come as we simultaneously put into practice the principles we've learned in this book.

I realize that when you are just starting out, you may have to combine two or three of the principles as a starting point. But as soon as you possibly can, initiate and utilize as many of the principles together as you possibly can. This is the law of synergy, which will empower you to get into the "wealthy place" much more quickly.

Let's look at the principles in order of priority, beginning with the spiritual principles and moving on to the practical principles. You must begin with the spiritual principles, at least in tithes and offerings (Malachi 3:8-12). This will ensure God's blessings on your money.

A. *Tithes* (Giving 10% of your gross income to the Lord)

B. *Offerings*

C. *Supernatural giving through faith promises*

D. *Radical Obedience to God and His Word*

E. *Vision* (The Wealth Book)

F. *Gaining knowledge and applying wisdom*

G. *Goals* (The plan)

H. *Coming out of debt*

I. *Establishing some investment storehouses*

J. *Applying tax laws to your advantage*

2. *Trusting in the wrong god.* Jesus said you cannot serve two masters because you will love one and hate the other, or vice versa. He said you cannot serve both God and money. It just can't be done.[18]

> **No one can serve two masters. For you will hate one and love the other, or be devoted to one and despise the other. You cannot serve both God and money.**
>
> **— Matthew 6:24 (NLT)**

Paul told Timothy that in the last days there would be counterfeit Christians who would act religious, but would love and trust only themselves and their money. He described them as having no self-control. For money, like Judas, they would even betray their friends. Paul said their faith is counterfeit, and even though they try to appear prosperous spiritually and financially, God calls them "Fools!"[19]

Jesus told of a man who trusted in his wealth instead of trusting in God. Just when he thought he had enough to take it easy and retire, God said to him, "You fool! You will die this very night." Then Jesus went on to explain, "Yes, a person is a fool to store up earthly wealth but not have a rich relationship with God." There's nothing wrong at all with investing and saving as long as you have a rich relationship with God.[20]

3. Living in iniquity. Iniquity is simply doing what we want to do without regard to God's will or purpose. It's worse than sin, because sin is simply missing the mark. Iniquity is when a person doesn't even care about the mark, God's laws, God's Word, or God's will. Basically, iniquity is independence.

That was Lucifer's downfall. Iniquity says, "I will . . ." "I will . . ." "I will . . ." (Isaiah 14:12-15).

4. Rejecing God's Covenant. God made a covenant with Abraham to multiply him and make him great (rich). The Lord blessed Abraham with riches. It is the Lord's blessing that makes people wealthy.

> **The blessing of the LORD, it maketh rich, and he addeth no sorrow with it.**
>
> **— Proverbs 10:22**

When we come to Jesus Christ in humble repentance from our sins, and with faith in God, we receive the blessings of Abraham.

> **Christ hath redeemed us from the curse of the law, being made a curse for us: for it is written, Cursed *is* every one that hangeth on a tree: That the blessing of Abraham might come on the Gentiles through Jesus Christ;**
>
> **— Galatians 3:13-14a**

Prosperity was promised to God's faithful people under the old covenant. We now, through Jesus Christ, have a better covenant with better promises (Hebrews

8:6). Now everything promised under the old covenant and the new covenant can be ours in Christ Jesus (2 Corinthians 1:20). Don't allow the devil to rob you of the full blessings of being in covenant with God.

Sometimes I am asked why some nations are so poor. My answer is always the same. It's because, by and large, they are not in covenant with God. The reason some Christians are not prospering is because they haven't believed and accepted God's wonderful covenant of blessings. They have accepted part of the covenant, eternal life through Christ, but they've failed to accept the deliverance from sickness and poverty as part of their covenant rights.

5. ***Withholding the tithe.*** The concept of tithing did not begin with Abraham or Moses. It began in the Garden of Eden when God said that He was reserving one tree for Himself. He told his creation, Adam and Eve, not to eat from His tree. They violated the law of the tithe and ate what belonged to God. Once multi-trillionaires, they were driven from their opulent, outrageously luxurious home, and sent off to make it the best they could elsewhere.

I have tried seriously to get this point across throughout this book. The tithe belongs to the Lord. To use the tithe for yourself in any way, brings a curse on your finances and may lead to serious consequences.

I remember an older couple standing in church one Wednesday evening as they confessed their sin to the entire congregation. They were weeping and holding each other, almost shaking. They said they had been missing church so they could build their retirement home on a lake in Northern Michigan. They confessed they had been using part of God's tithe to buy materials for their home. One Sunday, they drove up to find everything they had built in ashes. A fire destroyed the entire home. They lost all their family pictures, keepsakes, and everything that had any emotional and material value to them. They were going to get the home insured the next week, but now it was too late. They lost everything. They withheld part of the tithe from God, not remembering the Lord their God by not remembering His house and His tithe.[21]

Do you know what I have done for several years? I have given what I call a "faith tithe." I tithe on the income ***I want***, not the income I have. This practice has never failed me, because faith never fails. What do you want your income to be next year? Try "faith tithing" this year, based on what you expect next year.

6. Failing to choose prosperity. If you don't make a conscious choice for God's wealth, you are making a choice for lack by default. It's the same way with everything when it comes to the Kingdom of God. If you don't choose Jesus Christ, then by default, you are lost. If you don't choose prosperity, then by default, you are choosing whatever happens to come your way, in terms of wealth. It's that simple.[22]

7. ***Lacking knowledge.*** Hosea, the prophet, said concerning God's people, they are destroyed (fail, perish) for lack of knowledge. Jesus said that unregenerate people of this world are often wiser than the children of God (Luke 16:8). It's amazing that Jesus would say that, but it's true. Many people who don't know Christ will take the time to go to seminars and conferences that will help them realize their dreams. They will buy books to teach themselves how to get ahead.

Only a handful of believers ever take the time to go to a financial planner. Very few make an effort to search God's Word to find spiritual truth relating to wealth. They usually just parrot what they've heard someone else say. I conducted a solid year of scriptural research before I ever offered so much as an opinion about God's will concerning wealth and riches in the life of the believer.

Some Christians would rather drive a fancy car they purchased with borrowed money, than to invest in a financial library. This shows what they really respect. What you respect will come toward you, and what you don't respect will move away from you.

Your library will say everything that needs to be said about your respect for finances.

Ignorance is costly and can be deadly. Somebody knows something that you need to know. Somebody knows something that can help you move into the wealthy place more quickly. Pursue that somebody. It may be a financial planner or an investment advisor. It may be a person who has written a book to help you understand the principles of wealth. Invest in knowledge. Learn how to ignite that power to get wealth — that blessing that is already in you.

8. Following the wrong advice. You want to find places where you can get knowledge, but you want to go to the right places. Your broke, bankrupt cousin is not the fellow you should be going to for investment advice. The Psalmist wrote, "Blessed is the man that walketh not in the counsel of the ungodly." That's rule number one when it comes to getting advice. Don't go to the ungodly.

An insurance man who was a professing Christian was going over my finances years ago trying to sell me some insurance and investments. When he saw that my wife and I were giving 35% of our income to the Lord's work, he suggested that we cut it back to 7% and invest the savings. When I told him that I would certainly ***not*** cut back on our giving to the Lord, he accused me of not caring about my family. I showed him the door. My best investments have always been in the Kingdom of God, and one of the greatest things I could teach my children is to put God first in everything.

Don't listen to the advice of these salespeople who suggest you cut back on your giving to the Lord so you will have the money to buy their products. If you listen to them, you are a fool.

I attended an investor's conference a few years ago. I like to keep up with what the economy is doing, and which sectors the advisors are suggesting for investments. I heard Mark Skousen, an investment advisor, give a lecture.[23] He quoted Scriptures and seemed to reflect a decent moral image. I invested in one of his "picks" and doubled my investment in two months.

Doug Fabian and his father, Dick, are a couple of intelligent, well-prepared investment advisors. The Bible teaches us not to walk in the counsel of the ungodly. Doug and Dick are not ungodly men. In fact, I subscribe to Doug's newsletter and use it to review my investments every month. I have never heard Doug, or Dick recommend any investment that was socially unacceptable to me. They seem sensitive about this.[24]

I once wrote a quick note to Doug to tell him how much I enjoyed his presentation at an investor's conference, and I gave him a little word of blessing as I closed the letter. He sent me back a note of appreciation, thanking me over and over for that blessing.

On the other hand, I went to another workshop and ended up walking out. The man boasted about his track record for advising his clients. He then suggested to his attendees that they invest in a particular tobacco company and also in Playboy magazine. He thought these two stocks were going to be the next winners. I walked out. That's all I needed to know concerning his kind of counsel.

Then in another workshop I attended, I wanted to learn more about IPO's (initial public offerings). That's an area where I lacked knowledge. The presenter began to use unacceptable words and would frequently take the name of the Lord in vain. I listened to his presentation, but I never invested anything in his suggested companies. I don't trust people who do not respect God.

God will give you good discernment.

9. Failing to resist the devil. The devil came to steal, kill and destroy (John 10:10). Jesus came to give you an abundant life. Satan is roaming around the earth looking for someone to tear apart. He wants to steal your finances, kill your future, and destroy your wealth. He is seeking to devour you and your finances.[25]

The devil's nature is one of lies. He leaves in his path nothing but sin, sickness, and poverty. His tools are limited to temptation, deception, and accusation. He tempts people to withhold from God. He deceives people into thinking they can come into the wealthy place their own way, rather than God's way. He accuses you of loving money when you want more for your church, missions, and family. He accuses preachers of preaching the "Wall Street gospel" when they are only trying to lift God's people to their full rights and inheritance in Jesus Christ. He is a liar and the father of all lies.[26]

We are told to resist the devil steadfastly.[27] Don't give him an inch. If something breaks down, costing you money, demand a seven-fold return on your loss. The devil is a thief, and if you catch him, order him to pay seven times more than he stole (See Proverbs 6:30, 31).

The devil will tell you there is virtue in lack. If you don't believe he is a liar, just drive down to an area of town where poverty and lack are prevalent. You'll find no virtue or glory there. You'll find high crime, prostitution, X-rated movie houses, and hungry, hurt children.

Don't be afraid to engage in spiritual warfare over your finances. I've had to do this many times. I bind demons, loose angels and get violent with the devil.[28]

Bob Harrison took a dying Chrysler dealership in Southern California and by resisting the devil, engaging in spiritual warfare, and listening to God, turned that dealership into one of the great success stories of our generation. And he did it all during a time of recession when a dealership per week was going bankrupt. Today Bob leads some of the finest financial seminars available through Harrison International. He has produced tape albums such as "Spiritual Warfare in Your Finances," and "How You Can Cause Financial Increase." You may contact Bob Harrison at P.O. Box 701890, Tulsa, Oklahoma 74170 or by calling (800) 632-4653.

10. Living in disharmony and strife. Jesus said a house divided against itself cannot stand.[29] This is true in business, in the ministry, and in the home. St. James tells us that strife is found wherever there is envy and confusion.[30] In fact, strife brings confusion, which gives us a clue as to its source. God is not the author of confusion.[31] Paul said that those who get into strife can be taken captive by the devil at his will.[32]

There is synergistic power in agreement.[33]

Suppose you want a three-bedroom house, but your spouse wants a four-bedroom house. Unless you can agree on what you desire, it is fruitless to even pray. Faith does not work where there is strife or division. If you are facing a financial mountain, the first place I'd look into is the area of strife. Is the house divided?

Many couples miss out on countless blessings because of fighting in the home instead of agreement. What do you want? You must agree on it. And here's something that may not be too popular, nonetheless, I need to say it. If you cannot agree on something, then the wife, generally speaking, should submit graciously to her husband's plan, just for the sake of harmony. It may not be easy, but if you do it with a good attitude, you can prevent the devil from destroying your wealth.[34]

At all costs, protect your power of agreement. Strife is the devil's trap.

11. Underestimating the power of words. Few people realize the power of their words and the enormous impact these words have on their condition in life. I wish we could all tape record ourselves for one day and then listen to it. We might be shocked at what has slipped out of our mouths.

- Wrong words can poison your entire life, including your finances (Proverbs 7).
- You can protect your life with proper, faith words (Proverbs 13:3).
- Your words tell others whether you are wise or a fool (Proverbs 15:2).
- Failure can be the fruit of speaking improper and inappropriate words (Proverbs 18:7).
- Your words will determine whether or not your financial dreams will live or die (Proverbs 18:21).
- Your words can be a source of introducing major troubles into your life (Proverbs 21:23).
- Your words can become a trap; a snare that can destroy your wealth (Proverbs 6:2).
- Your words are more crucial to your success than possessing silver or gold (Proverbs 10:20).
- Your words can affect how quickly you will come into the wealthy place (Proverbs 18:20).

There is remarkable power in your words. In fact, the power of life and death is in the tongue.[35]

Yet listen to most people's words. "I can't afford it." "I don't have the right background." "I'm stupid when it comes to money." "I come from a poor family and I'll probably always be poor."

Make this your day to begin speaking the Word of God. Here are some good things to confess daily.

- "God wishes that I prosper and be in health," (3 John 2).
- "My storehouses are being filled with plenty because I put God first," (Proverbs 3:9,10).
- "All good things are being added unto my life because I seek first God's Kingdom and His righteousness," (Matthew 6:33).
- "I will come into the place of wealth regardless of my background," (Psalm 66:12).
- "God is blessing me with wealth! It is not because I have the right education, but because of His marvelous grace, I have been given the amazing power to get wealth," (Deuteronomy 8:18).
- "Regardless of my past mistakes, God is restoring me and making me wealthy," (Job 42:10; Joel 2:25).

- "The windows of Heaven are open to my life and the devourer is rebuked," (Malachi 3:8-12).

You get the idea. Every time you find a Scripture relating to wealth, start confessing it. Drive out that old vocabulary. When my kids were young, I never told them that we couldn't afford anything. If we were temporarily out of money and they wanted to go get an ice cream cone, I'd say, "Hey, I have a better idea. Let's whittle a stick!" That sounded like a great idea to them. They never knew when we were struggling financially in our early years of ministry because we always confessed prosperity, according to God's Word. In time, the prosperity followed our faith words.

Words are important.

I know a businessman who read Mark 11:23 and took Jesus seriously about speaking to the mountain. That's a good thing to do — take Jesus seriously. The man quit talking about how bad his business was doing. He put a watch over his mouth (Psalm 141:3) and stopped complaining about his losses and frustrations. He actually started commanding his business to start making money. He spoke to his mountain and within a few months his accountant announced that the business was out of the "red" and into the profit zone. You'll only come into the wealthy profit zone when you learn to speak to your mountains, watch your words, and say things according to God's Word, not according to the way things "appear."

> **For verily I say unto you, That whosoever shall say unto this mountain, Be thou removed, and be thou cast into the sea; and shall not doubt in his heart, but shall believe that those things which he saith shall come to pass; he shall have whatsoever he saith.**
>
> **— Mark 11:23**

Speak to your debts. But don't stop there. Start sopping them up. Speak to your accounts receivables and start receiving. Why not? Jesus spoke to a tree and made it do what He said. He did it to give us a lesson in faith.[36] Sound foolish? Remember, God is pleased to use the foolish things to confound the wise.[37]

Put the pressure on the devil. When Jesus wanted to send the devil away, He spoke simple WORDS from the Old Testament. When you want to send the devil away from your finances, speak God's Word continually. Confess God's promises of prosperity and wealth daily. Submit to God's Word, resist the devil with your faith words, and you'll find that you have just passed by another pothole in the road to radical wealth.

12. Listening to false teachers. Quit listening to the "sick, sorry, and broke" preachers who would love to hold you back from radical wealth. Quit listening to your critics who think you should be broke instead of wealthy. Little by little, if you keep listening to them, their words will sink into your soul. Solomon said, "Stop listening to teaching that contradicts what you know is right ," (Proverbs 19:27 TLB).

Jesus warned us to be careful what we listen to (Mark 4:24). Listen to men like Dr. John Avanzini, a man used in an extraordinary way to unveil God's truth's about wealth. Listen to preachers who refuse to compromise God's Word; preachers like Kenneth Copeland, or Dr. LeRoy Thompson. Get into a church where your pastor is interested in seeing you succeed in life, rather than holding you back. Find a place where the pastor encourages you to go after all that God has available for you.

13. Being unwilling to prosper. Believe it or not, some people are not willing to prosper. Some grown children think it will make their poor parents feel like failures if they excel in wealth. There are any number of reasons why some may not be willing to come into wealth, but usually the reasons are well camouflaged.

> **If ye be WILLING and obedient, ye shall eat the good of the land: But if ye refuse and rebel, ye**

> **shall be devoured with the sword: for the mouth of the LORD hath spoken *it*.**
>
> **— Isaiah 1:19,20**

How can you know if you are willing to prosper? It's easy to tell. Are you willing to spend four hours to carefully write out your wealth vision in your wealth book? Have you purchased your wealth book yet, or did that get pushed to the back of your priority list? Are you willing to take an hour a week to review your wealth plan? Are you willing to purchase the necessary books, tapes, and newsletters that will help you in your wealth attainment?

The answers to these questions will signal whether or not you are truly willing to prosper.

14. Having a poverty image. You will never rise above your inside image. In New York, a group of Christians went to a run down apartment building and, as a gesture of goodwill, fixed it all up. It was beautiful. The people should have been proud of their newly renovated home. Instead, in less than two years, it was all run down again. You can get a new set of clothes, but if you don't change your inside image, you'll be back in rags before long.

Until we change our image on the inside, we will stay the same as we are. That's why Paul told us to renew our minds (Romans 12:1-2). Don't be like the ten spies with a self-image problem. Be like Joshua and Caleb who knew that with God, they were more than winners.

Do you see yourself as a victim or as a conqueror? If you see yourself as a victim of your age, your background, your family history, your past failures, your environment, or your culture, ***change it now!***

> **For as he thinketh in his heart, so *is* he: Eat and drink, saith he to thee; but his heart *is* not with thee.**
>
> **— Proverbs 23:7**

Use God's Word to discover everything He has said about you. Find out who you are in Christ and take a few minutes every day, with your eye of faith, to see yourself as the conqueror God has created you to be.

15. Being unwilling to start where you are now. "Now faith is . . . ."[38] Some say, "Oh, I'll begin tithing when I have more money." No you won't. If you don't start now, you are cheating yourself out of the radical wealth God has planned for you. That's why God said, "Prove me ***now*** . . . ."[39]

You can start your wealth book ***now***. It will only cost you a couple of dollars and four hours of your time. You can begin to tithe ***now***! You can start buying your wealth library ***now***. You can do something *now*, while you are motivated. You can begin your plan for debt-reduction *now*. You can start a savings account or investment account *now*.

Don't wait another minute. Get off your easy chair and go to the store and buy yourself a notebook to begin your plan. Take one small action toward the wealthy place.

Send a note to your pastor and tell him you are going to begin tithing *now*, if you don't already. If you do tithe, start giving offerings too. Right *now* you can ask God where He wants you to plant a money seed to begin your money harvest. There is something you can do *now*.

These are just fifteen of the roadblocks on the road to radical wealth. In the next chapter, I'll give you more. Remember, these serve as a checklist. Go over them often, the way that a pilot checks over his aircraft each time before he flies.

And never forget this: ***You are destined for radical wealth.***

Why don't you insert your name, and sign this certificate *now*?

Radical Wealth Certificate

I, ______________________________

am destined for radical wealth. I will pray, plan, and prepare to come into the wealthy place.

Signed:___________________

Date: _____________

"Without clear-cut financial goals your faith will be unfocused, weak, and diluted."

CHAPTER 19

Roadblocks to Radical Wealth – Part 2

Let's continue with our checklist now. I like checklists. If something isn't working that is supposed to be working, I just go over the list to see if I have overlooked anything.

I find out where I am missing the mark and I take the corrective actions necessary to fix the problem.

We've discussed Roadblocks 1 to 15. Now let's look at more roadblocks on the road to radical wealth.

16. Having no specific financial goals. Goals are targets at which to aim. If you aim for nothing, you'll probably hit nothing. At best, without goals, you're taking a chance and wasting a lot of energy in the process.

Every sport has goals. In football, the goal is the touchdown. In basketball, the goal is the hoop. In baseball, it's the home run, or at least getting runs back to home plate. In hockey, the goal is the goal! Without goals, you have no way to measure your progress.

Jesus said, "What ***things*** soever ye desire, when ye pray, believe that ye receive them and ye shall have them," (Mark 11:24). I want you to focus on the word "***things***."

That word, "***things***," means objects or objectives. Objectives are goals. Specific targets. As I mentioned earlier in this book, faith cannot go after nonspecific, nebulous, obscure things.

"Faith is the substance (or substantiating) of ***things*** hoped for," (Hebrews 11:1). Faith needs a specific target.

Without clear-cut financial goals your faith will be unfocused, weak, and diluted. That's why I gave you a project in chapter seventeen to make a list of the ***things*** you really want, because faith can only pursue specific things. Without financial goals, you'll have to be satisfied with whatever life happens to bring to you, whether it be wealth or lack of wealth.

Ten Or Twenty Years From Now

Try to imagine yourself ten or twenty years from now. How do you see your financial condition? What would you like to have in life? What missions projects would you like to be supporting? What kind of a home would you like to be living in? How much money would you like to have in your "storehouses?" Write out your vision in your wealth book, and then begin to work backward setting goals for attaining the things you ***desire***. Remember, Jesus said, "What ***things*** soever ye ***desire*** . . .."

Make your goals big enough for God to work miracles on your behalf along the way.

One of my financial goals, about which I regularly pray, is to live on just the interest in one of my storehouse accounts. I desire to give 55% of my income to the Lord's work. It is all written out. What are your financial goals?

Some will tithe and give offerings as money seeds into God's work, then never set a goal for their harvest. Faith needs a specific target. Your financial goals will be the targets for your faith to go running after. Once you set your financial goals, you'll get a glimpse of how faith works, and you'll wonder why you didn't unearth this secret sooner.

Often times, a person will walk up to me and say, "I want more money. Will you pray that God will give me more money?"

I then ask, "How much more do you want?"

The response is typically the same. "Oh, I don't know. I guess, maybe enough to get out of debt, pay my bills, and live comfortably."

Again I ask, "How much is that?"

Rarely can a person tell me how much they really want. Prayer and faith, to be authentically powerful, and to bring results, must be specific and focused. If a person prays, "Oh, Lord, send me more money," and then finds a penny later that day, their prayer has been answered. They have more money. Prayer and faith must be focused like a laser to bring your desired outcome. Goals provide the specificity you need for faith to function successfully. Not only that, faith needs specific promises from God's Word in order to be activated for launching you into the harvest of wealth.

My book, *Faith Goals — The Secret Of Setting And Reaching Them,*[40] is available at your local bookstore, or you may write to us for information on how you can get a copy. This would be a great addition to your wealth-building library.

17. Being lazy. The Bible has nothing good to say about laziness and slothfulness. Laziness affects your wealth.

> **Take a lesson from the ants, you lazybones. Learn from their ways and be wise! Even though they have no prince, governor, or ruler to make them work, they labor hard all summer, gathering food for the winter. But you lazybones, how long will you sleep? When will you wake up? I want you to learn this lesson: A little extra sleep, a little more slumber, a little folding of the hands to rest — and poverty will pounce on you like a bandit; scarcity will attack you like an armed robber.**
>
> **— Proverbs 6:6-11 (NLT)**

This is God's message to lazy people. The promise for laziness is poverty and scarcity. Some folks are too lazy to go out and gather their harvest when it's staring them right in the face. Remember, God does not give you wealth; He gives you the power to get wealth. The wealth comes as a harvest. You have to go out and bring it in.

There is a common tendency in the human race toward laziness. It's easier ***not to*** learn something new than it is ***to*** learn something new. It's more comfortable ***not to*** work than it is ***to*** work. Laziness is a sin that each of us must combat if we are to come into the place of radical wealth.

Jesus spoke about an unfruitful servant in Matthew 25. The real reason that the servant was not productive or successful, Jesus revealed, was because he was "slothful!" In other words, he was just plain L-A-Z-Y!

May I make a recommendation to you? I recommend that you read the Book of Proverbs once a month for an entire year. Proverbs will give you wisdom, and wisdom will show you the action steps for getting wealth (Proverbs 8:17-21).

> **He becometh poor that dealeth *with* a slack hand: but the hand of the diligent maketh rich. He that gathereth in summer *is* a wise son: *but* he that sleepeth in harvest *is* a son that causeth shame.**
>
> **— Proverbs 10:4-5**

> **The hand of the diligent shall bear rule: but the slothful shall be under tribute. The slothful *man* roasteth not that which he took in hunting: but the substance of a diligent man *is* precious.**
>
> **— Proverbs 12:24, 27**

> **The soul of the sluggard desireth, and *hath* nothing: but the soul of the diligent shall be made fat.**
>
> **— Proverbs 13:4**

> **The sluggard will not plow by reason of the cold; *therefore* shall he beg in harvest, and *have* nothing.**
>
> **— Proverbs 20:4**

You can't humanly help a lazy man. He'll have an excuse for his failure every time you try to teach him principles of wealth.

> **The slothful *man* saith, *There is* a lion in the way; a lion *is* in the streets.**
>
> **— Proverbs 26:13**

Although neatly disguised, he's making an excuse for his laziness. Why doesn't he succeed and come into the wealthy place? There is something "in the way!" In this instance it was a lion.

Usually, the lazy man will not yield to godly reason. You see, he knows it all! He is wise in his own conceits. The best thing to do for this poor individual is to pray for him, asking God to help him see the destructiveness of being lazy.

> **The sluggard is wiser in his own conceit than seven men that can render a reason.**
>
> **— Proverbs 26:16**

Laziness breaks up relationships, disintegrates personalities, and causes untold family problems. Laziness will keep a person poor.

> **Yet a little sleep, a little slumber, a little folding of the hands to sleep: So shall poverty come . . ..**
>
> **— Proverbs 24:33-34a**

18. Failing to listen to God. How can you obey God if you won't listen to God? You begin to learn how to hear God's voice by first obeying His written Word, the Bible. Jesus said, "My sheep know my voice." God has a voice, and that voice will tell you where your harvest is located and how to reap it. God's voice will tell you what to give and where to give in order to produce the greatest harvest.

My Florida Home

I wanted to find a nice condominium in Florida. I desired a place where I could go five times a year so I could write my books and make plans for my church. If I have sixteen hours a day of uninterrupted time, I can accomplish more in one week than many people can in a whole year. So, I started calling realtors and searching for a condo.

I planned to rent the condo to short-term vacationers when I was back in Michigan. I figured that would pay for the home, and I would basically have the five weeks a year free. I am always thinking like that. But it seemed that every place I liked had some association rules that were unacceptable to me. For example, I found a terrific three-bedroom condo right on the golf course where the Nike World Open Golf Tournament is held every year. It was a spectacular condo, the price was right, and it was not far from the ocean. But the rules stated that I couldn't rent it for one year, and each renter after that had to be approved by the association board. That was terrible. So, I walked away from the deal.

This type of thing happened time and time again, almost to the point where I was getting frustrated. I even had listed "Florida Condo" as one of my faith goals. It had been on my list for nearly three years. But the last time I was in Florida, the Lord spoke to me. It wasn't an audible voice, but an impression. It was as if the Lord was saying, "Quit searching. I will provide." So I obeyed and quit searching.

Shortly after I quit searching for the perfect property, the Lord spoke to my heart about giving a certain amount of money to a particular mission. So I gave away the down payment I would have used for my new condo.

A few weeks later, a retired missionary called me and asked if I could meet him for lunch, so we made the arrangements. At lunch he told me that God had called him to spend six months a year back on the missions field in Africa so he could train young pastors to be successful in their calling.

"It doesn't make sense," he said to me as we ate our lunches. "My wife and I just built a brand new home in Florida and were planning on enjoying our retirement there. But now our beautiful, newly built home will be sitting empty six months every year. Dave, how would you like to have a Florida home absolutely free for a half year, every year?"

My spirit leaped within me. I told him about my faith goal and how nothing had seemed to be working out relative to the Florida condo. The missionary became excited and told me that the more I could use his house, the happier he would be.

Now I have a beautiful, brand new, three-bedroom home in Florida to work on my books and plans anytime during the six months he's in Africa.

When God speaks to you about giving something away from yourself, it's only because He has something bigger and better in store for you. Listen to God's voice.

I have written a book entitled, *Have You Heard From the Lord Lately?* The book explains all the different ways God speaks to His children and contains dozens of powerful examples and illustrations on the value of listening to God's voice. You can get a copy at your local bookstore or by writing to us. Listening to God's voice is priceless when it comes to receiving your harvest of wealth.

"I've Got A Mansion"

Several years ago, a highly esteemed Christian author and minister felt God speaking to his heart about starting a printing plant where millions of pieces of faith-building literature could be produced and sent around the world. He had the desire, he believed it could be done, but now he needed to know how to do it.

Being a man of faith and prayer, he diligently sought the Lord concerning the matter of "how?" Such a venture would cost many thousands of dollars, money he didn't have. In seeking the Lord's direction, an idea came to him, "We could sell our home and use the equity."

So the family sold their cozy home, bought a printing plant, and moved into the basement of the office.

After living there for nearly a year, a knock came at the door one Saturday morning. It was a Christian lady who attended the same church. Both she and her husband were contractors. She said, "My husband was awakened during the night. He told me that he wants to build you a home. He wants to donate his services free of charge and will ask his men to do what they can also."

The man kept his word. He built a lovely, large brick home with ample room to entertain the many evangelists and missionaries who were in the Lord's work.

On moving day, after the final load of furniture was delivered, the minister's wife stole away to her bedroom. Tears of gratitude ran down her cheeks. She prayed, "Lord, I expected to live in a place like this when I got to Heaven but You gave it to me on earth!"

God rewarded this family for obediently listening to His "still, small voice." They listened, they obeyed (even though it meant suffering inconvenience for a short while), and God rewarded them with a dream house. Today their presses are turning out millions of faith-building magazines and books! It pays to listen to God's voice.

> **Call unto me, and I will answer thee, and shew thee great and mighty things, which thou knowest not.**
>
> **— Jeremiah 33:3**

19. Lacking common sense. God never asks you to do foolish things that serve no purpose for His Kingdom or for your life. Beware of individuals who are always doing some unintelligent, preposterous thing, and then blaming it on the Lord.

You'll see advertisements that will try to entice you to believe you can make $16,000 a month in your spare time. Common sense should tell you something isn't right about that. You'll see "infomercials" on television claiming that if you buy their "system," you'll be making millions of dollars practically overnight. Some are legitimate. Most are not. But God gave you common sense. Use it.

> **Have two goals: wisdom—that is, knowing and doing right—and common sense. Don't let them slip away, for they fill you with living energy and bring you honor and respect. They keep you safe from defeat and disaster and from stumbling off the trail.**
>
> **— Proverbs 3:21-23 (TLB)**

Common sense tells me that if I throw a seed on a cement driveway the chances of it growing are pretty slim. Yet some Christians plant their money seeds in fly-by-night, pseudo ministries that spend the biggest percentage of their income on fund-raising and nonsense, rather than leading people to Christ, making disciples, and evangelizing the world. Just out of common sense, I won't plant my money seeds into any ministry that isn't winning souls, making disciples, and reaching out to the world through missions.

I was going over some reports on the accounting books of a church where the pastor had defected. He left the church and enticed about forty people, through deception, to follow his authoritarian ministry. My team and I were trying to clean up the mess he had left behind. I was incensed when I discovered that this pastor had spent more church money on his cell phone bill, and flagrant travel expenses, than what he had given to the work of evangelizing the lost. People who planted their money seeds into that ministry lacked common sense.

Before planting your money seeds in a ministry find out what that ministry is doing to evangelize the lost. What is it doing for world missions? That will tell you everything you need to know about whether or not your money seeds are going into good soil.

Sanctified common sense can keep you from making major money mistakes.

Some folks think it is "spiritual" to give cash anonymously in the offering plate at church. That's not spiritual. That's a lack of common sense. As long as your charitable contributions are deductible for income tax purposes, you should do it. For every dollar you give that is not recorded, you are paying an additional eighteen to thirty three cents in taxes.

It doesn't make sense to give God $100, then have to pay up to $33 additional in taxes just because you didn't use an offering envelope. Use common sense.

20. Working at a job you hate. Hating your work is no way to come into the wealthy place. Your work should be enjoyable and rewarding. God doesn't want you to be miserable. When you are miserable, you won't find the strength to bring in your harvest, because the joy of the Lord is your strength (Nehemiah 8:10).

Security Is Deceptive

Steve worked in a factory for 23 years and hated every minute. Whenever I asked him how he was doing, he'd have some complaint about his job. I asked him why he didn't leave the factory and begin to do what he loved, which was electronic work. "Oh, I only have seven more years before I can retire, so I'll stick it out for that much longer," he would say.

Security is a big factor in people's decisions. I know it was in Steve's decision to stay on a job he hated. Security can become a god. God wants to be your security and give you the desires of your heart. An independent study back in the 1970's revealed that more millionaires had become wealthy by doing what they love, than any other way.

What happened to Steve? He never got to enjoy much of his retirement. He left the factory after he had 30 years of service, just as he planned. They gave him a little watch with an inscription as a reward for 30 years of doing the work he hated for the sake of making someone else rich. Unfortunately, less than two years after he retired, Steve died at the age of 59. Doing what you hate causes terrific amounts of stress that you just were not designed to bear.

She Took A Chance

I know a lady who wasn't enjoying her job as an executive assistant. She didn't have the education necessary to do what she really loved, and that was teaching. She could teach Sunday school, and that was great, but she would have loved to be teaching full time.

One day she had an idea. "Maybe I could take some courses in public speaking and get a position as a seminar presenter."

She took some simple courses, joined a local Toastmasters club and became very proficient in public speaking. She took a chance and sent a resume to one of the nation's leading seminar companies. She auditioned and was accepted to head up seminars all across America. Now she is one of the most popular presenters in the company. She travels every week, doing exactly what she loves to do, and in the process is making a fortune compared to her salary as an executive assistant. And, oh, did I mention to you that she is nearly 70 years old?

God has given you certain gifts and talents for a purpose. He works a certain "desire" inside of you; a desire that leans toward a certain field of interest. Follow God's tug on your heart. You must enjoy your work. I'm not saying that every day will be perfect;

there will still be challenges. Doing what you love to do is an important key on the road to radical wealth.

Can you believe it? We've just talked about six more roadblocks on your journey into radical wealth. In the next chapter, we'll discuss even more.

"You are destined for colossal riches. You won't need to apologize to anybody for your abundance. You are about to enter into the domain of shameless wealth. But only if you qualify. That decision is yours."

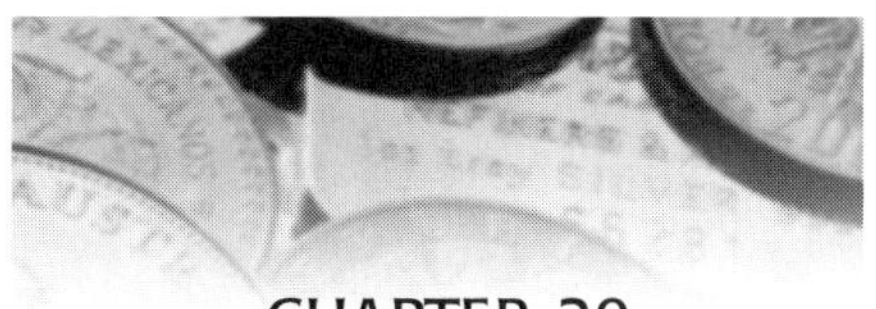

CHAPTER 20

Roadblocks to Radical Wealth – Part 3

When my son, David, was twelve years old, I took him on a surprise trip with me to Oklahoma. He loves Tulsa. That's where I learned to fly years ago, over at Riverside Airport, across the river from Oral Roberts University. Bill Spratt, my flight instructor, became like a dad to me and a grandfather to David. To this day, my son and daughter both call him "Grampa."

I was taking David out to Tulsa to see "Grampa." David loves to fly, so I planned to get him some flight instruction while we were there. When we boarded the airplane, David had no idea where we were going. He was delightfully surprised and excited when we landed at Tulsa International Airport. We checked into our hotel, and headed off to Riverside Airport to meet with "Grampa Bill."

Bill gave David some great flight lessons, teaching him lots of interesting things about flying, the most important being how to use a checklist.

One day during our stay in Tulsa, Grampa Bill was busy with other students, so I decided to take David flying around Oklahoma to give him a little mentoring. We flew to small airports around, stopping everywhere there was a soda machine. We had fun. But one time as we were taking off from the Okmulgee airport, we heard a banging sound on the side of the airplane. Clang, clang, clang! It was frightening. Something wasn't right. It sounded like our right wing was breaking off. That's not a good thing. All sorts of thoughts crossed my mind, as you can imagine. So I decided we had better go back and land the plane.

Before we landed, however, we found the problem. David had not fastened his seat belt. It was hanging out the door of the airplane and the buckle was intermittently slamming on the side of the airplane as we flew through the air. What a stupid mistake! We had flown so much that day, we thought we knew everything about checking over the airplane for our flights, but we had forgotten one fundamental thing —***fasten your seat belts***.

It's right there on the checklist. "Make sure your seat belts and harnesses are fastened securely." But we failed to go over the checklist, point-by-point, because we had done it a thousand times and thought we could do it without the list. We were wrong.

In our situation, no harm was done, but what about the situation where another pilot failed to follow the checklist before taking off and crashed his airplane? He and his passenger both were killed right here in my city. What was the problem? The pilot had simply forgotten to remove the rudder lock. But it was on the checklist. If he had gone over the written checklist, he would have discovered the rudder lock and could have prevented that tragedy.

That's what I'm giving you in these final chapters — a checklist. Go over this list often. Even if you think you know it by memory, go over it regularly. It could mean the difference between financial success and financial disaster. Let's move on now.

21. Failing to follow the Golden Rule. What is the Golden Rule? "Do unto others as you would have others do unto you."[41] It is called "love." Love is God's plan for success that is guaranteed to never fail.[42]

You don't want to be cheated. Don't cheat others. You don't want to be taken advantage of. Don't take advantage of others. You want to be forgiven. Forgive others.

You want your dreams to come true. Help others make their dreams come true.

This is the supreme principle for success. Jesus said that all the law and the prophets hang on this one commandment to love. All true faith operates and is motivated by love.[43]

Love your neighbor. Love your competitor. Love your enemy. For God so loved ***you*** that He gave His only begotten son, Jesus, to die on the cross for you. The Holy Spirit has put God's love in your heart, so spread it around.[44] You may be surprised at what an important key this is to coming into the wealthy place.

22. ***Seeking personal advancement over the advancement of God's Kingdom.*** How many people really put God first in everything? If you were offered a job that paid twice as much as you are earning right now, but you'd have to move to another state, or maybe even another country, what would your first consideration be? Would you consider first how this would advance you personally? Or would you think first how your move would affect God's Kingdom?

In Matthew chapter six, Jesus listed all the things the heathen are groping after. Money, clothes, material possessions, riches, substance — "things." He said that unbelievers make these a priority in their lives and go after them in hot pursuit. For His followers, however, He made an amazing, almost too-hard-to-believe statement, promising them everything they could ever dream about if they would do just one thing. What is that one thing? Simply this: Prioritize God's Kingdom.

> **But seek ye first the kingdom of God, and his righteousness; and all these things shall be added unto you.**
>
> **— Matthew 6:33**

I know many people who have failed in life and never found their wealthy place, because though they were Christians, they sought personal advancement over Kingdom advancement. They took jobs that were outside of their assignment in life for the sake of better pay or benefits. They didn't ask, "How will my decision affect God's work?" They thought only about their advancement. Consequently, they, like Esau, have given up their right to come into the place of radical wealth.

In Haggai chapter one, we are told the real reason some of God's people can never seem to open the door to the wealthy place. It was because they were building their homes, while ignoring God's House. Let's read it.

> **So the Lord sent this message through the prophet Haggai: "Why are you living in luxurious houses while my house lies in ruins? This is what the Lord Almighty says: Consider how things are going for you! You have planted much but harvested little. You have food to eat, but not enough to fill you up. You have wine to drink, but not enough to satisfy your thirst. You have clothing to wear, but not enough to keep you warm. Your wages disappear as though you were putting them in pockets filled with holes! This is what the Lord Almighty says: Consider how things are going for you! Now go up into the hills, bring down timber, and rebuild my house. Then I will take pleasure in it and be honored, says the Lord. You hoped for rich harvests, but they were poor. And when you brought your harvest home, I blew it away. Why? Because my house lies in ruins, says the Lord Almighty, while you are all busy building your own fine houses.**
>
> **— Haggai 1:3-9 (NLT)**

Allow me to comment on the highlights of these verses.

- The people were building luxurious homes while the Temple was in disrepair.
- The people planted much, but the harvests became smaller and smaller.
- The people's wages started to be eaten up by unforeseen problems. No wonder — the devourer was no longer being rebuked over their finances.

- The people seeking personal advancement without *first* remembering the Lord their God and His House ended up losing their wealth.

When you go on to verse 11 you find that everything they worked so hard to get for themselves ended up being ruined. They lost out on coming into the wealthy place because they sought first their own wealth, rather than seeking first the things that were on God's heart.

Then in chapter two of Haggai, God makes some outrageous promises to the people who truly would put Him and His House as a priority. He assures the people that all the silver and gold (wealth) belongs to Him.[45] He can control the flow of wealth into your life by turning it on or turning it off. He can open the throttle or close it. He promises that those who put His Kingdom *first,* will receive a divinely invoked blessing even before the normal harvest time.[46] The others, who put personal advancement as a priority, with no regard for God, will be overthrown and put into poverty.

True Promotion

True promotion comes only from the Lord. You can choose to promote yourself, or try to get man to promote you, and end up on poverty row. Or you can seek first the advancement of God's Kingdom and be placed in the land of wealth by God Himself.

> **For promotion *cometh* neither from the east, nor from the west, nor from the south.**
>
> **— Psalm 75:6**

Balaam, a one-time prophet of God, chose a promotion from man. The evil, worldly king promised him, "I will promote thee unto very great honor . . .." Balaam took the bait and gained some temporary wealth in so doing.[47]

This one mistake led the prophet down a dark, sinking road of soothsaying, fortune telling, and selling "prophesies" to make a living. His wealth was gone and so was his anointing. A few years later he was slain in a surprise attack right along with the people he looked to for his personal advancement. There is a high price for putting one's desire for personal advancement over the priority of God's Kingdom advancement.

Ask yourself a couple questions before making any major decision. "How will my decision affect God's Kingdom?" Ask yourself, "Am I seeking personal promotion? Or am I seeking God's will?" God wants you to come into radical wealth, not radical ruin. He leaves the choice to us, based upon our priorities.

23. Being hypocritical and insincere. Have you ever known someone who tried to appear rich when they actually were not? You see it all the time. And it's one of the roadblocks to real wealth.

In a book entitled *The Millionaire Next Door,* a study of millionaires in the 1980s showed that most true millionaires in America actually drive normal cars like Chevrolets and Buicks. Most of the people who drive the super luxury cars are not wealthy at all, but they'd like people to think they are. Most real millionaires live in normal homes in normal neighborhoods and you'd never know just how rich they really are.

It's interesting that Jesus was never too harsh on common, ordinary sinners. That's whom He came to seek and save. His wrath was unleashed, however, toward hypocrites — those who "played a role" but didn't really live the part they were playing. They were actors.

I know there are success gurus today who tell you that to gain great wealth you need to look the part. They tell you to go out and buy a luxury car, even if you cannot afford it. It will give you the feel of success. Do you want to know what the real feel of success is? It's when you are seeking God's Kingdom first, and driving a car for which you've paid cash —

a car you can actually afford. It's paying your bills, getting out of debt, opening your storehouse accounts, and moving into the wealthy place step-by-step. Once you are there, go ahead and buy a fancy car if that's what you want. Just make sure you can pay cash for it.

One of the Ten Commandments is "Thou shalt not bear false witness." If you are living a lie, that's "bearing false witness." If you are trying to appear rich when you're not, you are violating God's law. That's one form of hypocrisy.

What is really important to you: the short-term ego boost you'll get by looking rich, or the long-term peace of mind which assures you that you are genuinely on the road to radical wealth?

The High Price Of Hypocrisy

In Acts chapter five, we find a case of flagrant hypocrisy on the part of a husband and wife who had sold some property and brought some of the money from the sale to the church. They wanted to appear to be giving everything to Jesus, so they told the apostles they sold the property and brought all the money to the church. But they were lying. They were holding back a portion for themselves.

They weren't wrong for keeping some of the profits from that sale. The property was theirs to do with what they wanted. Their sin was in being hypocritical by saying they were giving everything when, in fact, they were not. The consequences of their hypocrisy cost them a lot more than just their wealth. You can read it in Acts 5:1-11.

Insincerity

When non-tithers come up to me and say, "When I win the sweepstakes and get that ten million dollars, I'm going to give five million to the church." I don't believe them. If they won't tithe to God and give offerings of the money they have in their wallet right now, they'll never give much to God, even if they win the big sweepstakes. They are not being sincere.

The story of the two boys that grew up together in the same town is a great example.[48] One went to Bible college and became a missionary. The other became a successful farmer.

The young missionary, as he was preparing to leave for the mission field, went back to his hometown to see his old friend. His friend said, "I'm so happy to see you and proud of you for answering the call to missionary service. You are going on the mission field and I am a successful farmer. I want you to know that I think it's terrific that you are obeying the call of God, and pray that He blesses you in your work.

"You know, if I had two cars, I would give you one. In fact, if I had two houses, I would give you one. If I had two tractors, I would give you one. Even if I had two million dollars, I would give one million dollars to you."

The missionary replied, "That's wonderful! Tell me, if you had two cows, would you give one to me?"

The farmer answered, "Now, that's not fair. You know I have two cows."

Insincerity and hypocrisy is a roadblock to radical wealth.

I think we've covered enough territory for this chapter. So let's move on now to the next chapter as we continue studying the roadblocks to radical wealth.

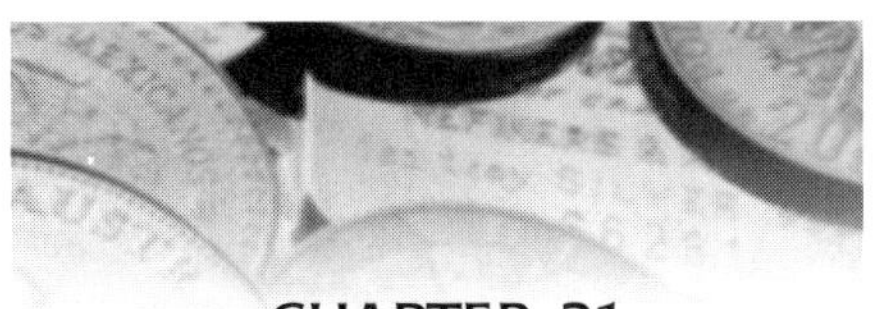

CHAPTER 21

Roadblocks to Radical Wealth – Part 4

I need you to understand something as we discuss these roadblocks. I'm not trying to be negative by highlighting these hindrances. I'm merely pointing out to you some of the potholes in the road to radical wealth so you can avoid them. I want you to be able to speed along the highway of wealth without wrecking your car along the way.

Get my point?

Okay, let's move on and look at some more enemies of your wealth.

24. Impulse buying. This is another roadblock on your road to radical wealth. One lady claims she has "accidental spending sprees." You'd be surprised at how many advertisers and chain stores intentionally ambush their customers with things that trigger the "buy-it-now" impulse. Impulse buying is when you see an advertisement and you "have to get that product now," so whether you need it or not, you buy it. I know people who have homes full of gadgets and gizmos they never even use. They bought them on an impulse when they saw the advertisement on television.

"I want this and I want it ***right now!*** I can't wait another minute. I have to get it." This is precisely what advertisers are hoping they can do to you. They need to break down your self-control to make you feel like you will be lost or left behind if you don't buy the product they are promoting. They want you to buy on emotions rather than on good sense. This is how the devil himself works. He seeks to wear down your will and pull your life out of control.

Self-control is a fruit of the Spirit. Impulsive and emotional decision-making stems from the works of the flesh.[49]

Anything that is out of control is sick. If the cells in your body grow out of control, you are really sick. An out-of-control government is a sick government. Nobody wants to be on a highway when a car goes out of control or in a forest when there is an out-of-control fire. When a person's spending is out of control it is more deadly to his wealth than a raging forest fire.

I have known people who have racked up thousands — and I mean ***thousands*** — of dollars worth of debt on multiple credit cards simply because of impulse buying.

Why not daily ask God to keep you from "accidental spending sprees?" Ask the Lord to deliver you from the temptation to buy anything on a sudden emotional whim. Don't sacrifice your future wealth for a little ego satisfaction now. This is a serious roadblock to your radical wealth. Make an agreement to wait three weeks before purchasing anything you think you "need to have right now."

25. Playing the blame game. This game is as old as creation itself. Adam blamed Eve for his sin. Eve blamed the devil. King Ahab blamed his problems on the prophet of God. Some blame the "gospel of prosperity" for their lack, if you can imagine that. They say, "That preacher got all my money. Now I'm broke."

Others blame a bad broker or a lousy investment consultant. But ***you*** are responsible for your own life and its outcome. Someday you will stand before God and give an account for your life. No excuses will be accepted on that day. No blame shifting will be heard.

Down in a southern state a few years back, a fellow took his shotgun into a brokerage firm and began shooting the stockbrokers. Several were killed. The man blamed his financial failures on the people who bought and sold his stocks. But these brokers were only acting on the man's orders to buy or sell. It wasn't their fault he picked mostly losers.

I know a man who has been broke financially for years. Twenty some years ago an investment venture went sour, and he is still blaming the other guys who invested with him. They went on with their lives, but this fellow, for some immature reason, just hasn't yet chosen to get past his failure and get on with his life. He keeps rehearsing the loss, over and over. No wonder he's always broke.

People cast blame as a means of protecting their own egos. "It's somebody else's fault." "If they had listened to me, we'd be rich." Blaming seems to be one of America's favorite pastimes. One political party blames the other, and the list goes on indefinitely.

If you ask fifty broke people why they have no money, not one of them will say, "It's because I didn't follow God's plan for wealth and take the right actions." No, they'll say, "My darn boss doesn't understand my needs. He doesn't pay me enough," or "I can't start a wealth plan now, I have too many expenses." "The government has wrecked the economy, preventing me from getting ahead."

Let me tell you the truth. The blame game is the lazy man's way of avoiding responsibility for his financial problems and the pain that goes into correcting those problems. It's hard to respect a man who is full of excuses. God is willing to turn your financial messes into financial miracles, if you will wholeheartedly get on His system for wealth.

Quit blaming, begin fixing, and start moving on if you want to come into the wealthy place.

26. Being dishonest with money. Dishonesty of any kind dishonors God.

St. Paul renounced the hidden things of dishonesty.

> **Therefore seeing we have this ministry, as we have received mercy, we faint not; But have renounced the hidden things of dishonesty, not walking in craftiness, nor handling the word of God deceitfully; but by manifestation of the truth commending ourselves to every man's conscience in the sight of God.**
>
> **—2 Corinthians 4:1, 2**

I don't think I need to take much time on this point. I'm sure you can think of all kinds of hidden ways people are dishonest with money. Let's just list a few.

• Not reporting some miscellaneous earned income in order to save a few dollars in taxes.

• Being undercharged for a service or product and never bringing it to the attention of the vendor.

• Receiving too much change from the lady at the cash register and never mentioning it to her.

• Failing to honor contracts with people you've hired to do a job. Nit-picking for the sake of reneging on your agreement.

I had a little accident in a rental car during one of my travels out-of-state. My insurance company dealt dishonestly with me for over a year. I finally called the state insurance bureau and discovered that this company had more complaints against it than any other company. I know dozens of people who canceled their policies with this company when they found out how rude and dishonest the adjusters were to me. Dishonesty will cost you business. People will find out.

We had an office machine salesman who came to sell us a new office machine. He let us try it out for a week to see if we liked it. He was offering us an amazingly good deal for a new machine, almost thirty percent cheaper than other company's prices for the same kind of machine.

Our accounting lady became suspicious and checked the serial number on the machine. She wasn't surprised to find out that it wasn't a new machine at all, but a rebuilt, used machine. She confronted the salesman about his dishonesty and he responded by saying, "That's what we call a new machine." After exchanging some words, he lost his temper and took his machine. Our savvy accounting lady then bought two used machines from another dealer for less than the price of the other salesman's one machine. People in our office building now know with whom *not* to do business.

Once you've been caught in dishonesty for the sake of money, word will get out and you'll eventually be drained of your wealth and your wealth potential. According to the "world's greatest salesman," Joe Girard, just one customer who discovers that you've been dishonest will affect 250 other potential customers. Imagine that! Dishonesty carries a high price tag.

27. Having indecision and double-mindedness. To be double-minded means to have two minds. One mind says, "Yes, God wants me to prosper." The other mind says, "Prosperity may be for others, but it is probably not for me." One mind says, "I will start my wealth plan today." The other mind says, "Tomorrow may be a better day to begin."

One mind says, "I will get out of debt." The other mind says, "Some debt is good, because you can get a tax deduction."

St. James tells us that the indecisive, double-minded man can receive ***nothing*** from the Lord. That includes wealth.

> **For let not that man think that he shall receive any thing of the Lord. A double minded man *is* unstable in all his ways.**
>
> **— James 1:7, 8**

You have two minds: the conscious and the subconscious. Both your subconscious mind and your conscious mind must be harmonized, in agreement, to eliminate the "double mind." That's why Paul said to be renewed in the spirit of your mind. I believe the spirit of your mind is referring to the subconscious mind.

> **And be renewed in the spirit of your mind;**
>
> **— Ephesians 4:23**

Meditating upon God's Word will help to renew the spirit of your mind (your subconscious mind). That's why, I'm sure, prosperity and success are rewards for meditating upon God's Word. It renews the inner mind, which must be in agreement with the conscious mind in order to produce effective results.

> **Blessed *is* the man that walketh not in the counsel of the ungodly, nor standeth in the way of**

> **sinners, nor sitteth in the seat of the scornful. But his delight *is* in the law of the LORD; and in his law doth he meditate day and night. And he shall be like a tree planted by the rivers of water, that bringeth forth his fruit in his season; his leaf also shall not wither; and WHATSOEVER HE DOETH SHALL PROSPER.**
>
> **— Psalm 1:1-3**

> **There shall not any man be able to stand before thee all the days of thy life: as I was with Moses, *so* I will be with thee: I will not fail thee, nor forsake thee.**
>
> **— Joshua 1:8**

The Christian's biggest area of hindrance, in terms of wealth, is not in the spirit, but in the mind. The mind is programmed, so to speak, by years of input. If that input includes things like "money is the root of all evil," then it has to be reprogrammed, or renovated, by God's Word. That happens as we listen to faith-building teachers and meditate upon the promises of God.

Just listen to the lyrics of songs that have helped to program many minds. "It's a hard world to get a break in." "I've got heartaches by the number, troubles by the score." There are many more like these, and even worse.

Your conscious mind can discern and reject false concepts. Your subconscious mind cannot. In other words, if you consciously listen to something or read something that you don't want to go into your subconscious, you can reject it consciously. But if, for instance, you are sleeping and the radio is playing softly in the background, your conscious mind, when it's not focused on discerning, cannot stop any evil, damaging, or harmful input.

Suppose the song is playing as you sleep, "I've got troubles, whoa oh, I've got worries, whoa oh." Your conscious mind cannot reject the concepts so the words of the song sink deeply into your undiscerning subconscious mind. The next day you'll begin to wonder why you seem to have so many troubles and worries. Your conscious mind doesn't want to worry but your subconscious mind is out of harmony, and thus, is setting you up for the feeling of troubles and worries. I'm sure, at some point in your life, you've had something similar to this happen to you.

The more quickly you can renew your mind, the more quickly you can come into the place of wealth.

Can I Be Wealthy Without Education?

Perhaps you've been told that because you have the wrong education you cannot do certain things. Your mind is programmed to think that you can never have wealth because of your lack of training. If you believe it, then that's what you'll experience. You need to renew your thoughts to the truth. The truth is, education is important, but lack of education cannot hold you back from the wealthy place. It's not education that brings you wealth; it's the power of God that brings you wealth.

Lee Braxton had only a sixth grade education. After becoming a mechanic, he realized he had reached the top of the ladder; he had risen as far as he could. Soon, a godly dissatisfaction developed in Lee's heart and he began to pray to God for guidance.

Lee read an inspirational book that got him to thinking that God really is a good God. He began to renew his mind by reading the Bible. He started believing that God is always a good God, contrary to the harsh sermons he had heard in his young life! He came to understand that there was a power working within him to accomplish the impossible regardless of how little education he had (Ephesians 3:20). Lee read and meditated on God's Word and realized that God had given him the power to get wealth. He always wanted to run a bank, but no bank would hire him because of his lack of education. So he started his own bank!

Lee organized and became the president of the First National Bank of Whiteville. Subsequently he established several successful business enterprises and was later elected as mayor of the city. Lee, having only a sixth grade education, became a wealthy man.

At the age of 44, Lee Braxton, a millionaire several times over, sold his businesses. Why did he sell out? So he could retire? So he could relax in the Florida sunshine for the rest of his life? So he could just lie down, roll up and die? Absolutely not! Lee Braxton invested the rest of his life helping the ministry of one of the nation's leading evangelists. He enjoyed every minute of it!

God is no respecter of persons. What He has done for others, He'll do for you — if you'll give Him a chance. A song writer, Stuart Hamblen so eloquently wrote:

> "It is no secret, what God can do, What He's done for others, He'll do for you!"

You cannot be double-minded or indecisive. Make a decision ***now*** to renew your mind and the spirit of your mind by listening to faith building messages, reading God's Word, and meditating on His Word. Begin moving up the road to radical wealth, fully committed, unswerving in your resolve, that God really does want you to enjoy wealth.

More potholes to avoid in the next chapter.

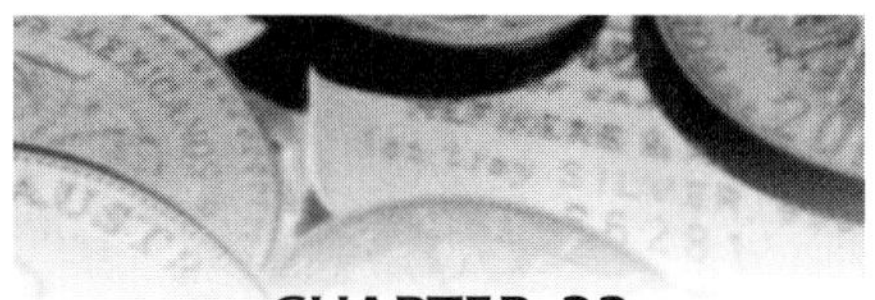

CHAPTER 22

Roadblocks to Radical Wealth – Part 5

We all yearn to be free of financial pressures. Yet so many of God's precious children are still living in bondage to lack. The scars of yesterday, the programming of the past, the false beliefs they hold to be true, and perhaps a hundred other things hold them back from enjoying God's wonderful promises of prosperity and wealth.

I'm pointing out to you some of the roadblocks, or potholes, on the road to radical wealth. Some of my readers have been on the wrong road for so many years. They need to race speedily down the road to radical wealth now that they are on the right road. By putting these "warning flags" by the "potholes" I can save you some time by helping you avoid an accident on the road.

I want to remind you that all the principles I have shared with you so far work synergistically together for far greater results than if you apply only one or two of the principles. Some of God's people tithe and give offerings but have never made a supernatural faith promise. Others have never opened a storehouse account. Still others fall into every pothole along the road. I hope you can feel my passion. At this moment I have a divine obsession to see you succeed and come into the promised "wealthy place."

So let's continue now to expose more of those speed-destroying potholes.

28. Looking to man as your source instead of to God as your source. Someone said, "My boss is so stingy, he hasn't given me a raise in two years!" May I be frank? That's why you're not receiving a financial harvest. You're sitting at the wrong door, waiting for a hand out.

> **The LORD *is* my shepherd; I shall not want (lack).**
>
> **— Psalm 23:1**

> **But thou shalt remember the LORD thy God: for *it is* he that giveth thee power to get wealth, that he may establish his covenant which he sware unto thy fathers, as *it is* this day.**
>
> **— Deuteronomy 8:18**

Your boss can give you a puny pay raise, if that's what you want. But he cannot give you the power to get wealth. Only God can do that. If you are disappointed with your boss, maybe God is trying to get your attention. Perhaps God is trying to show you that He wants to be your source of supply. Wealth is not a matter of luck. It's a matter of having the right source.

When God is your source, you can make radical, supernatural faith promises when He speaks. When God is your source, you are totally convinced that it's up to Him to bring the money through your life to meet that faith promise. Abraham trusted God as his source so much, "he was willing to do whatever God told him to do," (James 2:22 TLB). It is no wonder Abraham became one of the first millionaires. He kept God as his source. When God is your source, you are willing to trust Him with all your heart, and not depend upon your own human understanding.

For radical wealth, make sure you are looking to the right source.

29. Lacking patience. When a farmer plants his crop, he doesn't expect it to be ready for harvesting the next day. He patiently waits. The same is true with a financial harvest. You plant the seeds and patiently wait for your harvest.

Faith and patience go hand in hand. They are powerful links to your financial harvest. If, after you have planted money seeds into God's work, you find that your harvest is not parked in your driveway the next morning, don't be like the immature person and get all upset, saying things like, "This prosperity stuff doesn't work." If you do, it's like pouring poison on your crop and destroying it before it comes to fruition. Your harvest is coming.

The word patience in the Greek language implies ferocious tenacity — persistence.

In others words, patience stands firm in the face of opposition and situations that appear contrary to your faith. Patience will cause you to keep sowing those money seeds regularly and consistently, knowing that your financial harvest is on the way. Patience will remind you that there is a growing time for anything you plant.

> **For ye have need of patience, that, after ye have done the will of God, ye might receive the promise.**
>
> **— Hebrews 10:36**

> **And let us not be weary in well doing: for in due season we shall reap, if we faint not.**
>
> **— Galatians 6:9**

Patience won't allow you to give up. I sometimes call it patient determination. If a person plants money seeds into God's work then starts talking about how it probably won't work, patience is missing and that person will likely miss their harvest. When you have been faithful to stand firm, and you continue to sow your money seeds, your wait will one day be over and your harvest will have arrived!

Without patience — shameless tenacity — there is no hope of you coming into the wealthy place. But with faith, plus action, plus patience, the windows of Heaven will open and you will be roaring up the road to radical wealth.

Patience — not giving up — will always strengthen you.

> **My brethren, count it all joy when ye fall into divers temptations; Knowing *this*, that the trying of your faith worketh patience. But let patience have *her* perfect work, that ye may be perfect and entire, wanting nothing.**
>
> **— James 1:2-4**

There are those who have a tendency to uproot their planted seeds by their impatience. It becomes a way of life with them. They are sporadic in their giving, they run from place to place searching for blessings and then wonder why their harvest never seems to arrive. They never stay in one place long enough to realize or reap the reward of their sowing.

Consistency And Persistence

A good plan is to always write God the first check every time you receive any income or increase. Do it *first,* before you write out the checks to pay your bills. It's symbolic, I know, but it helps you focus on your priority money seeds. Also, do it consistently. Bring your tithes to the storehouse of your church. If you give offerings to evangelists or missionaries, do it regularly on a certain day each week or month. This will teach you persistence.

Patience will always provide a bridge to receiving the promises of God.

> **That ye be not slothful, but followers of them who through faith and patience inherit the promises. For when God made promise to Abraham, because he could swear by no greater, he sware by himself, Saying, Surely blessing I will bless thee, and multiplying I will multiply thee. And so, after he had patiently endured, he obtained the promise.**
>
> **— Hebrews 6:12-15**

Patience becomes a supernatural bridge that extends from the sowing side to the reaping side. Patience is a key ingredient to your faith. Those coming toward the wealthy place take hold of God's promises and just keep walking across the bridge of patience until they arrive at the promised harvest. They refuse to say anything contrary. They are determined to stay on that bridge unable to be swayed or budged. They won't speak a word against the promise. They just keep speaking, believing, and patiently walking until they reach their harvest.

Patience will always result in happiness (James 5:11).

Patience will always build character in your life (James 1:2-4).

When You Feel Like It's Not Working

When you feel like nothing is working, when you feel overwhelmed, defeated, or swallowed up by problems, patience will bring you over to the other side. When it looks like all is lost and you seem to be going down in flames, remember God is going to turn the situation around and make it your greatest victory or your biggest miracle. Be patient because the word "time" is right in the middle of seed time and harvest.

> **While the earth remaineth, seed time and harvest ... shall not cease.**
>
> **— Genesis 8:22**

Plant your seeds. Give them *time* to grow. Then *reap* your harvest.

30. Failing to take action! You can become wealthy regardless of who you are or what your background is. You can come into the wealthy place no matter what your level of education might happen to be. You can get on the road to radical wealth regardless of how young or how old you are right now. You can have your treasuries filled with riches no matter how many mistakes you've made in the past or what your current level of income may be.

The only thing that can stop you is ***inaction.***

The power to get wealth is a gift from God. Yet you have to take ***action*** to receive that gift.

This Is Your Miracle Moment

Perhaps once in a lifetime a book like this comes across your path to provide you with the anointing and the tools for acquiring an abundance of wealth. This is ***your*** moment — ***right now***. If you read this book then take action on the principles I've shared, you will come into the wealthy place. It's not the readers but the ***doers*** who will become radically wealthy. You can sit in church and listen to an anointed sermon and it will profit you nothing — until you put it into practice — unless you take ***action*** on the principles you've learned.

> **Therefore to him that knoweth to do good, and doeth *it* not, to him it is sin.**
>
> **— James 4:17**

Now Is Your Time

Some people are waiting for the right time to begin taking the action steps toward their radical wealth. They are waiting for perfect conditions, procrastinating. They are filled with "tomorrow words" like "Someday I'll start a wealth book." "When the conditions are better, I'll begin." "Next week, I plan to organize my finances." "One of these days my money ship will come in." Then they wonder why they must continually face the grave consequences of financial shortage. It's because they put off these important matters for the sake of "more important" matters.

Faith is not "someday." Faith is *now*. Faith is not "tomorrow." Faith is *now*. Unless you quickly overcome all the excuses for not acting on what you've learned, you'll be doomed to a life of just enough, probably no more, and perhaps even less.

> **If you wait for perfect conditions, you will never get anything done.**
>
> **— Ecclesiastes 11:4 (NLT)**

When Pastor Yonggi Cho started pastoring a small church in South Korea, the world's thirteenth most repressed nation in the world, he began teaching those poor people the principles of God's financial system. He taught them to tithe, give offerings, and obey the voice of God. Many of them owned nothing but chopsticks and little bowls, but they believed the man of God who was the key to their future prosperity. They gave their chopsticks and their bowls in offerings to the Lord.

Today, many of the members of Pastor Cho's church are millionaires even by American standards. But they started out very poor. They listened to their pastor and took *action* on God's plan for wealth. You too can begin to take *action* now. You have something to release into God's Kingdom. The Bible tells us that God gives seed to the sower. If you are willing to take what you have and give it to God then God is willing to take what He has and give it to you.

You must take *action now!* You may begin by simply sending your pastor a note, telling him that you are committing yourself to the biblical practice of tithing. Next look for something you possess to give to God's work. Start *now* to get into the rhythm of giving; consistently planting money seeds, time seeds, energy seeds — something. But start *now*.

Start your wealth book *now*. Begin to meditate on the wealth Scriptures *now*.

Start an investment account *now*. Get some storehouses upon which God can command His blessings. Get some treasuries God can begin to fill. Do it *now*.

Some precious believers have never set up a storehouse account because they believe Jesus is coming soon for His Church. Yet right in the middle of Jesus' discourse on the end times He talks about investing.

> **Again, the Kingdom of Heaven can be illustrated by the story of a man going on a trip. He called together his servants and gave them money to invest for him while he was gone. He gave five bags of gold to one, two bags of gold to another, and one bag of gold to the last—dividing in proportion to their abilities—and then left on his trip. The servant who received the five bags of gold began immediately to invest the money and soon doubled it. The servant with two bags of gold also went right to work and doubled the money. But the servant who received the one bag of gold dug a hole in the ground and hid the master's money for safe-keeping.**
>
> **After a long time their master returned from his trip and called them to give an account of how they had used his money. The servant to whom he had entrusted the five bags of gold said, 'Sir, you gave me five bags of gold to invest, and I have doubled the amount.' The master was full of praise. "Well done, my good and faithful servant. You have been faithful in handling this small amount, so now I will give you many more responsibilities. Let's celebrate together!'**
>
> **Next came the servant who had received two bags of gold, with the report, 'Sir, you gave me two bags of gold to invest, and I have doubled the amount.' The master said, 'Well done, my good and faithful servant. You have been faithful in handling this small amount, so now I will give you many more responsibilities. Let's celebrate together!'**

> **Then the servant with the one bag of gold came and said, 'Sir, I know you are a hard man, harvesting crops you didn't plant and gathering crops you didn't cultivate. I was afraid I would lose your money, so I hid it in the earth and here it is.' But the master replied, 'You wicked and lazy servant! You think I'm a hard man, do you, harvesting crops I didn't plant and gathering crops I didn't cultivate? Well, you should at least have put my money into the bank so I could have some interest. Take the money from this servant and give it to the one with the ten bags of gold.**
>
> **— Matthew 25:14-28 (NLT)**

I'm quite certain that Jesus is coming soon. This is all the more reason to start moving into radical wealth *now*, so we can send more missionaries, print more Bibles, and finance the building of more churches and evangelistic outreach stations.

Some are afraid that the economy is going to crash and they will lose their investments. First of all, God owns all the wealth. Secondly, if He owns it, He can certainly tell you where to put it regardless of what happens to the world economy. Besides, I believe that when Jesus comes for His Church it won't be bad economic times. Why do I believe this? Because Jesus said he would come suddenly at a time when it was "business as usual" on the earth.

> **But of that day and hour knoweth no *man*, no, not the angels of heaven, but my Father only. But as the days of Noe *were*, so shall also the**

> **coming of the Son of man be. For as in the days that were before the flood they were eating and drinking, marrying and giving in marriage, until the day that Noe entered into the ark, And knew not until the flood came, and took them all away; so shall also the coming of the Son of man be.**
>
> **— Matthew 24:36-39**

Notice, people were doing all the normal things, getting married, eating, and drinking. It was "business as usual." In fact, it sounds like perhaps it might be a fairly prosperous time just before the Lord comes for His Church.

Just by virtue of the fact that Jesus gave us the illustration of investing right in the middle of His talk on the last days tells me that we should be investing ***now***. The servant who wasn't investing was the one sternly rebuked as "lazy and wicked."

There is no better time than ***now*** to begin your wealth plan.

> **The hand of the diligent shall bear rule: but the slothful shall be under tribute (bondage).**
>
> **— Proverbs 12:24**

You have a choice ***now***. You can be in bondage to "Egypt's" system of finance by doing nothing, just staying in debt and lack. Or you can be loosed from "Egypt" by your ***action*** of stepping into God's financial system. "Egypt's" system seems attractive but it's only for a short season. Greed, covetousness, control, and slavery are a part of "Egypt's" system of finance. Tithing, giving, obeying, liberty, and radical wealth are all a part of God's financial system. It's your choice, but you must choose ***now***.

Dream all you want. Confess all you want. That's good. But until you take ***action***, you will remain the same, you'll be in the same general condition year after year, until one day it dawns on you that you lost all those years and cheated yourself and your family out of the wealth God had prepared for you.

"Faith without works (actions) is dead," St. James tells us (James 2:26).

Add to your dreams ***action***. Add to your confession ***action***. Add to your faith ***action***. But do it ***now***. Right ***now*** do something, maybe just one little thing, toward your future wealth. Start the wealth book. Open the storehouse account. Take one ***action each*** day toward coming into the wealthy place (Psalm 66:12).

Nobody can do this for you. It must be your decision. And you must be faithful, consistent, and persistent once you begin. The master said to the servant who invested and profited, "Well done thou good and faithful servant. Thou hast been faithful over a few things, I will make you ruler over many things" (Matthew 25:21). Be faithful with the wealth God has entrusted to you and He'll entrust more wealth to you.

Have you failed in the past and are now afraid? Let faith drive out your fear.

> **Remember ye not the former things, neither consider the things of old. Behold, I will do a new thing; now it shall spring forth; shall ye not know it? I will even make a way in the wilderness, *and* rivers in the desert.**
>
> **— Isaiah 43:18-19**

> **Brethren, I count not myself to have apprehended: but *this* one thing *I do*, forgetting those things which are behind, and reaching forth unto those things which are before...**
>
> **— Philippians 3:13**

You are not too young. You are not too old. You are not undereducated.

You are not too *anything* to begin *now*.

> **Do not despise these small beginnings, for the Lord rejoices to see the work begin . . .**
>
> **— Zechariah 4:10a (NLT)**

Where will you be financially five years from now if you don't begin your wealth plan *now*?

What are you going to do right *now* about your finances? You have the anointed equipment found in this book. I have never in my life been more anointed to write on any topic than I am right now as I write this book for you. Perhaps not everything in this book pertains to your situation but much of it does. I know it.

God is a great and mighty God who loves you. He wants you to enjoy wealth and riches but He wants you to have the proper perspective on money. Wealth is not designed to make you arrogant and high-minded. Wealth is not designed to be your security or your source. Wealth is for you to enjoy and to provide the means for doing good things for others and for advancing His Kingdom. That's His plan.

There is a powerful anointing on my life right at this moment. I'm going to pray for you ***now***.

> *"Father, I come to you in the Name of Jesus Christ, confessing Him as the True Prosperity Giver. I come on behalf of my dear friend reading this right now.*
>
> *"Dear Friend, I pray a special blessing and anointing of increase over your life and home. I pray a powerful anointing of multiplication to come to your finances as you obey God and His Word.*
>
> *"I command, dear friend, a total release from every hindrance and roadblock in your life that has prevented you from enjoying the wealthy place.*
>
> *"I pray that the power that is within you will rise up like a flood causing you to know beyond a doubt that God Almighty has put within you the power and*

anointing to get wealth. I command blessings on your storehouses as you act upon God's conditions.

"I speak words of prosperity and abundance over everything God has entrusted to you. I call for a divine empowerment to come upon your life ***now*** *that will enable you to supernaturally see the harvest, and supernaturally know how to reap your harvest as it comes into maturity.*

"I pray that the first radical money seed you plant ***now*** *will bring you a one hundred-fold return* ***now*** *and in this time. I pray God will protect you from the things that block wealth and I command the spirit of poverty, and the foul spirit of mammon to be loosed from your life and your finances* ***now****.*

"I pray a blessing of peace, anointing, and radical wealth over you ***now****, my friend. I pray it. I speak it. I decree it for you* ***now*** *while I am under this heavy anointing.*

"In the Name of the Father, and of the Son, and of the Holy Spirit. I see it and I call it ***done****! Amen!"*

Now, I want you to take a very special action. Will you sit down and write to me? Will you jot me a short note and let me know what you are going to do toward your radical wealth? I'd love to hear from you. I'd love to pray for you. Please write to me today. Your letter is so important to me. Write to me at: ***P.O. Box 80825, Lansing, MI 48908-0825***

"Radical riches are restricted for those who meet the qualifications."

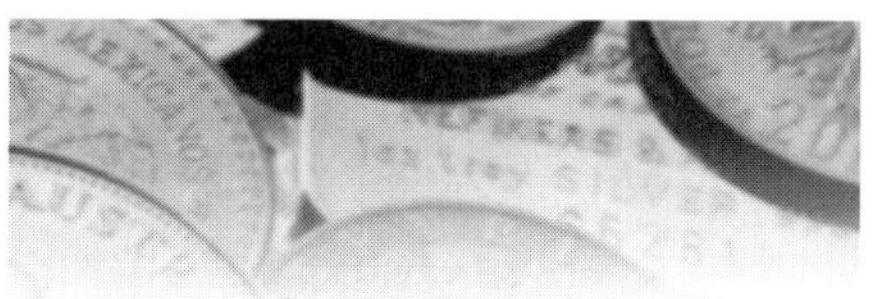

CHAPTER 23

On The Road To Wealth – Yes Or No?

You are destined for radical, outrageous wealth.

God has given you the power to get wealth.[50]

God wants you to come into the wealthy place.[51]

God's will is for your prosperity.[52]

The opulence of Heaven is staggering to the human imagination.[53] Jesus taught us to pray, "Thy kingdom come, Thy will be done, on earth as it is in Heaven."[54] This fact alone assures me that God's will for you on earth is not poverty but plenty.

You are among the few chosen people who have been given the astonishing secret to radical riches. This secret has been hidden from the eyes of those claiming to be wise in this world, but are in reality fools.

It is true the Bible gives us many warnings about the deceitfulness of riches and the improper handling of money, but these warnings were not meant to turn us away from wealth. They were designed to inspire us to use our wealth wisely and appropriately.

Radical riches are restricted for those who meet the qualifications. Just as the gift of salvation has requirements — repentance from dead works, faith in God, public confession of Jesus Christ as Lord, and receiving Jesus Christ. Likewise the gift of power to get radical wealth has some requirements. Throughout this book we have pointed out those requirements.

In this chapter I'm going to give you another checklist. It's interesting to me how many times the Bible gives us checklists. Peter gives us a checklist of attributes to add to our faith.[55] Paul gives us a checklist to identify the works of the flesh and the fruit of the Spirit.[56] In 1 Corinthians 6, Romans 1, and Galatians 5, Paul gives us a check list of those who are deceived, thinking they are going to Heaven when in fact they are not.[57]

Lists are important. I hope that you, after reading this far, have made a detailed checklist of actions you are going to take toward your radical riches. I am going to provide you with a simple, straightforward checklist of statements to which you may answer either "yes" or "no." The number of "yes" answers will determine how close you are to coming into the wealthy place spoken of in Psalm 66:12. Be honest with yourself and with God. Nobody is grading you on your answers. This list is designed to provide you with a point of reference for your benefit.

If you are married, you may want to make a photocopy of these pages and take the "test" together. Or you can do it with an accountability partner if you wish. However you choose to do it, be sure you are brutally honest. Think about each statement before you check your answer.

Please remember, you are checking "*yes*" if the statement is true concerning you.

Well, turn the page and let's get started.

YOUR WEALTH CHECKLIST

YES	NO		
❐	❐	1.	I believe money is important.
❐	❐	2.	I believe that part of Jesus Christ's work was to redeem me from, not only sin, but also poverty.
❐	❐	3.	I believe that nobody has to be poor.
❐	❐	4.	I believe that God wants me to be debt-free and prosperous.
❐	❐	5.	When I give to God, I always expect a harvest in return.
❐	❐	6.	I am willing to give all my worldly possessions — everything — if God asks me to do it.
❐	❐	7.	I am willing RIGHT NOW to sell everything I have and give it all to God's work or to the poor, if the Lord so instructed me.
❐	❐	8.	I have, in the past, given to God more than I could afford, when I sensed that He was prompting me.
❐	❐	9.	I am fully convinced that God has a plan for getting his people out of debt and into radical prosperity.
❐	❐	10.	I have dreams about a more prosperous financial future.
❐	❐	11.	There is plenty of wealth available in this world for me.
❐	❐	12.	I believe God owns all the wealth in the world and is willing and able to show me how to get my share.
❐	❐	13.	I have read this book entirely, as the author instructed in the first chapter, not picking and choosing what I wanted to read.
❐	❐	14.	I have meditated day and night upon the Scriptures pertaining to wealth the author has shared throughout this book.

YES	*NO*		
❐	❐	15.	I plan to read this book again, and carefully seek to understand all the principles and Scriptures given.
❐	❐	16.	I am willing to be corrected if I have a wrong attitude about wealth and riches.
❐	❐	17.	I have already followed many of the instructions the author of this book has shared.
❐	❐	18.	I believe the power to get wealth is in me now.
❐	❐	19.	I refuse to believe the negative economic and financial input offered by this world.
❐	❐	20.	I refuse to quote people who report bad news about money.
❐	❐	21.	I reject any teaching about the virtue of poverty or lack.
❐	❐	22.	If the world was in a depression and everyone was saying, "There are no jobs" and "times are bad," I would be confident that I would not only survive, but thrive through it.
❐	❐	23.	I believe there is outrageous wealth available today.
❐	❐	24.	I have made the conscious decision to come into God's "wealthy place."
❐	❐	25.	I always tithe the first ten percent of my gross income.
❐	❐	26.	The first check I write after being paid or receiving some form of income or increase, is the check to God's work.
❐	❐	27.	I am convinced that the tithe belongs to God, not me.
❐	❐	28.	Ten percent of all my income and increase belongs to God and I faithfully make sure that He gets it.
❐	❐	29.	I have given radically beyond the tithe in the past three months for a desired result; a desired harvest.

YES	NO		
❐	❐	30.	I regularly, consistently, and persistently give offerings beyond the regular tithe.
❐	❐	31.	I take God at His Word and claim His promises daily.
❐	❐	32.	I am willing, like David, to lay something important to me on the "altar" in order to have God send me prosperity now.
❐	❐	33.	When it comes to money, I do what I can, and always trust God to do what only He can do. And I really believe it works.
❐	❐	34.	I understand that faith is always NOW and have proven that I believe it by my faith actions today.
❐	❐	35.	I have combated and beat covetousness and greed in my life.
❐	❐	36.	I understand that faith gives, and greed hoards.
❐	❐	37.	I have faced and done warfare against the wicked principality of mammon.
❐	❐	38.	I am happy when others are blessed financially, even when I may be going through a difficult time.
❐	❐	39.	I never criticize others for their wealth or riches.
❐	❐	40.	I am totally free from the fear of what others may think about me if I drive an old car I paid cash for.
❐	❐	41.	I never intentionally do anything to try to impress others with my wealth, position, or status.
❐	❐	42.	I make my decisions in prayer, and base them upon God's Word and God's Spirit, not money.
❐	❐	43.	I refuse to listen to the spirit of mammon.
❐	❐	44.	God controls my decisions; money does not.
❐	❐	45.	Money does not motivate me; God's will does.

YES	NO		
❐	❐	46.	I have made faith promises in the past year that have been beyond my personal ability to meet.
❐	❐	47.	I understand the law of seed time and harvest.
❐	❐	48.	I am absolutely confident that when God calls me to give in a radical way, it's only because He is preparing and open door of radical opportunity for me.
❐	❐	49.	I understand that I cannot have two Gods or two masters.
❐	❐	50.	I know that money matters and spiritual matters are intertwined and related to each other, based upon Jesus' teachings.
❐	❐	51.	I believe money has a spiritual significance.
❐	❐	52.	I love it when the preacher talks about God's financial plan for my prosperity.
❐	❐	53.	I rejoice when I have the opportunity to give.
❐	❐	54.	I know that how I handle money will largely determine my success or failure in life.
❐	❐	55.	I rejoice when I see another Christian prospering and being blessed financially.
❐	❐	56.	I love it when I see a man of God who has riches.
❐	❐	57.	I realize that Mammon can stop the flow of my wealth if I make decisions based solely on money.
❐	❐	58.	I know the devourer is rebuked over my home and my finances.
❐	❐	59.	I believe a non-tither is a thief, stealing someone else's money.
❐	❐	60.	I have seen a progressive change for the better in my finances over the past five years.
❐	❐	61.	I am convinced that God's principles play no favorites. They will work for anyone who will put them to work.
❐	❐	62.	It is possible to have a mammon-controlled church.

YES	NO		
❐	❐	63.	Everyone can afford to tithe and give offerings.
❐	❐	64.	The tithe is a test to prove that we are putting God first.
❐	❐	65.	I believe tithing opens the windows of Heaven, but offerings provide the "containers" to catch what is coming out of those windows.
❐	❐	66.	Whatever measure I use in my offerings is the measure that I will have to contain my own blessings of wealth.
❐	❐	67.	It is never okay with God for a person to tithe to a family member in want, or to a soup kitchen, or other charitable organization. We are to provide for these needs through offerings and giving.
❐	❐	68.	It's not how much a person makes that will determine his future wealth, but what he does with the money he earns.
❐	❐	69.	I remember several times in my life when I put my own personal desires on "hold" for the sake of giving to God's work.
❐	❐	70.	Mammon, the principality over greed, covetousness, and financial deceit will always come to collect from his followers.
❐	❐	71.	Many of God's promises are reserved only for those who are faithful tithers and radical givers.
❐	❐	72.	The love of money is the taproot into all sorts of evil things.
❐	❐	73.	I am functioning in my God-ordained, assigned role in life.
❐	❐	74.	When a person prioritizes money over God's will, he puts a siphon that extends into the cesspool of filth and wickedness.
❐	❐	75.	When I pursue God's will and Kingdom first, I inherit the promise of protection and the guarantee of prosperity.

YES	NO		
❐	❐	76.	When I give, I always do it cheerfully, and I always have a desired harvest in mind.
❐	❐	77.	I can actually increase the fruit of my righteousness by giving generously.
❐	❐	78.	God's blessing are chasing me every day.
❐	❐	79.	I believe it is possible to go from poverty to prosperity in a short time.
❐	❐	80.	A pastor can cheat his flock by not allowing them to financially bless him.
❐	❐	81.	The man of God is a key to my wealth.
❐	❐	82.	I can open the door to radical miracles in my life by the way I treat the man of God.
❐	❐	83.	Blessing the man of God should be done in a tangible way.
❐	❐	84.	The man of God should be blessed financially, above and beyond his salary, even if he makes a good salary.
❐	❐	85.	I have blessed my pastor in a tangible way in past year.
❐	❐	86.	In the past year, I have given an offering to some Bible teacher who has particularly helped me and blessed me, whether on television, radio, print, or in person.
❐	❐	87.	The pastor's pay can affect the total church income.
❐	❐	88.	My radical wealth is somehow connected to the man of God.
❐	❐	89.	I regularly pray for my pastor to be blessed financially.
❐	❐	90.	Some people need to give their way out of poverty.
❐	❐	91.	Those who cheat a man of God are walking on dangerous turf.
❐	❐	92.	The higher my pastor goes in finances, the higher I can go.

YES	NO		
❐	❐	93.	I refuse to allow the spirit of poverty to control my life.
❐	❐	94.	I refuse to use phrases like, "money doesn't grow on trees."
❐	❐	95.	It is possible to become a millionaire on $12,500 a year.
❐	❐	96.	Money is like a seed. It must be planted in order to produce.
❐	❐	97.	The spirit of poverty is recognized by the feeling of hopelessness it brings to its victims.
❐	❐	98.	When we put God first with our money, that is an indicator that we are putting God first in other areas of our lives too.
❐	❐	99.	There was a time in my life when I cast everything I had into the church offering.
❐	❐	100.	It is possible to give so violently, that the spirit of poverty is actually cast off of the giver's life, and out of the giver's finances.
❐	❐	101.	Money is a wonderful servant but a terrible master.
❐	❐	102.	The spirit of poverty causes people to be underachievers.
❐	❐	103.	Those controlled by the spirit of poverty are more likely to focus on the "cares of life" than the person walking in divine prosperity.
❐	❐	104.	It's wonderful to talk about money in church.
❐	❐	105.	I appreciate ministers who have the courage to tell the people the truth about money, based upon God's Word.
❐	❐	106.	I am totally out of debt.
❐	❐	107.	I have drawn up a plan for getting out of, or staying out of debt.
❐	❐	108.	When I use credit cards, I always pay them off each month and never incur any interest charges or fees.

YES	NO	
❒	❒	109. It irritates me when I hear someone call God's financial plan, "the gospel of prosperity," or "the Wall Street gospel."
❒	❒	110. I fully expect a financial harvest every single time I plant a money seed into God's Kingdom.
❒	❒	111. The earth is the Lord's and the fullness thereof.
❒	❒	112. Everything the devil has on earth, he has obtained through illegal means.
❒	❒	113. God wants me to have financial power, not financial pressure.
❒	❒	114. I am not a slave to any financial institution because I owe nothing.
❒	❒	115. I paid cash for my car.
❒	❒	116. I have no debts on depreciating assets. (Checking "Yes" means I have no debts.)
❒	❒	117. God wants me to be the lender, not the borrower.
❒	❒	118. I refuse to operate my finances on "Egypt's" system, because it is leveled against the average person.
❒	❒	119. I have made less than $500 in interest payments in the past year.
❒	❒	120. Debt is enslaving millions of people today.
❒	❒	121. My assets outweigh my liabilities.
❒	❒	122. I have demonstrated my willingness to delay gratification in the past year, by refusing to borrow money on something I really wanted.
❒	❒	123. I spend less than I earn.
❒	❒	124. I can pay off my home loan in seven years or less.
❒	❒	125. I always pay more on the principle than I do on the interest when I make a house payment.
❒	❒	126. I realize that when I am faithful over little, God will entrust more to me.
❒	❒	127. I have been faithful to live below my means, and never borrow money for cars and other depreciating items.

YES	NO	
❐	❐	128. I was not created for poverty. I was created for radical prosperity.
❐	❐	129. I am moving from the land of "just enough" to the land of outrageous wealth. I have seen progress over the past three years.
❐	❐	130. I have determined to go after everything God has promised to me.
❐	❐	131. I read the entire Book of Proverbs every month.
❐	❐	132. I read through the Bible every year and meditate upon God's promises to me.
❐	❐	133. I always honor God with the firstfruits of everything I get, including what I get in my vegetable garden (if I have one) and in my financial accounts.
❐	❐	134. All that I have is on loan from God. I am a steward of God's wealth, and the better I handle it, the more He will let me manage.
❐	❐	135. I know nothing multiplies until I release it to God.
❐	❐	136. God wants me wealthy. I am totally convinced of this fact.
❐	❐	137. God wants me to provide for missionaries to go to people who have not heard the gospel.
❐	❐	138. God wants me wealthy so I can help get His True Covenant established throughout the world.
❐	❐	139. I have given at least five percent of my gross income to missions endeavors in the past year.
❐	❐	140. All in all, I regularly give on the average of 23% or more of my income to God each year in tithes, offerings, and supernatural faith promise giving.
❐	❐	141. I have determined to not neglect the power of wealth that is in me.
❐	❐	142. I have made an active, firm, unwavering decision to come into the wealthy place.

YES	*NO*	
❒	❒	143. I never cheat on my taxes. Never.
❒	❒	144. I have asked God to provide me with supernatural tax money in the past two years.
❒	❒	145. I have studied the tax laws or talked to an estate planner or certified financial planner about it in the past three years.
❒	❒	146. I always use an envelope when I tithe and give offerings so I can take advantage of the legitimate tax deduction.
❒	❒	147. God wants me to give good gifts to my children.
❒	❒	148. I have a plan for leaving an inheritance to my grandchildren.
❒	❒	149. I have a legal will and trust in place right now.
❒	❒	150. I have helped the poor in some way during the past month.
❒	❒	151. I know that when I prosper, it brings pleasure to God's heart.
❒	❒	152. Prosperity is God's perfect will for my life.
❒	❒	153. I know that debt and lack are not God's best for my life.
❒	❒	154. I know God gets no pleasure when I go into debt.
❒	❒	155. I realize that as I prosper, I'll be criticized.
❒	❒	156. I know that critics are those who complain the most and do the least.
❒	❒	157. I believe the hundred-fold principle can be activated today.
❒	❒	158. All the promises of God in both the Old and the New Testaments belong to me in Christ Jesus.
❒	❒	159. If God told me to give something to a wealthy man, I wouldn't argue. I would just give it.
❒	❒	160. I am confident that when someone means something for my harm, God will turn it around for my good.
❒	❒	161. I know it is possible to give more than I can give, when I listen to God's voice.

YES	NO	
❐	❐	162. When God channels money through me, and I give it, He counts it as a seed for my own personal harvest.
❐	❐	163. I realize that the more I prosper, the more critics I will attract.
❐	❐	164. I believe the "poverty gospel" has held back many Christians from coming into their rightful place of wealth.
❐	❐	165. I read Proverbs every month because God promised me that wisdom will cause my treasuries to be full.
❐	❐	166. I have opened at least one storehouse account since reading this book.
❐	❐	167. I have a 401(k) or 403(b) in place and I am putting the maximum I can into these accounts.
❐	❐	168. I have opened a tax-deferred IRA and have set a goal for a specific amount I will deposit each year.
❐	❐	169. I have adequate insurance on my life (five times my annual income).
❐	❐	170. I have opened a tax-deferred variable annuity and set a goal for what I will deposit into it each year.
❐	❐	171. I know how much money I want in my storehouse accounts twenty years from now, if Jesus tarries. I have planned it all out.
❐	❐	172. I know exactly how much money I owe and have prayed specifically to God for that amount so I can get out of debt.
❐	❐	173. I have called some investment companies in the past month to get information on what they offer.
❐	❐	174. I have started to build my wealth library and have at least five books pertaining to finances now.

YES	*NO*	
❐	❐	175. I have, in the past year, ordered a financial newsletter from a credible consultant.
❐	❐	176. I have, in the past three days, asked God to bless my storehouse accounts with a specific amount.
❐	❐	177. I know approximately what my financial needs and desires are for next year and have prayed specially for God to meet them.
❐	❐	178. I love it when I see a preacher driving a nice car.
❐	❐	179. I have determined that God is my Source, nobody else, and nothing else.
❐	❐	180. I refuse to complain about my boss or my company, because I do not look to them for my wealth.
❐	❐	181. I never worry about my resources drying up, because I have made God my real Source.
❐	❐	182. I have not complained about a minister asking for money in the past three years.
❐	❐	183. I know it is no sin for someone to face a financial need.
❐	❐	184. I have not sinned with my tongue in a long time, because I know that sins of the tongue can stop the flow of blessings into my life.
❐	❐	185. I understand and fully realize that if I am to come into the wealthy place, I must first come out the place I am currently.
❐	❐	186. I know God doesn't automatically give me wealth, but He gives me the power to get wealth.
❐	❐	187. Whenever I am facing any problem, I remember the Lord first.
❐	❐	188. I have put nothing ahead of my relationship with God in the past year.
❐	❐	189. I have everything I need already in me to come out of bondage and into the wealthy place.

YES	NO	
❐	❐	190. I have always done things God's way, not my way, for the past three years.
❐	❐	191. God has given me a covenant of increase because of my relationship with His son, Jesus.
❐	❐	192. I know the Lord is never magnified in debts and bills.
❐	❐	193. I am functioning in my assignment from God right now, and not looking for "greener pastures."
❐	❐	194. I have written out my financial vision on paper.
❐	❐	195. I have a special book, just for my financial dreams, goals, plans and prayer matters.
❐	❐	196. I have listed all the reasons why I want God's radical wealth in my life.
❐	❐	197. I have listed fifty things I really want in life.
❐	❐	198. In the past month, I have cut out pictures from magazines to paste in my wealth book to help my vision.
❐	❐	199. In the past year, I have attended a financial conference or seminar.
❐	❐	200. In the past five years, I have attended an estate planning seminar, or made an appointment with a certified professional to go over my plans.
❐	❐	201. In the past month, I have taken at least one specific action toward my wealth goals.
❐	❐	202. I have itemized all my assets and liabilities and know exactly where I stand in terms of my so-called net worth.
❐	❐	203. I have laid specific, reasonable but challenging, financial goals and put them all on paper in my special wealth book.
❐	❐	204. If someone were to ask me exactly where I want to be financially in ten years, I would be able to answer with a specific, concrete amount. I would not answer in vague terms, like "to have enough to live on."

YES	NO	
❐	❐	205. I make extra house payments at least five times a year.
❐	❐	206. I have listened to an audio cassette on finances in the past week.
❐	❐	207. I have started turning off the television and started listening to financial teaching cassettes, and reading books that will bring me closer to realizing my financial dreams.
❐	❐	208. I have ordered John Cummuta's *Debt Free and Prosperous Living Course.*
❐	❐	209. I have studied the law of compound interest, and have put it to use in my storehouse accounts.
❐	❐	210. I have opened storehouse accounts for my children.
❐	❐	211. I have ordered a subscription to the *Tax Hotline* so I can keep abreast of the tax laws.
❐	❐	212. I understand the law of synergy and have used it in applying the principles in this book.
❐	❐	213. I know God wants me to store up treasures in Heaven and on the earth, but I know it's only a fool who stores up wealth on earth and doesn't nurture a rich relationship with God.
❐	❐	214. In the last days many counterfeit Christians will be in the church, who love and serve only themselves and their money.
❐	❐	215. Iniquity — doing things my way instead of God's way — is a roadblock to radical wealth. This is what caused Lucifer's fall.
❐	❐	216. I, as a believer in Jesus Christ, can have the same blessings that Abraham had. I am in covenant with the God who owns all the wealth in all of creation.
❐	❐	217. I know that if withhold the tithe for any reason, God requires me to pay it with 20% interest the next week.

YES	NO	
❐	❐	218. Adam and Eve violated the principle of the tithe and were driven out from their beautiful home, and lost their status as "trillionaires."
❐	❐	219. I have made a conscious decision to live prosperously.
❐	❐	220. I would rather get knowledge and wisdom than rubies or diamonds, because wisdom can bring me wealth.
❐	❐	221. I have invested more in my storehouse accounts, financial library, and financial planning, this year than I have paid in interest payment.
❐	❐	222. I seek out and listen only to the advice from people who are godly, and have proved that they know what they are talking about.
❐	❐	223. I have never cut my giving to God for the sake of buying anything for me or my family.
❐	❐	224. I actively resist the devil so he cannot get his hands on the wealth God has entrusted to me.
❐	❐	225. I have engaged in spiritual warfare over my finances within the past year.
❐	❐	226. I guard against strife in my home, realizing the power it has to hinder wealth.
❐	❐	227. I speak words of life, power, health, and wealth; never words of poverty, sickness, or failure.
❐	❐	228. I understand the power of my words, and always speak them in harmony with God's Word.
❐	❐	229. Regardless of my past mistakes, I know God can still bring me into the wealthy place.
❐	❐	230. I turn off the television or radio whenever a preacher comes on with words that damage my faith more than inspire my faith.
❐	❐	231. I have changed my image to one of success, prosperity, and radical wealth.
❐	❐	232. I am a conquero r, not a victim.

YES	*NO*	
❐	❐	233. I practice the Golden Rule daily.
❐	❐	234. I have made the commitment to never seek my personal advancement over God's Kingdom advancement.
❐	❐	235. I have renounced all forms of hypocrisy and insincerity.
❐	❐	236. I have committed myself to refrain from impulse buying.
❐	❐	237. I am learning the amazing secret of patience, and have determined to never give up on my seed-planting and harvesting.
❐	❐	238. I have taken at least five new actions since reading this book.
❐	❐	239. I realize that now is the right time to begin, and I have begun by taking action on coming into my wealthy place.
❐	❐	240. A new day has arrived for me. I am coming out of bondage and into the freedom of God's miracle financial system.

You probably noticed that each of these 240 statements were taken right from the previous chapters in this book and each has a Scripture to back it up. Why don't you make a copy of these pages and put them into your wealth notebook? As you read through the Bible, place the Scripture reference next to each statement. This will be a faith-building practice and will help you to concentrate on God's promises for your radical wealth.

"We don' t need more empty words, more lifeless sermons, more depthless philosophies. We need power."

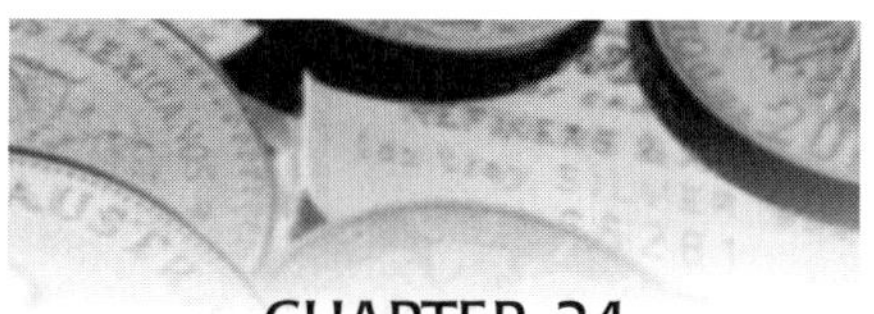

CHAPTER 24

Your Day Of Destiny

Only once in a lifetime it happens. Something so precious and priceless comes along that has the power to change your destiny. You can accept it or reject it. That is your choice.

I've shared with you in this book principles for radical riches — ideas and concepts that have the power, when activated, to change your financial destiny. You have the right to choose to believe these principles and to act on them, or to just go on as you are now. It's your choice. God respects your human will so much that He will not force His blessings on you. If you decide that either you don't want His promised blessings or you are unwilling to do what is necessary to experience them, God respects your decision.

For example, Jesus Christ came to seek and save lost humanity. Yet He never forces Himself upon anyone. Jesus came to offer eternal life to all who would qualify for it through faith. He came to destroy the works of the devil (sin, sickness and poverty). He came to lavish upon His creation an abundance of good things far beyond anything we have ever known.

> **For God so loved the world, that he gave his only begotten Son, that whosoever believeth in him should not perish, but have everlasting life. For God sent not his Son into the world to condemn the world; but that the world through him might be saved.**
>
> **— John 3:16 - 17**

> **For this purpose the Son of God was manifested, that he might destroy the works of the devil.**
>
> **— 1 John 3:8b**

> **The thief cometh not, but for to steal, and to kill, and to destroy: I am come that they might have life, and that they might have *it* more abundantly.**
>
> **— John 10:10**

Some reject Jesus.

> **And this is the condemnation, that light is come into the world, and men loved darkness rather than light, because their deeds were evil.**
>
> **— John 3:19**

But everyone who receives Him is given a special privilege — a special power greater than any other power in the universe.

> **But as many as received him, to them gave he power to become the sons of God, *even* to them that believe on his name.**
>
> **— John 1:12**

I still look back to the day in 1971 when two young men had the courage to invite me to go to church with them. They never gave up on me. They were determined to lead me to Jesus Christ. They prayed for me, and they put action to their faith by loving me, talking to me, and continuing to invite me to church.

One night, their car was broken down and they asked if I'd drive them to church, so I did. We drove 85 miles to a church in Costa Mesa, California. The pastor was teaching from Daniel chapter two that night and somehow wove into his message the clearest presentation of the gospel I had ever heard in my life. That night I became a follower of Jesus.

I didn't know until that night that the wages of sin is death.

> **For the wages of sin *is* death.**
>
> **— Romans 6:23a**

I didn't know until that night that everybody has sinned and fallen short of God's standards and expectations.

> **For all have sinned, and come short of the glory of God.**
>
> **— Romans 3:23**

I thought believing in God was good enough. But I learned that even the devil believes in God. But the devil will never have a place in Heaven, just because he believes in God. Many who merely "believe" in God will spend eternity in hell with the devil.

> **Thou believest that there is one God; thou doest well: the devils also believe, and tremble.**
>
> **— James 2:19**

In order to be qualified for this gift of eternal life, I had to do something. I had to repent from my sins (Acts 2:38; 3:19; Luke 13:3). Next I had to express faith toward God by trusting in His only plan to get me into Heaven. Jesus said, "I am the Way, the Truth, and the Life. No man comes to the Father but ***by Me***," (John 14:6). St. Paul said that Jesus is the only Mediator between God and man. In other words, everybody is hopeless apart from the Creator's only way to be forgiven, made new, and made fit for Heaven.

Generally speaking, I love the right side of the "buts" in the Bible. A moment ago I quoted part of Romans 6:23. Let's look at the rest of the verse.

> **...but the gift of God *is* eternal life through Jesus Christ our Lord.**
>
> **— Romans 6:23**

Ah, there it is, ***the gift of God*** is eternal life, but ***only*** through Jesus Christ.

God created no "Plan B" to get us into Heaven or make things right with our souls. When we receive Jesus Christ as Lord, believing that He died on the cross for our sins, and that God raised Him from the dead, and we publicly confess that He is Lord, we are given a covenant with God. Part of that covenant is a unique power.

We are given power over sin and the devil, and a great power that can bring us exceedingly and abundantly more than anything we could ever ask, think, dream, or imagine.

> **Now unto him that is able to do exceeding abundantly above all that we ask or think, according to the power that worketh in us,**
>
> **— Ephesians 3:20**

This is the power that can be activated to get wealth and even radical riches beyond anything we can pray about or imagine.

Jesus died for you. He hung on an executioner's cross for six torturous hours to purchase your right to be forgiven, have a home in Heaven someday, experience peace with God, and receive the power necessary for everything you can imagine within the framework of God's plan, purpose and destiny for your life.

But, you have to qualify. You have to be willing to turn from your selfish life and turn to Christ's life of selflessness and humility. You must come to Christ, just as you are, and ask Him to forgive you, change you, and empower you. You must look to Him alone as your only hope of ever having a true covenant with the Creator, who gives only His covenant children the power to get wealth.

This gospel of Jesus Christ is not for sissies. This gospel of Jesus Christ is a gospel of ***power***. This gospel is not one of mere words but of ***power*** and ***demonstration.*** Look at what St. Paul said concerning the message of the gospel.

> **And my speech and my preaching *was* not with enticing words of man's wisdom, but in demonstration of the Spirit and of power: That your faith should not stand in the wisdom of men, but in the power of God.**
>
> **—1 Corinthians 2:4-5**

We don't need more empty words, more lifeless sermons, more depthless philosophies. We need ***power***. It is He that gives us the ***power*** to get wealth.

> **But thou shalt remember the LORD thy God: for *it is* he that giveth thee power to get wealth, that he may establish his covenant which he sware unto thy fathers, as *it is* this day.**
>
> **— Deuteronomy 8:18**

Many today are forgetting the Lord God and wondering why they are working harder, while still seemingly going backwards. They skip church, missing the corporate anointing of Christ's body, so they can work overtime to get more money, or so they can attend motivational rallies that inspire their desire for greater riches. Their intentions may be good, and many times they promise more money to God's work. But in their hearts, oftentimes, greed has slowly and subtly replaced God and consequently they miss the true ***power*** from God to get wealth. There is nothing more important to your wealth than "remembering the Lord your God, for it is ***He*** that gives you the power to get wealth."

Jesus gave His disciples a four-point plan for success: (1) make a personal choice, by your will, to come to Jesus, (2) deny yourself, (3) take up your cross, (4) follow Jesus. He then made an interesting statement a few moments later. Let's look.

> **For what shall it profit a man, if he shall gain the whole world, and lose his own soul? Or what shall a man give in exchange for his soul?**
>
> **— Mark 8:36-37**

What a question! What does it profit a man if he gains not only radical riches, but the whole world, then lose his own soul? Time is passing. Eternity is forever. We must, while using the power God placed within us to get wealth, always remember to set our affections on Heaven, not the earth (Colossians 3:1-5). That's easy to do when you are laying up more treasures in Heaven than you are here on earth.

Money can't save us on Judgement Day. Only a rich relationship with Jesus will be able to help us then.

Money can't buy an extra breath when it's time to leave this life.

Lowell Lundstrum sings a song about sending treasures to Heaven. He sang it in our church nearly twenty years ago and I never forgot the gist of it.

"Many people have been living,

For this life below.

They don't do much giving,

their canceled checks do show.

But if death should call, they'll leave it all,

Behind them when they're dead.

Transfer your riches while you can

You better send them on ahead.

Oh, You've never seen a hearse with a U-Haul trailer

Truckin' on down the road.

And you've never seen a coffin with a vault inside it

It would be a heavy load.

And you never hear a mention of the Wall Street Journal

By any man of means that's dead.

No, you can't take it with you when it comes to dying,

So you better send it on ahead."

God created you. That means you are His creation, subject to His laws. But you, like me, and like everyone else in the world, have violated those laws. If you've ever told a lie, even a little "white lie," you are worthy of hell. If you've ever failed to honor God's day, you've messed up. If you've ever thought about money more than God, you've violated God's law, making you fit for hell. Any time you've broken any of the laws on God's checklist you are lost. When your heart quits beating, and three seconds later, you are thrust into eternity, you will know you are lost forever and ever.

The only solution is a Savior. God gave only one Savior in all of history and that is Jesus Christ, His eternal Son. Receive Him and no matter how wealthy or how poor you may be, when your life is over, angels will carry you from this life to your new luxurious home in Heaven.

Perhaps you'd like to pray right now. I'd be happy to pray with you. Say this prayer with me right now:

Dear Lord Jesus,

Please forgive me of all my sins. I have broken Your laws in many ways. I have lived selfishly and have ignored Your Word, the Bible. I cannot save myself. I need a Savior. Jesus, I believe You died on the cross for me, and I believe You were raised from the dead. Please come into my life and cleanse away all my sins, and give me the power to be free from sin, and the power over all the power of the devil. I receive You, Jesus Christ, as my only Hope of ever having a home in Heaven. I confess You now as my Lord. I will live for You from this day forward.

*Thank You, Jesus, for You have forgiven me of all my sins and have brought me into a relationship with God, the Father. I now have eternal life, and peace with God. My sins are gone. I have a home in Heaven, and a fresh **power** from above. I am Your covenant child and I have a brand new start in life ... beginning **now**! Amen!*

Signed: ___________________________________

Date: __________

If you prayed that prayer and really meant it, call someone right now and tell them that Jesus has forgiven you and given you a new life. Tell someone that you now have ***power*** from Heaven because you are a covenant child of God.

If you don't have anyone to talk to, call us at the Global Prayer Center at (517) 327-PRAY. Or sit down and write me a letter, so I can write you back and rejoice in your decision to make peace with God. Also, I'd be honored to send you a free copy of my best-selling *New Life* book, if you request it. It's free and you have no obligation to me whatsoever. When you call the prayer center, ask about a church you can attend in your area.

God will never forsake you. Jesus said, "I am with you always, even unto the end of the age."

Now . . . actively pursue everything God has destined for your life, including those radical promises of radical wealth!

"Don't be afraid to uncompromisingly teach God's people the principles for God's prosperity."

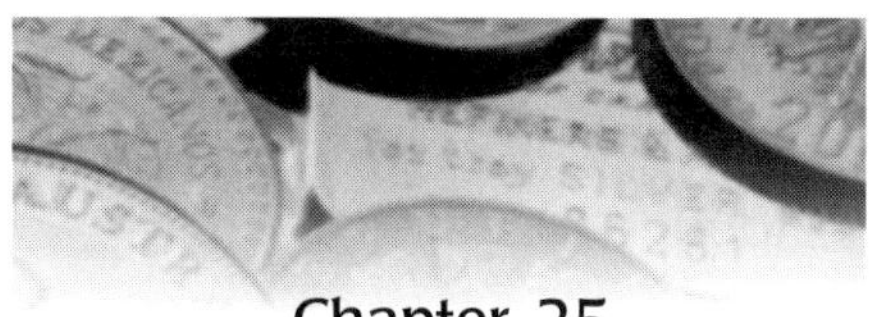

Chapter 25

A Special Word To Pastors

This chapter is especially written for my dear pastor friends. I have a heart for these men of God who are so deeply committed to Christ, dedicated to God's people, and totally sold out to God's Kingdom. You are precious, pastor. I know the difficulties you face in the ministry and I'd like to address a few things here.

Teach The Word Of God

First of all, don't be afraid to uncompromisingly teach God's people the principles for God's prosperity. You are responsible to God for the flock over which He has entrusted to your care. Prosperity is not a dirty word. It is a biblical word and is God's express wish for His children.

It's not easy to talk about money in church. You begin to wonder if you will lose members. You will face the ringing voices of critics. Yet, from Genesis through Revelation, God has given us principles and examples concerning money, wealth, and riches. As a pastor, you must teach the whole counsel of God's Word if you expect your flock to be well balanced, Kingdom-minded, and full of faith.

When I first did a six-week series entitled, "Genuine Prosperity," I received notes telling me that I was going to hinder the revival God was bringing to our church by talking about money in the church. Some people walked out of the services accusing me of teaching the so-called "Wall Street gospel." I endured endless negative comments from fellow pastors in my city. It was painful, nonetheless, I continued with my series.

It wasn't easy, having a small church, watching as some walked out the door. But, after a solid year of studying God's Word on the subject, I was convinced that I had to preach God's plan for prosperity. I had no choice if I was going to walk in radical obedience.

After the six-week series our attendance had gone up by over thirty percent. Eighty five percent of those were new converts. That's right, brand new Christians. Our church decided to give more to missions projects than ever. The attendance continued to rise and the church income tripled within six months. Not only that, the people who were out of work began to find good jobs and stared actually experiencing God's financial blessings.

We started as a small church with a dream of giving big to world missions. Today we have over 4,000 happy people in our Lansing church and thousands more in our national and foreign churches which we have planted and established. We have ten daughter (branch) churches that are winning souls and making disciples for Christ. We are among the top missions giving churches in the nation, helping to support over 200 missionaries and missions projects in 160 different nations.

God has even blessed us by helping us to establish dynamic churches in foreign lands. Each of them is successful, growing, and the people are learning to prosper regardless of the social conditions, the culture, or the style of government. God's principles are universal.

God's Principles Work In Poor Countries, Too

A pastor just told me the other day that he led a Haitian man to Christ a few years ago. That man went back to Haiti, an impoverished nation, and began a ministry to the people there. He invited the American pastor to Haiti to preach. Thousands gathered, and the church did something you rarely see done in poor nations. They took an offering for the American pastor. This was a real step of faith. Normally, we would take an offering to them rather than from them because of their poverty. But they believed, like Neville McDonald said in South Africa, "These people need to learn to give their way out of poverty."

The American pastor brought the money back to his church and purchased a new pulpit. On the pulpit he placed a small engraved plaque that read, "This pulpit was a gift from the prosperous church in Haiti." That was a faith statement based upon God's will for the people in Haiti.

The next time he returned to that country the testimonies were incredible. Many testified that after they had given that offering to the American pastor the government started canceling their debts. Financial miracles started erupting for the Christians in that church. And . . . the church had grown so much that they built a baseball stadium style facility in order to accommodate all the precious souls coming into Christ's family!

So, dear pastor, please don't be afraid to teach your flock these powerful principles. Not only will the church be blessed corporately, but your wonderful people, as they learn to make God their source, will begin to magnificently prosper as well.

Let me give you another example. A pastor ordered several copies of my book entitled *Genuine Prosperity.* He distributed a copy to each member in his church.

Within two weeks the church income doubled and God began to bless the people financially in many personal ways.

The Care And Treatment Of Ministering Guests

Second, I want to encourage you to always bless your guest ministers and missionaries. Treat them like royalty. I guarantee you that it will be a rare treat for many of them.

My evangelist friend canceled a meeting in Texas because a pastor of a church in the north had an "emergency" and begged him to come that next weekend. So the evangelist arranged a flight to the church which needed him that weekend. When he finished two days of ministry the pastor gave him $500, which didn't even cover the evangelist's plane fare.

Another friend of mine took his whole family to a southern state to minister for a pastor who had called and wanted a series of meetings. My friends packed up their family and headed for this southern state. They ministered for three days in this church and the people seemed to be blessed. When they left, the pastor thanked them and handed them a check for $500. It didn't even cover their expenses.

Yet another minister preached in a church where the pastor agreed to receive a love offering for him. After the service, the pastor handed the evangelist a check and said, "This is only half of the love offering. We didn't know the offering would be so large so we kept back half of it."

God will not honor this blatant violation of integrity.

When you invite a guest speaker, evangelist, singing group, or missionary, make sure you cover all their expenses and establish a prearranged agreement on the finances. Whether you chose to give an honorarium or to receive a love offering, make sure you keep your word. Don't deduct "administration fees" from their offering. Don't deduct "expenses" from their offering. If you received the offering for them, make sure it goes to them. And I mean all of it!

Provide a nice hotel for traveling guests. Have a fruit basket in the room when they arrive. Pay all the expenses involved in advertising the meetings, unless something else was prearranged. After you count the love offering, add some to it. Go the extra mile and God will bless you pastor.

Always give a guest the offering before they leave town. The nightmare of all statements for a traveling minister is, "We'll mail you the check." Many jokes have circulated among evangelists concerning "the check's in the mail." It's something nobody wants to hear. Make sure your church has the style and class of a winning enterprise. Always present the guest with a check before he leaves.

If you don't give your speaker the check before he leaves, he won't have the opportunity to pray a blessing of increase over your church. Many traveling ministers that minister at Mount Hope church will take their check, lay one hand on me and their other hand on their check, and pray a fabulous prayer of increase over me on behalf of my church. I wouldn't want to miss that blessing by telling them, "We'll mail you the check."

Do you know what I do with any honorarium or love offering I receive from my personal outside speaking? First, I tithe. Next, if the check is given to me the evening of my ministry, I will normally give ten percent to the pastor who invited me. The rest will typically go into our missions ministry.

> **Dear friend, you are doing a good work for God in taking care of the traveling teachers and missionaries who are passing through. They have told the church here of your friendship and your loving deeds. I am glad when you send them on their way with a generous gift. For they are trav-**

> **eling for the Lord and take neither food, clothing, shelter, nor money from those who are not Christians, even though they have preached to them. So we ourselves should take care of them in order that we may become partners with them in the Lord's work.**
>
> **— 2 John 5-8 (TLB)**

Remember Your Source

The third thing I feel compelled to share with you is this: always remember your source. Do not become embittered toward people because some stingy deacon has cheated you out of a pay raise. You must keep a clean heart before God and before the people when you preach. It disturbs me when I hear pastors griping constantly about how the "board" doesn't take care of them. My friend, the "board" is not your source, God is.

It's not how much money you make that determines your radical wealth. It's what you do with that money that will make all the difference in the world. Remember the pastor who never made more than $250 a week yet retired a millionaire? Remember the UPS employee that never made more than $270 a week yet today is worth over $70 million? It wasn't how much they made, but what they did with their money that made the difference.

I started pastoring a church where most of the board members believed it was good stewardship to keep the pastor humble and poor. I kept a good attitude. I tithed on what I wanted to earn, not what I was earning. I gave offerings regularly and consistently. Sometimes, my wife and I gave everything we had to the Lord, because we needed financial miracles. God always came through, just as He promised, and just as we believed He would.

You see, if you don't believe God wants you to prosper, there isn't a prayer for you being able to prosper. You must activate the power to get wealth by applying the principles both corporately and personally. If you are constantly complaining rather than magnifying the Lord, you probably won't experience an abundance of wealth in your life or your ministry. But if you grab hold of the power God has given you and activate that power, you will see outrageous riches running your way.

There was time I was having trouble supporting my family. I was one hundred percent committed to God's work. I refused to allow my wife to go to work to help support the family because I wanted her with our children. Then God showed me how to get some money. I found an insurance policy with a $500 cash value. I learned about investing, cashed the policy in, tithed on it and put the $500 into an investment I was comfortable with. That's how I started.

Now, twenty years later, I have a godly church board that loves to bless me financially. But most of my increase came by keeping out of debt, giving big to God, and wisely investing that original $500, both in God's Kingdom and in good storehouse accounts here on earth.

Today I have the resources to do practically anything I want. My family can travel anywhere we dream about. I could live almost anywhere I'd choose and drive any kind of vehicle I'd want. But we have made the decision to live simply, conservatively, and modestly. We do so because our first priority is God's Kingdom. We give thirty five percent of our income to the Lord and have set a goal to be giving fifty five percent to the Lord's work in the next ten years.

You Can Be Practical, And Still Enjoy Some Luxury

Just because I live simply it doesn't stop me from enjoying a two-week trip to Hawaii or the Caribbean with my wife. I live modestly but enjoy a little luxury now and then. I think Jesus enjoyed a little luxury, too, at times. When the lady anointed him with the expensive perfume from her alabaster box, He didn't stop her. The value of that ointment was a whole year's salary. The only one who complained about that luxury was Judas Iscariot, the thief and betrayer.

Jesus rode into Jerusalem on a donkey, which was considered a luxury in that time, since the vast majority of people walked wherever they traveled.

Sometimes a deacon board, or whoever sets your salary, needs to simply understand God's principles. Get them each a copy of my book, *The Pastor's Pay*. Every pastor that I know who has given a copy of this book to the church board has received a nice pay raise. Sometimes lay people do not know God's guidelines for taking care of the man of God. Contact us for a quantity discount on these books.

Don't Build A New Building Without Counting The Cost

The final thing I want to share with you is this: Don't build a new church building for the sake of building a new building, especially if you must borrow heavily to do it. You need to be concerned about how much of God's money you are sending to "Egypt" on interest payments.

We were worshipping in a 450-seat building fourteen years ago. That was fine as long as our attendance was only 226. But when the attendance grew to 450, I was tempted to launch a building program. After weighing out how much it would cost and how much interest we'd have to pay, I decided to add a service instead. So we went to two services, then three, then four, and finally five Sunday services before we considered building. It gave us time to raise money.

You can borrow some money, if you can quickly pay it back. My rule is this: If the interest will cost more than the building will appreciate in value over the time of the loan, I won't borrow. I will never borrow for church operations. That's a death rattle.

Today we have beautiful facilities on forty-three lovely acres of property. We enjoy our 3,000 seat worship center, and have three Sunday morning services. It would be nice to have a 5,000 seat church, but I won't build a bigger building until we are having five packed-out Sunday services. We are debt-free and it just doesn't make sense to spend God's money on construction when I can work a little smarter and get the same results. I am building other things, like our newly completed Global Prayer Center in Lansing, but I'm not building a new church building until I absolutely have to.

If you are not comfortable speaking about finances in your church, at least invite somebody to speak in your church who will. Perhaps Dr. John Avanzini, Bob Harrison, or Dr. LeRoy Thompson would be willing to come for a Sunday evening and share the principles of God's financial system. I take a limited number of Sunday evenings each year to minister these principles in churches across the country. The point is, don't cheat your people out of a God-given blessing by keeping them in the dark concerning their power to get wealth.

I hope you have sensed my concern for you as I shared these things with you, my pastor friend. My prayer is that you will set the example by coming into the place of radical wealth and passing that anointing onto the precious people in your church.

> **And it shall come to pass in that day, *that* his burden shall be taken away from off thy shoulder, and his yoke from off thy neck, and the yoke shall be destroyed because of the anointing.**
>
> **— Isaiah 10:27**

"These resources can point you to the ladder of wealth but they can't make you climb it. That's something you will have to do yourself."

Chapter 26

Wealth Building Resources

Jesus made an interesting statement in Luke chapter 16, verse 8. He said, "The children of this world are in their generation wiser than the children of light."

It is true that often times the ungodly seem to possess a greater savvy concerning wealth than the children of God do. The children of this world often set monstrous goals, gather all the information they can find, make huge commitments, and walk away with incredible riches, while God's children sit back and wait for something to happen.

Nothing Is Impossible

When the Tower of Babel was being built, the children of this world had to be stopped. God said, "Nothing will be restrained from them, which they have imagined to do."[58] That's why God was forced to stop them from constructing their devil-honoring tower.

All ungodly wealth-gainers will likewise one day be stopped.

These worldly-minded people used their imaginations. They laid plans, set goals, established unity, and unless God stopped them, He said, nothing would be impossible for them. But you are ***not*** ungodly. You are not a child of this world. You are God's chosen family member. Jesus said, "Nothing shall be impossible unto you."[59]

Solomon said, "The prudent (wise) man dealeth with knowledge: but a fool layeth open his folly."[60]

What is he saying? Simply this: If you are wise, you will seek knowledge concerning a particular subject. The wise person, if he wants to activate his power to get wealth, seeks to uncover knowledge about wealth. The fool says, "Oh, I don't need any knowledge. If God wants me to be wealthy, He'll just come down and make me rich." The fool expects God to not only give him the power to get wealth, but expects God also to do all the work.

Can you imagine a farmer saying, "God has given me seed. If He wants it to be planted, He'll just come down and plant it"? Or can you picture a farmer saying, "The harvest is now ripe. If God wants me to have it, He'll come down and reap it for me"? You would say, "That farmer is crazy."

Yet many of God's children, the children of the light, act in a similar manner by saying in either words or attitude, "If God wants me to have a financial harvest, He'll go out and reap it for me and bring it all into my barns." That's as ridiculous as a farmer expecting God to go out and pick the corn after it has grown and matured.

In this final chapter I want to give you a list of resources that will help you gain some practical knowledge concerning finances. Many of these resources can point you to the ladder of wealth but they can't make you climb it. That's something you will have to do yourself.

When you start learning about investments, it may seem like a maze at first. It was to me. But month after month, and year after year, it all will become clearer to you as you gain more knowledge. It is exactly like the prophet Isaiah said:

> **Whom shall he teach knowledge? and whom shall he make to understand doctrine?** *them that are* **weaned from the milk,** *and* **drawn from the breasts. For precept** *must be* **upon precept, precept upon precept; line upon line, line upon line; here a little,** *and* **there a little:**
>
> **— Isaiah 28:9, 10**

Don't get discouraged. Start building your wealth library today. Here are some resources that I believe can help you. These experts can be your support team of wealth consultants.

Dr. John Avanzini

Dr. Avanzini is one of the most inspirational speakers I've heard on biblical economics. He has authored many books on the subject, tape albums, videos, and even makes available an entire course entitled *The Debt-Free Army*. You may contact Dr. Avanzini at Harrison House Books / P.O. Box 35035 / Tulsa, OK 74153 or by writing directly to: P.O. Box 1057 / Hurst, TX 76053

Peter J. Daniels

Peter J. Daniels came from a broken home, failed every grade in school, and was a third generation welfare recipient. He met Jesus Christ at a Billy Graham crusade and then went on to become a multi-millionaire land developer and one of the most sought after speakers in Australia. His book, *How to Be Happy Though Rich*, is a real inspiration to the person who feels like they don't have the right background for radical riches. You may write for information to: Mr. Peter J. Daniels / The House of Tabor Publishers / 84 Northgate Street / Unley Park, South Australia 5061.

Billy Joe Daugherty

Billy Joe is one of America's great pastors. He pastors Victory Christian Center in Tulsa, Oklahoma. His book, *Living in God's Abundance,* would be a great addition to your wealth library. You may write to Billy Joe Daugherty at Victory Christian Center / 7700 South Lewis Avenue / Tulsa, OK 74136

Dr. LeRoy Thompson

Dr. Thompson has written some terrific books about escaping from the bondage of poverty and moving into God's prosperity. His classic, *Money Cometh,* teaches the reader how to get into the flow of the God kind of prosperity. His subsequent book, *Money: Thou Art Loosed,* is an expose on Psalm 66:12 — coming out of the place of financial hardship and into the place of wealth. You may write for a current catalog: Dr. LeRoy Thompson / Ever Increasing Word Ministries / P.O. Box 7 / Darrow, Louisiana 70725

Bill Swad

Bill Swad is the builder of one of America's greatest automotive enterprises. In his simple, easy to understand book, *How I Got Millionaire Mentality,* Bill takes you on a journey through his life and how God taught him the principles of wealth. You may write to Bill Swad, Sr. at: Christian Center / 298 South Rocky Fork Drive / Gahanna, OH 43230

Larry Burkett

Larry Burkett is perhaps one of the best known writers on the subject of Christian finances. His book entitled *Debt-Free Living* is incredibly powerful and would make a great addition to your wealth library. Please check your local bookstore.

Look for books by Bill Staton and Mark Skousen also. They are easy to read, understandable, and provide some real financial and economic insight to the readers.

Joe Gandolfo, Ph.D. and Associates

You read about Joe in this book earlier. Dr. Gandolfo will help you with estate and financial planning. For a one-time fee, you have Joe as your coach for life. You can call him anytime for a little consultation. Joe is an amazing man. You can reach him at: 5214 South Florida Avenue / P.O. Box 6989 / Lakeland, FL 33807 or call (863) 646-8586 or (800) 553-1008.

Bob Harrison

Bob Harrison took a dying Chrysler Dealership in the 1970's and turned it into one of Southern California's biggest success stories. Bob leads Harrison International now and offers tapes sets, seminars for business people, and Hawaiian leadership conferences. Bob has some tape sets that every business person needs including *Spiritual Warfare and Your Money*. You may contact Bob Harrison at: Harrison International / P.O. Box 701890 / Tulsa, OK 74170 or by calling (800) 632-4653.

Oral Roberts Ministries

Oral Roberts Ministries has published several books to show you God's plan for sowing and reaping finances. The classic by Oral Roberts is *The Miracle of Seed Faith*. Also written by Oral Roberts is the hardbound book entitled, *How I Know Jesus Wasn't Poor.* Richard and Lindsay Roberts have a book called *Debt Blasters* which includes writings from several authors, showing you the principles of transforming your finances God's way. You may write to Oral Roberts Ministries, Tulsa, OK 74171 for information.

John Cummuta, CSL, CFIC

John Cummuta is the author of the *Debt-Free and Prosperous Living* course. John publishes a newsletter and videos as well as the original course. I encourage you to get the basic course simply entitled, "Debt-Free and Prosperous Living." John shows you how the system is leveled against you unless you learn the rules. You may write for information to: Financial Independence Network / 310 2nd Street / Boscobel, WI 53805.

Genuine Prosperity and The Pastor's Pay

Two books I have written that will bless you are *Genuine Prosperity* and *The Pastor's Pay*. *Genuine Prosperity* is a "wealth primer" based upon God's biblical laws of wealth. *The Pastor's Pay* is my heart-to-heart talk with those who are responsible for determining the pastor's salary. Both books are available by writing to: Decapolis Publishing / 202 S. Creyts Rd. / Lansing, MI 48917 or by calling (517) 321-2780, extension 222.

Tax Hotline

This publication keeps you up to date on tax law changes that affect you financially. The monthly publication is designed to alert readers to both opportunities and traps in the broad range of tax laws. Several tax experts make up the *Tax Hotline's* team of writers. To me, it's like getting a tax lawyer for less than a hundred dollars a year. You may write for information to: Tax Hotline / Box 2714 /55 Railroad Ave. / Greenwich, CT 06836-2614 or write to Tax Hotline Subscription Service / P.O. Box 58477 / Boulder, CO 80328-8477.

Mutual Fund Forecaster

This was the first investment publication that I ever subscribed to. It is simple, easy to understand, and each month gives you projections as well as historic earning of hundreds of mutual funds. The newsletter also publishes the most recent telephone numbers of the mutual fund companies so you can contact them directly without paying a broker's fee.

Call toll free and ask for a free sample copy of the *Mutual Fund Forecaster* (800) 442-9000

They also publish the *Mutual Fund Buyer's Guide,* which is an investment scoreboard for America's mutual funds.

Doug Fabian

I like Doug Fabian. He is affectionately known as the "Maverick Investor." His goal is to give you the knowledge and advice each month that will bring you a return of 17% to 24% on your mutual fund investments. Doug has produced a compact disc with an entire seminar on Maverick Investing. My kids listen to Doug Fabian. He makes it easy to understand. You may contact Doug at www.fabian.com or by calling (800) 950-8765 for more information.

Louis Navellier

If you like to pick individual stocks over other investments, Lou Navellier comes with a high rating from Hulbert. Navellier has a *Blue Chip Growth Letter* you can subscribe to by writing to: Navellier / 7811 Montrose Road /Potomac, Maryland 20854 or you may check the web site at www.Navellier.com or www.bluechipgrowth.com.

If you ever want to check the success of a financial newsletter, you can contact the *Hulbert Financial Digest*, which rates over 500 newsletters. You can call (888) HULBERT for information.

I am not a financial planner or advisor. I can give you spiritual principles and biblical truths, but please contact the experts for assistance on the practical side of investing.

Finally . . . I'd like to give the numbers of four mutual fund families that I particularly like for storehouse accounts. I like investing in a family of mutual funds which allows you to switch from fund to fund over the telephone or on the web. These fund families I will list here have done well for me. You must, however be sure you are invested in the right fund at the right time. The market changes. That's why it's good to have a service like Doug Fabian's *Maverick Advisor* or the *Mutual Fund Forecaster*.

You can call any of these investment companies for an account application and prospectus.

Fidelity Investments	(800) 544-8888
Janus Investments	(800) 525-3713

Invesco Investments (800) 525-8085

Vanguard Investments (800) 523-1154

For an all-purpose brokerage account, I use Fidelity and Charles Schwab. They are my favorites, although, there are some great ways to invest on-line now if you are brave enough. Schwab's number is (800) 435-4000. Ask about their "One Account."

Also, there are several associations you can join, like the National Association of Individual Investors. Go to your local bookstore and buy some magazines like *Mutual Funds Magazine*, or *Individual Investing*. In these magazines you'll find plenty of information, web pages, phone numbers, and clubs you can call to start your quest for knowledge.

Go ahead! Start now! Get your storehouse accounts open so God can begin to command His blessings on them.

Always remember: ***You are destined for outrageous wealth.*** Go for it!

APPENDIX A

A Quick Reference Checklist

Qualifications For Activating The Power To Get Wealth

- ❒ Putting God first in your life .... Matthew 6:33
- ❒ Making Jesus Christ Lord of your life .... Acts 16:31
- ❒ The Tithe (10% of your gross income) .... Malachi 3:8-12
- ❒ The Firstfruits (10% of your income and increase) .... Proverbs 3:9, 10
- ❒ Offerings as "seeds planted" .... 2 Corinthians 8 & 9
- ❒ Supernatural faith promises .... 2 Corinthians 9:10
- ❒ Blessing the Man of God .... 1 Kings 17:8-24
- ❒ Remembering the Lord in everything .... Deuteronomy 8:18
- ❒ Fully believing God's will concerning prosperity .... 3 John 1:2
- ❒ Asking God, as your Source, for your desires ..... Mark 11:24
- ❒ Laying plans and goals in writing .... Habakkuk 2:2
- ❒ Gaining knowledge .... Proverbs 3:21-23
- ❒ Debt elimination .... Deuteronomy 28:12
- ❒ Establishing storehouse accounts .... Deuteronomy 28:8
- ❒ Applying tax laws to your advantage .... Mark 12:17
- ❒ Meditating upon wealth Scriptures and promises .... Joshua 1:8
- ❒ Speaking to wealth and commanding it to come .... Mark 11:22-24
- ❒ Taking action .... James 2:26
- ❒ Reading Proverbs through monthly .... Proverbs 4:20-22
- ❒ Renewing the spirit of your mind .... Ephesians 4:23-24
- ❒ Being willing and radically obedient to God ..... Isaiah 1:18-20
- ❒ Discovering and staying in your God-ordained assignment .... 1 Corinthians 7:7
- ❒ Activating the power to get wealth .... Deuteronomy 8:18
- ❒ Developing patient determination .... Galatians 6:9
- ❒ Conducting spiritual warfare over finances .... Ephesians 6:12-18
- ❒ Agreement and harmony in the home .... Matthew 18:18-19
- ❒ Practicing the "Golden Rule" of love .... Matthew 22:37-39
- ❒ Doing an excellent job where you work now ..... Ephesians 6:5-7
- ❒ Establishing a will and trust .... Proverbs 13:22
- ❒ Ruthless self evaluation and correction .... 1 Corinthians 11:31

APPENDIX B

Your Personal Balance Sheet

WHAT YOU OWN:

CASH

1. Cash on hand	$ ___________
2. Savings account	$ ___________
3. Checking	$ ___________
4. Money Market	$ ___________
5. Life ins. cash value	$ ___________
6. _______________	$ ___________

LIQUID INVESTMENTS

7. Stocks	$ ___________
8. Bonds	$ ___________
9. Govt. securities	$ ___________
10. Mutual funds	$ ___________
11. Precious metals	$ ___________
12. C.D.'s	$ ___________
13. _______________	$ ___________

PERSONAL PROPERTY

14. Automobiles	$ ___________
15. Furniture	$ ___________
16. Collectibles	$ ___________
17. Clothing	$ ___________
18. Jewelry	$ ___________
19. _______________	$ ___________

REAL ESTATE

20. House	$ ___________
21. _______________	$ ___________
22. _______________	$ ___________

NON-LIQUID INVESTMENTS

23. I.R.A.	$ ___________
24. Pension	$ ___________
25. Keogh or 401(k)	$ ___________
26. Annuity value	$ ___________
27. _______________	$ ___________

TOTAL	$ ___________

Your Personal Balance Sheet (cont.)

WHAT YOU OWE:

CURRENT BILLS

1. *Rent* $ ____________
2. *Utilities* $ ____________
3. *Charge accounts* $ ____________
4. *Credit cards* $ ____________
5. *Insurance premiums* $ ____________
6. __________________ $ ____________
7. __________________ $ ____________

TAXES

8. *Federal* $ ____________
9. *State* $ ____________
10. *City* $ ____________
11. *Property* $ ____________
12. *On investments* $ ____________
13. __________________ $ ____________
14. __________________ $ ____________

MORTGAGES

15. *House* $ ____________
16. __________________ $ ____________

LOANS

17. *Auto* $ ____________
18. *Education* $ ____________
19. *Home improvement* $ ____________
20. *Life insurance* $ ____________
21. __________________ $ ____________
22. __________________ $ ____________

TOTAL $ ____________

WHAT YOU OWN: $ ____________
MINUS WHAT YOU OWE: — $ ____________

EQUALS YOUR NET FINANCIAL WORTH $ ____________

APPENDIX C
Fifty Things I Desire

Go ahead, make your dream list now. (Mark 11:24; Proverbs 10:24)

1. ____________________
2. ____________________
3. ____________________
4. ____________________
5. ____________________
6. ____________________
7. ____________________
8. ____________________
9. ____________________
10. ____________________
11. ____________________
12. ____________________
13. ____________________
14. ____________________
15. ____________________
16. ____________________
17. ____________________
18. ____________________
19. ____________________
20. ____________________
21. ____________________
22. ____________________
23. ____________________
24. ____________________
25. ____________________
26. ____________________
27. ____________________
28. ____________________
29. ____________________

Fifty Things I Desire (cont.)

30. ______
31. ______
32. ______
33. ______
34. ______
35. ______
36. ______
37. ______
38. ______
39. ______
40. ______
41. ______
42. ______
43. ______
44. ______
45. ______
46. ______
47. ______
48. ______
49. ______
50. ______

APPENDIX D
Compound Interest Example

Because of the amazing law of compound interest, every dollar you spend wastefully now can cost you upwards of $600 or more over a forty-year period in lost gains in your storehouse accounts.

For money to grow, you need three things:

CAPITAL — some starting amount; either a one-time deposit or a continuing, regular deposit weekly, monthly, quarterly, or annually into a mutual fund, shares of stock, or some other good investment storehouse.

TIME — this is where your patience will be tested.

RATE OF RETURN — interest or growth on your money. Interest would include dividends. Growth is when you buy a stock for, say $3 and it goes up to $5. Your growth is $2 per share.

Here is the power of compound interest. Let's say you make a one time deposit of $50,000 into a storehouse account. The higher the rate of return (interest, dividends, or growth) you can get, the faster the wealth grows. This table is for educational purposes.

Scenario: One time deposit of $50,000.

Rate of return	*20 year value:*	*30 year value:*	*40 year value:*
5%	*$ 132,100*	*$ 215,200*	*$ 350,000*
10%	*$ 333,700*	*$ 865,600*	*$ 2,250,000*
12%	*$ 477,800*	*$ 1,480,000*	*$ 4,600,000*
15%	*$ 808,900*	*$ 3,272,000*	*$ 13,250,000*
20%	*$ 1,890,000*	*$11,700,000*	*$ 40,000,000*
25%	*$ 4,250,000*	*$40,000,000*	*$ 370,000,000*

You can see how important it is to:

- Set up your storehouse account as soon as possible
- Get the best rate of return you possibly can

APPENDIX E

Discount Brokers

Below is a list of a few of the better-know discount brokers

Brokerage Firm	Phone Number	Web Address
Accutrade	*(800) 882-4887*	www.accutrade.com
Ameritrade	*(800) 669-3900*	www.ameritrade.com
*E*Trade*	*(800) 786-2575*	www.etrade.com
Fidelity	*(800) 544-8888*	www.personal.fidelity.com
Schwab	*(800) 435-4000*	www.eschwab.com
T. Rowe Price	*(800) 225-7720*	www.troweprice.com
Waterhouse	*(800) 934-4430*	www.waterhouse.com

APPENDIX F
Buying Stocks Direct

If you buy stocks, you can cut the middleman buy purchasing stocks directly from the company if they participate in the direct buy program. Many no-load stocks are available for purchase. You can buy stocks each month as you are able, using dollar cost averaging as your investment strategy. Information is available on many no-load stocks through the following clearinghouses:

Direct Stock Purchase Plan Clearinghouse	*(800) 774-4117*
First Chicago	*(800) 446-2617*
Computer Shares Direct Stock Purchase Plan	*(800) 286-9178*
Bank of New York (Global Buy Direct)	*(800) 345-1612*
J.P. Morgan	*(800) 749-1687*
Netstock Direct on the Internet	*www.netstockdirect.com*
The DRIP Investor on the Internet	*www.dripinvestor.com*

You can call the companies to learn about the advantages of buying stocks directly. Here is a sampling of companies that offer stocks directly to the public.

AFLAC	*(800) 227-4756*
Amoco	*(800) 774-4117*
Atmos Energy	*(800) 774-4117*
Bell South	*(800) 631-6001*
Bob Evans Farms	*(800) 272-7675*
BRE Properties	*(800) 368-8392*
Chevron (Chase Melon)	*(800) 842-7629*
CMS Energy	*(517) 788-1868*
Dominion Resources	*(800) 552-4034*
Duke Realty	*(800) 278-4353*
Exxon	*(800) 252-1800*
Ford Motor Company	*(800) 955-4791*
Gillette	*(800) 643-6989*
Home Depot (Equiserve)	*(800) 730-4001*
McDonalds	*(800) 228-9623*
Merck	*(800) 613-2104*
J.C. Penney	*(800) 565-2576*
Sears	*(888) 732-7788*
Wal-Mart	*(800) 438-6278*
Wisconsin Energy	*(800) 558-9663*

APPENDIX G
Variable Annuities

While variable annuities have some drawbacks, they provide a wonderful storehouse account after you have fully funded your IRA (Individual Retirement Account) and your 401(k), Keogh, SEP, and other qualified tax deferred investment vehicles.

If you set up a variable annuity account, stick with the low cost annuities. Here are a few of the best, in my opinion. There are other good annuities, but you will want to check them out for yourself.

Fidelity Investments	*(800) 634-9361*
Janus Funds	*(800) 504-4440*
T. Rowe Price Associates	*(800) 469-6587*
Charles Schwab	*(800) 838-0650*
USAA Life Insurance	*(800) 531-4265*
Vanguard Group	*(800) 462-2391*

End Notes

[1] Strategic Global Mission is a Dave & Mary Jo Williams Charitable Ministry which provides scholarships for pioneer pastors and grants to inner city children's ministries. P.O. Box 80825, Lansing, MI 48908-0825

[2] *The Making of a Leader* by Ralph Mahoney World MAP, 1985

[3] *Tithing — God's Financial Plan*, Robertson, Norman, 1994, Norman Robertson Media, Matthews, NC 28106

[4] *Angola*, by Joel Kilpatrick, PENTECOSTAL EVANGEL, September 3, 2000, Springfield, MO 65802

[5] *The Pastor's Pay* by Dave Williams, DAVCO Publishing, PO Box 80825, Lansing, MI 48908-0825

[6] *Money Cometh*, by Dr. LeRoy Thompson, PO Box 7, Darrow, Louisiana 70725

[7] *Sell & Grow Rich* by Joe Gandolfo, PhD. and Donald Jay Korn, 1993 Dearborn Publishing, Chicago, IL 60610

[8] Illinois Society of Architects research, 1929

[9] *The Ministry of Greed* by Larry Martz, 1988 Newsweek, Inc. New York, NY

[10] *How to Be Happy Though Rich* by Peter J. Daniels, Revell, 1984 Old Tappan, New Jersey

[11] *The Desires of Your Heart,* by Dave Williams, Decapolis Publishing, 1998 Lansing, Michigan

[12] Deuteronomy 28:1-8

[13] *Money, Thou Art Loosed* by Dr. LeRoy Thompson, Ever Increasing Word Ministries, PO Box 7, Darrow, Louisiana 70725

[14] EP News 8/3/00

[15] *Mutual Fund Forecaster*, P.O. Box 1330, Newbrugh, NY 12551-9806, (800) 442-9000

[16] All the examples in this book are for educational and informational purposes only. Please consult a licensed professional prior to implementing or adjusting any changes to your present investment, tax, debt, mortgage, insurance, legal, estate, or any financial position.

[17] Deuteronomy 32:30.

[18] Matthew 6:24

[19] 2 Timothy 3:1-9

[20] Luke 12:16-21

[21] Deuteronomy 8:18; Malachi 3:8-12; Leviticus 27:30-32

[22] Deuteronomy 30:19; Joshua 24:15; Luke 11:23

[23] *High Finance on a Low Budget*, 7811 Montrose Rd., Potomac, MD 20854

[24] Fabian Resources, P.O. Box 2538, Huntington Beach, CA 92648

End Notes (cont.)

[25] 1 Peter 5:8
[26] John 8:44
[27] James 4:7; 1 Peter 5:9
[28] Matthew 18:18; 2 Corinthians 10:4; Ephesians 6:12
[29] Luke 11:17
[30] James 3:16
[31] 1 Corinthians 14:33
[32] 2 Timothy 2:24-26
[33] Matthew 18:18-19
[34] Ephesians 5:22; Colossians 3:18
[35] Proverbs 18:21
[36] Mark 11:12-14; 20-26
[37] 1 Corinthians 1:27
[38] Hebrews 11:1
[39] Malachi 3:10
[40] Faith Goals, MHC books, 202 S. Creyts Road, Lansing, MI 48917 (800) 888-7284
[41] Matthew 7:12
[42] 1 Corinthians 13
[43] Galatians 5:6; John 15:12; Matthew 22:37-40; Romans 13:10
[44] Romans 5:5
[45] Haggai 2:8,9
[46] Haggai 2:19
[47] Numbers 22-24; 2 Peter 2:15; Jude 11; Revelation 2:14
[48] *Thoughts on Stewardship* by R.H. Browne, 1993 RHBEA, Louisville, KY
[49] Galatians 5:13-26
[50] Deuteronomy 8:18
[51] Psalm 66:12
[52] 3 John 2
[53] Revelation 21
[54] Matthew 6:10
[55] 2 Peter 2
[56] Galatians 5
[57] Romans 1:28-32; 1 Corinthians 6:9,10; Galatians 5:19-21
[58] Genesis 11
[59] Matthew 17:20
[60] Proverbs 13:16

About The Author

Dave Williams is pastor of Mount Hope Church and International Outreach Ministries, with world headquarters in Lansing, Michigan. He has served for 20 years, leading the church in Lansing from 226 to over 4,000 today. Dave sends trained ministers into unreached cities to establish disciple-making churches, and, as a result, today has "branch" churches in the United States, Philippine Islands, and Africa.

Dave is the founder and president of Mount Hope Bible Training Institute, a fully accredited institute for training ministers and lay people for the work of the ministry. He has authored 39 books including the fifteen-time best seller, The New Life . . . The Start of Something Wonderful (with over 2 million books sold), and more recently, The Miracle Results of Fasting.

The Pacesetter's Path telecast is Dave's weekly television program seen over a syndicated network of secular stations. Dave has produced over 90 audio cassette programs including the nationally acclaimed School of Pacesetting Leadership which is being used as a training program in churches around the United States, and in Bible schools in South Africa and the Philippines. He is a popular speaker at conferences, seminars, and conventions. His speaking ministry has taken him across America, Africa, Europe, Asia, and other parts of the world.

Along with his wife, Mary Jo, Dave established The Dave and Mary Jo Williams Charitable Mission (Strategic Global Mission), a missions ministry for providing scholarships to pioneer pastors and grants to inner-city children's ministries.

Dave's articles and reviews have appeared in national magazines such as Advance, The Pentecostal Evangel, Ministries Today, The Lansing Magazine, The Detroit Free Press, and others. Dave, as a private pilot, flies for fun. He is married, has two children, and lives in Delta Township, Michigan.

OTHER BOOKS BY DAVE WILLIAMS

A,B,C's Of Success And Happiness
Aids Plague
Beauty Of Holiness
Christian Job Hunter's Handbook
Desires Of Your Heart
Depression, Cave Of Torment
Genuine Prosperity, The Power To Get Wealth
Getting To Know Your Heavenly Father
Gifts That Shape Your Life And Change Your World
Grand Finale Revival
Grief And Mourning
Growing Up In Our Father's Family
Have You Heard From The Lord Lately?
How To Be A High Performance Believer In Low Octane Days
How You Can Be Filled With The Holy Spirit
Laying On Of Hands
Lonely In The Midst Of A Crowd
The New Life . . . The Start Of Something Wonderful
Pacesetting Leadership
The Pastor's Pay
Patient Determination
Revival Power Of Music
Remedy For Worry And Tension
Secret Of Power With God
Seven Signposts On The Road To Spiritual Maturity
Slain In The Spirit — Real Or Fake?
Somebody Out There Needs You
Success Principles From The Lips Of Jesus
Supernatural Soulwinning
The Miracle Results Of Fasting
The World Beyond — The Mysteries Of Heaven
Thirty-six Minutes With The Pastor
Understanding Spiritual Gifts
What To Do If You Miss The Rapture

The Power To Get WEALTH

"I gave evey member in my church a copy of "Genuine Prosperity." In two weeks our church income doubled, and the people started experiencing God's real financial blessings."

– Rev. S. Davis
Jackson, MIchigan

Let Dave Williams show you the Scriptural way to get on the road to complete financial victory in your life. You'll learn about the economic trouble just ahead, and how to prosper in spite of it. Just look at a few of the chapter topics:

- *The Power To Get Wealth*
- *New Covenant Prosperity*
- *Objections To Wealth*
- *Causes of Poverty*
- *The Threat Of Debt*
- *What Your Future Holds*

$9.95 Each (10 copies 7.95 each, 30 copies $5.95 each)
Available at your favorite bookseller, or by calling (800) 888-7284
Prices good while supplies last.

Mount Hope Ministries

Mount Hope Missions & International Outreach
Care Ministries, Deaf Ministries & Support Groups
Access to Christ for the Physically Impaired
Community Outreach Ministries
Mount Hope Youth Ministries
Mount Hope Bible Training Institute
The Hope Store and Decapolis Publishing
The Pacesetter's Path Telecast
The Pastor's Minute Radio Broadcast
Mount Hope Children's Ministry
Sidewalk Sunday School
The Saturday Care Clinic

When you're facing a struggle and need someone to pray with you, please call us at (517) 321-CARE or (517) 327-PRAY. We have pastors on duty 24 hours a day. We know you hurt sometimes and need a pastor, a minister, or a prayer partner. There will be ministers and prayer partners here for you.

If you'd like to write, we'd be honored to pray for you. Our address is:

MOUNT HOPE CHURCH
202 S. CREYTS RD. LANSING, MI 48917
(517) 321-CARE or (517) 321-2780
FAX (517)321-6332 TDD (517) 321-8200

www.mounthopechurch.org
www.gospelmedia.com/davewilliams.asp
email: mhc@mounthopechurch.org

SAGINAW
CANAL
CREYTS RD.
MICHIGAN AVE.
W. ST. JOSEPH
LANSING MALL
I-96
I-496
N

West of the Lansing Mall, on Creyts at Michigan Ave.

For Your Spiritual Growth

Here's the help you need for your spiritual journey. These books will encourage you, and give you guidance as you seek to draw close to Jesus and learn of Him. Prepare yourself for fantastic growth!

HOW TO BE A HIGH PERFORMANCE BELIEVER
Pour in the nine spiritual additives for real power in your Christian life.

SECRET OF POWER WITH GOD
Tap into the real power with God; the power of prayer. It will change your life!

THE NEW LIFE . . .
You can get off to a great start on your exciting life with Jesus! Prepare for something wonderful.

MIRACLE RESULTS OF FASTING
You can receive MIRACLE benefits, spiritually and physically, with this practical Christian discipline.

WHAT TO DO IF YOU MISS THE RAPTURE
If you miss the Rapture, there may still be hope, but you need to follow these clear survival tactics.

THE AIDS PLAGUE
Is there hope? Yes, but only Jesus can bring a total and lasting cure to AIDS.

These and other books available from Dave Williams and:

For Your Spiritual Growth

Here's the help you need for your spiritual journey. These books will encourage you, and give you guidance as you seek to draw close to Jesus and learn of Him. Prepare yourself for fantastic growth!

THE ART OF PACESETTING LEADERSHIP
You can become a successful leader with this proven leadership development course.

GIFTS THAT SHAPE YOUR LIFE
Learn which ministry best fits you, and discover your God-given personality gifts, as well as the gifts of others.

GROWING UP IN OUR FATHER'S FAMILY
You can have a family relationship with your heavenly father. Learn how God cares for you.

SUPERNATURAL SOULWINNING
How will we reach our family, friends, and neighbors in this short time before Christ's return?

THE GRAND FINALE
What will happen in the days ahead just before Jesus' return? Will you be ready for the grand finale?

GENUINE PROSPERITY
Learn what it means to be truly prosperous! God gives us the power to get wealth!

These and other books available from Dave Williams and:

For Your Spiritual Growth

Here's the help you need for your spiritual journey. These books will encourage you, and give you guidance as you seek to draw close to Jesus and learn of Him. Prepare yourself for fantastic growth!

SOMEBODY OUT THERE NEEDS YOU
Along with the gift of salvation comes the great privilege of spreading the gospel of Jesus Christ.

SEVEN SIGNPOSTS TO SPIRITUAL MATURITY
Examine your life to see where you are on the road to spiritual maturity.

THE PASTORS PAY
How much is your pastor worth? Who should set his pay? Discover the scriptural guidelines for paying your pastor.

DECEPTION, DELUSION & DESTRUCTION
Recognize spiritual deception and unmask spiritual blindness.

THE ROAD TO RADICAL RICHES
Are you ready to jump from "barely getting by" to Gods plan for putting you on the road to Radical Riches?

THE DESIRES OF YOUR HEART
Yes, Jesus wants to give you the desires of your heart, and make them realities.

These and other books available from Dave Williams and:

For Your Successful Life

These video cassettes will give you successful principles to apply to your whole life. Each a different topic, and each a fantastic teaching of how living by God's Word can give you total success!

HOW TO BE A HIGH PERFORMANCE BELIEVER
Pour in the nine spiritual additives for real power in your Christian life.

THE UGLY WORMS OF JUDGMENT
Recognizing the decay of judgment in your life is your first step back into God's fullness.

WHAT TO DO WHEN YOU FEEL WEAK AND DEFEATED
Learn about God's plan to bring you out of defeat and into His principles of victory!

WHY SOME ARE NOT HEALED
Discover the obstacles that hold people back from receiving their miracle and how God can help them receive the very best!

BREAKING THE POWER OF POVERTY
The principality of mammon will try to keep you in poverty. Put God FIRST and watch Him bring you into a wealthy place.

HERBS FOR HEALTH
A look at the concerns and fears of modern medicine. Learn the correct ways to open the doors to your healing.

These and other videos available from Dave Williams and:

Running Your Race

These simple but powerful audio cassette singles will help give you the edge you need. Run your race to win!

LONELY IN THE MIDST OF A CROWD
Loneliness is a devastating disease. Learn how to trust and count on others to help.

HERBS FOR HEALTH
A look at the concerns and fears of modern medicine. Learn the correct ways to open the doors to your healing.

HOW TO GET ANYTHING YOU WANT
You can learn the way to get anything you want from God!

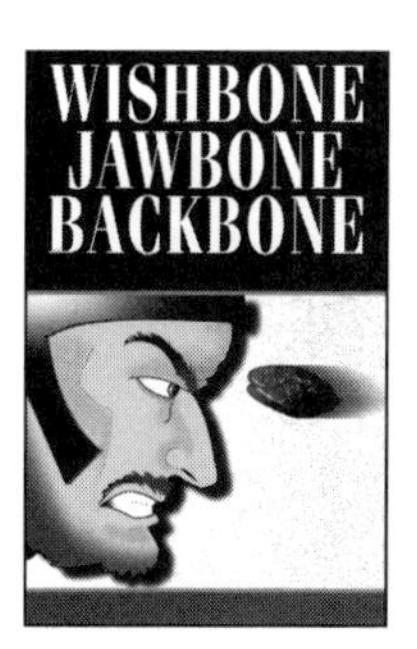

WISHBONE, JAWBONE, BACKBONE
Learn about King David, and how his three "bones" for success can help you in your life quest.

FATAL ENTICEMENTS
Learn how you can avoid the vice-like grip of sin and it's fatal enticements that hold people captive.

HOW TO BE A WALL BREAKER AND A CITY TAKER
You can be a powerful force for advancing the Kingdom of Jesus Christ!

Expanding Your Faith

These exciting audio teaching series will help you to grow and mature in your walk with Christ. Get ready for amazing new adventures in faith!

WHY DO SOME SUFFER
Find out why some people seem to have suffering in their lives, and find out how to avoid it in your life.

SIN'S GRIP
Learn how you can avoid the vice-like grip of sin and it's fatal enticements that hold people captive.

FAITH, HOPE, & LOVE
Listen and let these three "most important things in life" change you.

HEALING PRINCIPLES FROM THE MINISTRY OF JESUS
Determine to walk in healing! "By HIS stripes, we are healed."

DEVELOPING THE SPIRIT OF A CONQUEROR
You can be a conqueror through Christ! Also, Find out how to *keep* those things that you have conquered.

YOUR SPECTACULAR MIND
Identify wrong thinking and negative influences in your life.

These and other audio tapes available from Dave Williams and: